INTERNATIONAL POLITICAL ECONOMY SERIES

General Editor: Timothy M. Shaw, Professor of Political Science and International Development Studies, and Director of the Centre for Foreign Policy Studies, Dalhousie University, Halifax, Nova Scotia

Recent titles include:

Laura Macdonald
SUPPORTING CIVIL SOCIETY: The Political Role of Non-Governmental
Organizations in Central America

Stephen D. McDowell
GLOBALIZATION, LIBERALIZATION AND POLICY CHANGE: A Political
Economy of India's Communications Sector

Juan Antonio Morales and Gary McMahon (*editors*)
ECONOMIC POLICY AND THE TRANSITION TO DEMOCRACY: The Latin
American Experience

Ted Schrecker (*editor*)
SURVIVING GLOBALISM: The Social and Environmental Challenges

Ann Seidman, Robert B. Seidman and Janice Payne (*editors*)
LEGISLATIVE DRAFTING FOR MARKET REFORM: Some Lessons from
China

Kenneth P. Thomas
CAPITAL BEYOND BORDERS: States and Firms in the Auto Industry,
1960–94

Caroline Thomas and Peter Wilkin (*editors*)
GLOBALIZATION AND THE SOUTH

Geoffrey R. D. Underhill (*editors*)
THE NEW WORLD ORDER IN INTERNATIONAL FINANCE

Henry Veltmeyer, James Petras and Steve Vieux
NEOLIBERALISM AND CLASS CONFLICT IN LATIN AMERICA: A
Comparative Perspective on the Political Economy of Structural Adjustment

Robert Wolfe
FARM WARS: The Political Economy of Agriculture and the International Trade
Regime

International Political Economy Series
Series Standing Order ISBN 0–333–71110–6
(*outside North America only*)

You can receive future titles in this series as they are published by placing a standing order.
Please contact your bookseller or, in case of difficulty, write to us at the address below with
your name and address, the title of the series and the ISBN quoted above.

Customer Services Department, Macmillan Distribution Ltd
Houndmills, Basingstoke, Hampshire RG21 6XS, England

Human Rights in the Emerging Global Order

A New Sovereignty?

Kurt Mills
Assistant Professor
Department of Political Science
The American University in Cairo
Egypt

First published in Great Britain 1998 by
MACMILLAN PRESS LTD
Houndmills, Basingstoke, Hampshire RG21 6XS and London
Companies and representatives throughout the world

A catalogue record for this book is available from the British Library.

ISBN 0–333–72127–6

First published in the United States of America 1998 by
ST. MARTIN'S PRESS, INC.,
Scholarly and Reference Division,
175 Fifth Avenue, New York, N.Y. 10010

ISBN 0–312–21468–5

Library of Congress Cataloging-in-Publication Data
Mills, Kurt.
Human rights in the emerging global order : a new sovereignty? /
Kurt Mills.
p.   cm. — (International political economy series)
Includes bibliographical references and index.
ISBN 0–312–21468–5
1. Human rights.   2. Sovereignty.   I. Title.   II. Series.
JC585.M7793   1998
320.1'5—dc21   98–5591
                                                          CIP

This book is printed on paper suitable for recycling and made from fully managed and
sustained forest sources.

10   9   8   7   6   5
07   06   05   04   03   02   01   00

Printed and bound in Great Britain by
Antony Rowe Ltd, Chippenham, Wiltshire

Contents

Preface

The year 1998 marks the 50th anniversary of the Universal Declaration of Human Rights. This seminal document was a conceptual sea-change in global politics. Its scope was breathtaking. The international community had agreed that citizens of all countries should be guaranteed certain rights. No longer could states engage in the genocide of Nazi Germany. No longer could they torture their citizens, or deny them a wide range of social, political and economic rights. No longer, in other words, were individuals subject to the sovereign whims of the state in which they resided. These rights were further codified in the ensuing decades in conventions and covenants and declarations, but the Universal Declaration formed the core of a modern theory of human rights.

Theory, of course, gave way to reality as a Cold War grew out of the ashes of a World War, and as states continued their old ways of doing business. Millions of people have been imprisoned, tortured, and killed in the latter half of the 20th century. Genocides have occurred, and the international community has sat by passively, sometimes expressing outrage, and sometimes not even doing that.

Yet the idea of human rights has gained increasing normative salience worldwide. And, in practice, the international community has taken a few tentative steps to recognize the reorientation of rights and responsibilities embodied in the Universal Declaration. This book tells that story.

That story, however, is a rather ambiguous one, as reflected in the title of this book. The first part of the title indicates a less than firm conviction about how the world is developing and where it is heading. President George Bush popularized the phrase 'New World Order', which seemed to refer to a dramatic and irreversible shift in global politics, away from East-West conflict, to a single vision of a more peaceful world where democratic capitalism would flourish, and the rule of law would be upheld. Instead, after a few heady years when everything seemed possible, communal conflict and genocide appeared in unimaginable forms; the global community was prevented from responding to many crises by the same countries which had proclaimed a new era only months or years earlier, and old ways of doing business seem to continue unaltered. The term 'Emerging Global Order' indicates that while the world may be changing, it is still in a process of flux which will likely continue for a long time to come. The second part of the title – 'A New Sovereignty?' – is intended to indicate that the actual extent to which one can point to a commonly

vii

accepted revised concept of sovereignty is also ambiguous. While signs, indications and trends may be identified, the answers to the fundamental questions in global politics are still up for grabs.

This book began as my doctoral dissertation at the University of Notre Dame. Thus, I wish to express my supreme gratitude and thanks, first, to my dissertation committee: my adviser, Gil Losecher, who provided direction and support, even from 'across the pond'; George Lopez, who acted as director when Gil was out of the country; and Bob Johansen and Sharon O'Brien who provided useful comments and insights. Second, I wish to express my gratitude to all the people in Geneva who, in the autumn of 1993, provided me with their time and insights which put some of the big issues in a new light and added immeasurably to this book. Their names and affiliations are listed at the end of the bibliography. They are not cited specifically in the text because while some people were comfortable with being identified, others were less so and so all of my references to my interviews are somewhat anonymous. The Zahm Travel Grant Fund at Notre Dame helped make the trip to Geneva possible. Recognition is also due, not to a person, but to a barely definable concept – the Internet. This decentralized network of computers, which is at the forefront of challenging sovereignty, made parts of my research possible. It would have been almost impossible to keep up with the rapidly developing global scene without access to news and discussion groups on the Internet; in particular, the members of the PSRT-L and forced-migration mailing lists responded rapidly to last minute pleas for information.

Portions of this book have appeared elsewhere, including *The Netherlands Quarterly of Human Rights, Global Society,* and *The Journal of Humanitarian Assistance,* as well as in occasional papers from the Joan B. Kroc Institute for International Peace Studies at the University of Notre Dame and the Centre for International Security Studies at York University. I gratefully acknowledge the permission granted to use material published in the above journals.

The Thomas J. Watson, Jr. Institute for International Studies at Brown University provided a congenial place to finish revising my manuscript. At the Institute, Tom Weiss provided helpful comments on a portion of the manuscript. My colleagues Bill DeMars and Tony Lang at The American University in Cairo read parts of the manuscript and made valuable comments and suggestions and my research assistant, Dina Hussein, helped me compile the index.

Thanks are also due to my mother, Shirley, and all my friends who provided support during the various phases of this project. These include

Karen Slawner, who provided friendship and the occasional insight on early versions of this work, Michelle Madelien, who kept me going by e-mail, Sherine El-Ghatit, Liza Bobo, and Harriette Walker, who provided immeasurable friendship and support in Cairo, and Tristan Anne Borer, who has been a friend, confidant, and colleague since before this project ever began.

Finally, special thanks are due to Timothy Shaw at Dalhousie University, general editor of this series, and Aruna Vasudevan from Macmillan, who had faith in this book. Also thanks to Linda Auld Associates for copy-editing and editorial services.

List of Abbreviations

CSCE	Conference on Security and Cooperation in Europe
DHA	UN Department of Humanitarian Affairs
DPKO	UN Department of Peacekeeping Operations
ECOMOG	ECOWAS Cease-fire Monitoring Group
ECOWAS	Economic Community of West African States
EC	European Community
EU	European Union
GATT	General Agreement on Tariffs and Trade
HCNM	High Commissioner for National Minorities
ICRC	International Committee of the Red Cross
IDP	Internally Displaced Person
IGO	International Governmental Organization
IMF	International Monetary Fund
ITU	International Telecommunications Union
MSC	Military Staff Committee
NATO	North Atlantic Treaty Organization
NGO	Non-governmental Organization
OAS	Organization of American States
OAU	Organization of African Unity
ORC	Open Relief Centres
OSCE	Organization for Security and Cooperation in Europe
TNC	Transnational Corporation
UDHR	Universal Declaration of Human Rights
UN	United Nations
UNAMIR	United Nations Mission in Rwanda
UNDP	United Nations Development Program
UNFICYP	United Nations Force in Cyprus
UNHCR	United Nations High Commissioner for Refugees
UNPO	Unrepresented Nations and Peoples Organization
UNTAC	United Nations Transitional Authority in Cambodia
US	United States

Introduction

In recent years, a debate has emerged, or at least the volume of the debate has increased, regarding the theory and practice of state sovereignty. Sovereignty, which encompasses elements of power and authority has, for at least the last few hundred years, been identified with the territorial state. Traditional views of sovereignty regard these territorial entities as more or less independent and holding the requisite power and authority to provide for the security of the territory and the people within the territory. Some of the outlines and boundaries of sovereignty have been debated, but mainstream international relations discourse has more or less identified state sovereignty as *the* key reality of international politics.

However, this view has increasingly come into question. For a wide variety of reasons, increasing numbers of people are realizing that the current system of independent states which allows states to do basically whatever they want within their borders and does not compel them to address global problems which require global solutions is becoming dangerously outmoded.

The 1992 Rio Conference on the environment demonstrates this state of affairs very forcefully. Most of the world community recognized that environmental degradation is a serious issue which must be faced immediately and squarely. Yet, because one particularly strong state (which also makes the greatest contribution to environmental degradation) would not agree to binding agreements, significant advances in environmental protection were stymied. Refugees are another transnational problem which affects many states. However, the international community has been unable to come to grips with the underlying problems that cause cross-border migration, including civil war and famine.

Both of these examples point to the increasing permeability of borders. We are realizing just how ephemeral the borders we construct around ourselves are. Problems spill over and there is little we can do to insulate ourselves from their effects. However, it is not only concrete problems such as environmental degradation or masses of humanity which cross borders. Borders are the most permeable to ideas, including ideas pertaining to democratic participation in government and general issues of human dignity. A growing interest in human rights is spreading over the globe. There is an increasing realization that states do not have free reign in the way they treat their citizens and that the world community has a responsibility to address human rights abuses.

1

Yet, the world community has failed to adequately respond to many dire humanitarian circumstances. This failure has resulted partly from the array of political forces during the Cold War and partly because of a misconceptualization of the relationship between individual and state, state and world community, and individual and world community. However, the Cold War is over, and while some of the forces which propelled the ideological and military competition still exist, there are new openings for global cooperation rather than competition. And, there are also changes in how we think about power and authority and rights. Stale rhetoric about conflict between capitalism and socialism, democracy and totalitarianism is starting to give way to more serious discussion of participation and human rights.

This trend is by no means clearly defined. There are actually many conflicting trends. Some cannot free themselves from Cold War-speak. Others argue that we need to look inward and deal with the problems that arise within artificially constructed boundaries. And some want to create even more boundaries. Still others, however, are recognizing that these borders are, indeed, artificial constructs and that people and institutions are becoming more connected to each other in numerous ways which cross state boundaries.

A renewed focus on the greater problems of humanity and issues regarding the legitimate loci of power and authority, as well as the resulting recognition that international cooperation is required to address some of these issues, is contributing to an empirical, theoretical, and normative erosion of traditionally defined state sovereignty. This book focuses on the evolution of what I call the New Sovereignty – a recognition of this increasing interdependence and a reconceptualization of sovereignty, moving both downward and upward, inward and outward from the state, incorporating human rights as a legitimating factor in the emerging global order. It includes three themes of analysis. The first theme is normative in nature. I examine traditional state-centric concepts of sovereignty and argue that they are outmoded in that they ignore the fact that, ultimately, legitimate state authority derives from the individuals within the state and that the state can lose legitimacy if it abuses the sovereignty which is on loan from the people. I argue for a reconstructed notion of sovereignty which recognizes individual rights, group and global interests, and the obligations states and the international community have in responding to these rights and interests. Any claim to the authority and power associated with sovereignty must include respect for a wide variety of rights and interests, as well as a recognition that those claims cannot be nearly as absolute as some conceptualizations of sovereignty have maintained.

The second theme of analysis is more empirical. I document how state sovereignty has been, and continues to be, undermined through increasing interdependence and changing perspectives on humanitarian issues. I argue that this interdependence necessitates, first, a redefinition of sovereignty and second, new regional and global institutions and mechanisms. Further, I argue that definitions of sovereignty *are* changing; that it is truly a concept in transition. State and international elites and others increasingly perceive sovereignty as encompassing responsibilities as well as rights, responsibilities which include respect for human rights. In addition, there is a growing recognition that the domestic realm is becoming increasingly intertwined with the international realm. In other words, the idea that 'final and absolute authority'[1] resides in the state is increasingly coming into question. Further, the notion that there *can* be 'final and absolute authority' in any particular community is becoming increasingly problematic.

The third theme is policy oriented, examining recent and possible future international institutional developments in the area of human rights. The question, is who will ensure that the values of the New Sovereignty are upheld. Should it be regional organizations, which might have the greatest direct interest in, for example, regional refugee flows? Or, should it be a global institution which could claim that only it can speak with authority on the issue of fundamental human rights? More likely, there will be some sort of division of labour, interests, and authority among these levels of integration.

Taking these three themes as a whole requires a multi-level, multi-centric, and multi-textured notion of sovereignty which recognizes a constellation of interests, forces, and legitimating factors. That is, rather than relying on an absolute, unitary notion of sovereignty, legitimate sovereign authority is recognized as emanating from individuals, as well as groups. Further, the power to carry out these multiple sovereign wills is located in several centres simultaneously, having some territorial but also some functional aspects. That is, while territorial entities called states will still exist, other types and levels of aggregation also need to be factored into the equation. The implications for the theory and practice of sovereignty are far reaching. The days of sovereignty as an absolute ordering principle are over. State authority is becoming increasingly problematized. The way this authority is constructed is more subtle, requiring more complex discussions of what individuals and groups of individuals are relevant authority providers in what contexts. Thus, while in my reconstruction of sovereignty I still talk about it in terms of authority and power, the discussion is separated somewhat from the traditional territorial focus. The way authority and power are constructed and interact are more ambiguous than in traditional notions of sovereignty.

These three themes are linked in crucial and fundamental ways. Theory can never be wholly separated from practice, nor the normative from the empirical. Concrete practices help to form theoretical constructions, and these practices also provide the context for normative perspectives. It would be impossible to talk about tensions between state sovereignty and human rights if the ongoing practice called the state did not permeate almost every aspect of life on this planet. Yet, theoretical and normative perspectives colour the way we interpret empirical observations. Those who accept traditional views of international relations tend to discount to a large degree the role non-state actors play in international relations, while others see an emerging network of state and non-state actors and processes as increasingly important in determining how relations between, among, and within a wide variety of levels and actors occur. Further, those with different normative perspectives will view human rights abuses and other actions by governments in widely varying ways.

In addition, both empirical observations and normative perspectives impact one's policy prescriptions. A commitment to human rights and a recognition that state practices are interfering with this commitment will lead to certain types of conclusions regarding what different processes, institutions, and actors are necessary to uphold human rights. Those with a state-centric view of the world will come to very different conclusions. Thus, the realms of theory, practice, and prescription are intimately linked.

These three themes appear in various degrees in the following chapters. Chapter 1 provides an overview of the traditional concepts of sovereignty and the many challenges to these formulations. These challenges range from the technological and environmental to the social and humanitarian, from the empirical to the normative. I argue that once we recognize that states, like everything else, are social creations and not natural entities arising out of a predefined natural order of things, we can interrogate the social function of states to see what limits on states can be derived from that function. In fact, we see that the idea of human rights is inherent within the socially constructed reality of states, and thus a state's legitimacy rests, partly, on how well it upholds human rights. In addition, the authority of a state is related not only to its relationship with people as individuals, but also to people in the aggregate – 'the people'. This is the notion of popular sovereignty – rulers rule in accordance with the will of the people. Furthermore, a third building block of sovereignty relates not to 'people' or 'the people' but 'peoples'. That is, some form of self-determination and autonomy must be recognized for those groups who self-identify themselves as being distinct in some way from other members of society. Thus we have three constitutive principles of sovereignty from below the state level.

Moving upward from the state we see that in certain instances, the international community as a whole may be the only centre of authority which can ensure that these principles are upheld. Further, as with the relationship between individual and state within the context of recognizing the social purpose of the state, we can make similar connections between people and the international community. In other words, the international community has a responsibility to ensure that human rights and humanitarian standards are upheld. I thus argue for a reconceptualization of sovereignty which is a significant departure from traditional formulations and suggests a realm of social arrangements which will be increasingly ambiguous.

The ensuing three chapters look more closely at three aspects of the challenge to sovereignty – self-determination, human migration, and humanitarian intervention. Within each issue area there lays a challenge to the traditional concept of sovereignty in either a normative or physical/empirical aspect. Each illuminates a way sovereignty is being undermined and point to a particular aspect of the reformulation of the New Sovereignty. In addition, each issue area has certain international institutions and mechanisms associated with them, and the way the issue area is challenging sovereignty will indicate what changes might be needed in the future to deal with the challenges to sovereignty. All of the issue areas can be put under the broad heading of humanitarian issues, and are thus highly interrelated.

Chapter 2 examines the explosion of ethnonationalism which is threatening the sovereignty of a number of different countries, and, indeed, is calling into question some fundamental ideas about the traditional conceptualization of sovereignty. Communal conflict, including calls for autonomy or secession, as well as so called 'ethnic cleansing', is tearing apart countries worldwide. Traditional formulations of sovereignty identify it with the ability to execute supreme authority within a given territory. In a number of instances, internal rebel groups and secessionist movements have made this impossible. Does this then mean that the territory identified with the state is no longer a sovereign entity because there is no supreme authority? In addition, either directly or indirectly, the legitimacy of a government, or at least its control over a certain part of the territory of a state is called into question. This raises the issue of *de facto* and *de jure* control over territory. Is this distinction still useful in dealing with these issues? What is the link between legitimacy and sovereignty? In a number of states, groups are asking for some sort of autonomy from the central government. Is this the same thing as asking for partial sovereignty, and does such a concept make sense? Can one talk about partial sovereignty, variable sovereignty, levels of sovereignty, or even multiple sovereignty within a given territory?

Chapter 3 addresses some of the problems which arise, at least partly, from communal conflict – refugees. A large portion of humanity is on the move. Approximately 40 million people are displaced by war, famine, environmental degradation, economic depression, and persecution. Most of this movement has occurred in the Third World, both between Third World countries and from Third World countries to more developed countries. However, because of recent developments, especially in Eastern Europe and the former Soviet Union, more and more people are moving between more developed countries. To a large extent, states have been unable to cope with these massive waves of migration. Even when states desire it, they are frequently unable to physically prevent people from crossing borders. In addition, these migrant populations – both legal and illegal – are having disruptive effects within states. Refugee movements also affect the security considerations and calculations of many states. The inability on the part of states to stop or deal with human migration in the manner in which they want implies a weakening of their sovereignty. Further, from a normative perspective, I argue that, on the basis of an array of human rights concerns, state borders should be more open to migration than they currently are.

The New Sovereignty is premised on a recognition that individuals have fundamental human rights and that these require concomitant responsibilities on the part of states. Once this is granted, the questions then become at what point do these rights supersede internal sovereignty, who should step in to defend human rights, and how should this be accomplished? What role should force play to ensure that human rights standards are upheld? These are the questions addressed in Chapter 4. By claiming and acting upon a right of humanitarian access and intervention, – which is the logical outcome of the normative reorientation mentioned above, – the global community would signal an effective end to a traditional cornerstone of sovereignty, namely that the coercive apparatus of the state has final and supreme authority within its borders. Humanitarian intervention would also require new institutional arrangements in order for it to be carried out in a timely and effective manner within the bounds of the New Sovereignty.

In Chapter 4 I approach these questions, as in the previous chapters, from two perspectives. First, I examine the international legal setting and recent practice to investigate how the global community as a whole has been dealing with this issue. Second, incorporating arguments made in previous chapters, I look at how a normative commitment to human rights leads to the conclusion that the norm of non-intervention does not have the kind of normative force many ascribe to it and that it may be overridden in cases of extreme humanitarian distress. Finally, I put forward a number of criteria which I argue should be used when evaluating the balance between human rights and non-intervention.

All of these problems and questions lead us to a very practical question – what institutional arrangements are needed to deal with these issues? In Chapter 5 I argue that certain changes need to be made, especially within the UN, to deal with this reconceptualization of sovereignty. A few steps have already been taken to address some of the problems associated with communal conflict. However, a more coherent and unified strategy is necessary to deal with situations of intractable communal conflict or 'failed states'.

With regard to problems of displacement, I examine a few recent innovative activities on the part of United Nations High Commissioner for Refugees, such as providing aid to a variety of vulnerable populations in the midst of a civil war. Even with some expanded and innovative activities, there is still no focal point for dealing with the internally displaced, and the UNHCR may need an expanded mandate, or else a new organization may be required which would assist a wide range of victims of conflict. Further, I argue that to ensure that refugees get fair asylum hearing, and to ensure that the burden of dealing with refugees is spread more evenly among the states which can most afford it, a system may need to be created where the determination of asylum claims is taken out of the hands of states and where the developed states take more responsibility both in terms of resources and admitting asylum seekers.

Dealing with human rights abuses may necessitate several changes. I argue that a small, permanent UN police force should be established so that a quick initial response can be made in situations of immediate and dire humanitarian crises. In addition, to add a higher degree of legitimacy to forceful action, perhaps the General Assembly should become more involved in such decisions. All of the changes need to be thought of in the context of a revitalized view of a positive relationship between the individual, state and international community, and the concomitant recognition that sovereignty cannot be a shield for abuse of human and people's rights. Before more forceful action is taken, however, there may be instances where NGOs may play an increasingly important role in gaining access to affected populations, particularly insofar as they are perceived as separate from a politicized UN. Such a mixed system of NGOs and UN organs will probably continue to deal with human rights protection and delivering humanitarian aid.

Chapter 6 includes some final thoughts on the trajectories that thought and action regarding sovereignty may take in the coming years as the world becomes a village and as humanitarian crises are seen not as occurring somewhere out there but within a community – albeit a large one – of which we are all part. I conclude that the concept of sovereignty, with its concomitant aspects of legitimate authority and ability to carry out that authority, and the possibilities for the location and exercise of power and authority, will seem much more ambiguous in the future.

1 Reconstructing Sovereignty

[T]he further history of the concept [of
sovereignty] will be a history of its use and
misuse in varying political conditions and not
restatement of it in different or novel terms.   F. H. Hinsley[1]

It may be that the contemporary period is one
of considerable fluidity, when the most
fundamental questions regarding the exercise
of power and authority have been thrown
back into the crucible of history.   Joseph A. Camilleri[2]

For three or four centuries, and certainly by the Peace of Westphalia end-
ing the Thirty Years War, state sovereignty has been the guiding principle
of international relations. The state has been the way people have organized themselves, and has been seen as the natural or inevitable end product in the evolution of international society. F.H. Hinsley characterizes
sovereignty as 'final and absolute authority in the political community',[3]
and notes that it has been intimately associated with the state: 'the origin
and history of the concept of sovereignty are closely linked with the
nature, the origin and the history of the state.'[4] He talks about the 'inexor-
able' consolidation of the state and the 'victory of the concept of sovereignty'.[5] Harold Laski notes, however, that 'there is historically no limit to
the variety of ways in which the use of power may be organized'.[6] Mary
Catherine Bateson, too, sees more room for human agency and change:
'The state is not a fact of nature, however, but the solution to a problem[7] –
a modern and Western solution, recently generalizable to the rest of the
world, which is, in turn, itself a source of problems.'[8]

   The previous paragraph, as well as the two quotes at the beginning of the
chapter, paint two radically different pictures of the world. The first por-
trays state sovereignty as natural, as a realistic description of contemporary world politics, and as the way the world will be organized far into the
future. The second view recognizes the need to rethink some of our most
basic ideas and thus poses direct challenges to state sovereignty as a contemporary and future organizing principle. As Walter B. Wriston notes,
'When major tides of change wash over the world, power structures almost
inevitably reject the notion that the world really is changing, and they
cling to their old beliefs.'[9] Indeed, the world has changed, is changing, and

9

will continue to change in dramatic, yet ambiguous, ways in the future, and while those with a stake in the old order may 'cling to their old beliefs', there is a need to recognize this change. The concept of sovereignty is at the core of change and turbulence in global politics today. It is under assault from many quarters – the environment, communications technology, nuclear weapons, massive movements of people across borders, and increasing acceptance of human rights norms around the world have radical implications for the concept of sovereignty to which many would like to hold on. As Joseph Camilleri and Jim Falk note: 'Given the far-reaching transformation of the social and political landscape we have witnessed this century, and especially these past several decades, there is a pressing need to rethink the concept and practice of sovereignty.'[10]

This chapter is an attempt to come to grips with broad changes in the emerging global order and their effect on sovereignty. I will make reference to a wide array of challenges to sovereignty; however, the main focus, as with the book as a whole, will be on humanitarian issues. To place the discussion in historical context, I will begin with a brief discussion of the way in which some of the major theorists of sovereignty have conceived of sovereignty over the past few hundred years. Then, I will put my analysis in the context of what is becoming a major critical perspective in international relations – the postmodern condition. While reserving judgment on much of what the postmodern critique proposes, I will argue that this perspective is useful in 'denaturalizing' the state. Next, I will present an overview of the various challenges to state sovereignty, from the economic and technological to the environmental and humanitarian. The humanitarian issues will take centre stage and form the core of my critique and reconstruction of sovereignty. Finally, I will propose a framework for understanding these challenges and put forth a reformulation of sovereignty which encompasses a renewed view of human rights as the standard in assessing sovereignty.

THE CONCEPT OF SOVEREIGNTY[11]

The concept of sovereignty was formulated in conjunction with the founding of the modern state system in the 16th and 17th centuries. By the end of the 15th century there were up to 500 semi-independent political units in Europe, although the trend was toward centralization under monarchs. At the same time, these units 'saw themselves as the municipal embodiments of a universal [Christian] community'[12] under the Pope. Medieval Europe was 'a cosmopolitan patchwork of overlapping loyalties and allegiances, geographically interwoven jurisdictions and political enclaves',[13] with no sharp line between the internal and the external.

Yet, this period was characterized by significant religious unrest and threats to papal authority. The Renaissance contributed to the secularization of society, and the Reformation undermined papal authority. The secular state was viewed as the best remedy for religious and political disorder. Some point to the Treaty of Augsburg of 1555, which led to the right of each German principality to determine whether it would be Catholic or Lutheran, as the beginning of the modern state system. Others take the Peace of Westphalia in 1648 as the defining moment of the sovereign state system. While it may be hard to pinpoint the exact moment of birth for the current system of states, political community was associated with territory by the 15th century, and the idea of sovereignty was firmly entrenched by 1648. The move was made from a hierarchy of authorities to a decentralized system of independent – that is *sovereign* – political entities called states.[14] Thus, the sovereign state system came about as a response to specific historical circumstances, namely the disjunction between the development of an increasingly secular society in Europe and the continuing hold of religious authority on state (or pre-state) authority, or, rather, between secular particularism and Christian universality. This idea of the sovereign state as a product of specific cultural and political milieu contradicts Hinsley's idea of the state as a necessary end product.[15]

There are two sides to sovereignty traditionally conceived – internal and external. Internally, states are considered to have supreme authority within their borders. That is, there are no higher authorities and no entities with the authority to take coercive, or any type of, action within the territorial limits of the state.

Yet, the limits to which this authority is subject have been debated. Machiavelli felt that the ruler must be freed from moral and customary constraints in order to benefit the community or body politic as a whole. For Hobbes the ruler was supreme. Yet, while he has been characterized as saying that people had no inalienable rights,[16] Hobbes did, in fact, recognize three such rights: life, liberty, and the right to live so as not to grow weary of life.[17] Bodin, who was the first to put forward a coherent concept of sovereignty,[18] rejected the idea of Christendom as the universal society. Like Hobbes, he also believed that a central authority should have almost unlimited power, and used the French term *souveraineté* to describe this political arrangement. In addition, divine and natural law on the one hand, and customary laws of the political community one the other, were limits on the exercise of sovereign power. Rousseau formulated popular sovereignty as the basis of state sovereignty, and the state was connected to the people through a contract. This contract was not, however, a contract in the Hobbesian sense where the people give their complete submission without receiving anything in return. Rather, it was a contract which required that the ruler rule in the interest of the people, rather than for *raison d'état*. Locke, too, relying on natural law, and undermining the supremacy of power and authority in Bodin and Hobbes, viewed the government as holding a public trust.[19]

The link between the internal aspects of sovereignty and the external aspects is nonintervention. This principle has only come to be regarded as sacrosanct this century.[20] Certainly by the end of World War II and the founding of the United Nations non-intervention had become an overriding international norm. The contention of this book is that this principle is being eroded by increased concern for human rights even as it has reached ascendancy.

Externally, states have the right to engage in international activity – trade, exchange diplomats, take part in diplomatic conferences, and so on. Each state is regarded as equal in relation to all other states. However, this is a fallacious assumption. Many states, including mini-states such as Samoa or Monaco, do not have the same capabilities as other states such as the United States of America or France, to participate in international activities; yet, they have the right.

Alan James has taken a slightly different tact by defining sovereignty in terms of constitutional independence. That is, if there is no higher constitutional authority than domestic constitutional arrangements then an entity is a sovereign state.[21] Again, this says nothing about a state's abilities to engage in international activity.

Robert Keohane makes a distinction between two aspects of sovereignty – 'formal sovereignty' and 'operational sovereignty'. The former relates to autonomy – the legal ability of a state to decide policy for itself – and the equality between states. The latter concerns a state's actual ability to implement policy – its effectiveness – which is limited by external constraints.[22] Ruth Lapidoth, on the other hand, does not make a distinction between these two types of sovereignty, but does note that sovereignty – which includes Keohane's 'formal' sovereignty – can, indeed, be shared or divided.[23] She argues that there are three elements of state sovereignty: (1) the sovereign state is subject to international law, (2) it is not under any other state's control, and (3) it is able to exert power.[24] All three of these elements are problematic. First, international law and its ability to bind, especially its customary aspects, are still in dispute. Second, while a state may not be under the control of another state, it may, nonetheless, be unable to actually control portions of its territory or various processes within its borders. Third, there are many recognized sovereign states which are not able to exercise state power in any meaningful way.

Lapidoth notes, further, that there are a number of implications for the relations between states of this construction of state sovereignty. First, all states possess 'sovereign equality'.[25] Second, states cannot intervene in the affairs of another state.[26] Third, states have 'exclusive territorial jurisdiction'. Fourth, states are presumed competent. In other words, '[t]he sovereign state possess the totality of powers without a need for enumeration, except for those expressly excluded, such as the lack of jurisdiction over foreign countries and diplomats.' Lapidoth notes, however, that this rule is contested. Indeed, this presumption is also dubious in fact. Fifth, states can only be bound by adjudication with their consent. Sixth, states have the almost unlimited right to wage war. This has, for the most part, been discredited. Seventh, positivist international law is the source of binding rules between states, rather than natural law which is beyond the free will of states.[27] These implications are also problematic. Indeed, a number of them do not correspond to actual practice. In addition, they prevent the international community from addressing many emerging global problems. These conceptual and practical problems lead to the conclusion that the concept of sovereignty is, as Leibniz characterized it, 'thorny and little cultivated'.[28]

Thus, we have the (problematic) traditional formulation of sovereignty tied to a state defined by territoriality. States are portrayed as more or less self-contained units which are not subject to outside interference. Internally, states carry on their various economic and social functions. Authority to carry out these functions lies in the state, or, more precisely, the government of a state. But where does this authority actually come from? Hobbes would say that 'might makes right', that those with the power make the laws. This view, however, as I will demonstrate below, with the essentially universal recognition of the concept of human rights, has been discredited. Rather, there is increasing recognition of a relationship between the way a government treats its people and its authority. However, this relationship and the consequences for a state's ultimate standing and rights in the international community have not been resolved. This will be the focus of the latter parts of this chapter, as well as other sections of this book.

First, however, I will put this analysis in the context of an increasingly important perspective in international relations: postmodernism.

A POSTMODERN PERSPECTIVE

The 'post' in postmodern denotes an evolution or a break from something else called 'modern'. Thus, I will begin with a description of the modern.

Modernity is characterized by the idea of progress and scientific rationality. Camilleri and Falk describe the idea of progress as 'a belief that civilization has moved and will continue to move in a direction which is desirable and determined by natural law.'[29] In other words, there is some natural progression within which societies are embedded and through which they must move. The market with its 'invisible hand' and technology are important aspects of progress. Rationality, positivism, and a belief in absolute truth are other aspects of modernity. Modernity, in other words, is characterized by the belief that universal truth can be arrived at by science and reason. Habermas thus characterized the 'project of modernity' as an effort, on the part of Enlightenment thinkers, 'to develop objective science, universal morality and law, and autonomous art according to their inner logic.'[30]

Onuf points to three main aspects of modernity. First, it is human-centered. That is, interpretation of the world is focused on humanity and its implications for humanity. Second, reason and the individual are emphasized. Third, one finds a 'preoccupation with method, the differentiation of tasks, and material prosperity, all in the name of progress.'[31] Camilleri incorporates these various aspects and characteristics in what he calls the 'ideology of modernity', which includes:

> growth of codified knowledge as a way of controlling the physical environment; political centralization accompanied by the development of highly specialized bureaucracies; continuous increases in economic production and productivity; rapid rate of technological change; and introduction of social and cultural mechanisms designed to achieve the necessary psychological adjustments to these processes.[32]

This ideology is related to the state being regarded as necessary and inevitable. Yet, the logic of modernity also challenges state sovereignty

The modern impulse to control and master the environment has led to a contradiction. Material prosperity (for at least a portion of humanity) has increased at a dramatic rate, with no regard for the limits imposed by the natural environment. There has been increasing global convergence in both the technological and ideological (that is the ideology of modernity) realms.[33] Yet, as the world economy has modernized, one finds not only globalizing tendencies, but also fragmentation, resulting from the 'alienation and anomie that arise from the uniformity and reduced emphasis on spiritual values which appears to be characteristic of modern mass consumerist society.' One of the most significant fragmentations is that between the increasingly rich North and the poverty-stricken South.[34] All of this has resulted in what Richard Falk calls the 'crisis of modernism':

the complex modern project to apply science and technology to human problems has encountered several severe challenges that are undermining both its legitimacy as a creed and its coherence as a basis for action. Simplistically put, modernism as practiced has given us nuclearism and an overwrought encounter between human activity and ecological viability. Normative and spiritual blinders have not well served the species, at least not in this century. Of course, the modernist logic continues to lure many of us with its promises to overcome *with* technology the difficulties that technology has created: more modernization for the Third World, computerized democracy, electronic weaponry. But the crisis of modernism is generating nonmodernist responses as well. To cope successfully, we are urged to look backward (a heroic premodern antecedent) and to strive for a far greener future (a heroic postmodern prospect).[35]

The response to this crisis has been the incorporation of a postmodern perspective in analysis. Postmodernism (or constructivism), in its most basic form, is a realization that the reality we experience is socially created. That is, the way we perceive and interact with the world is continually created, recreated and changed through ongoing social processes. It is a repudiation of the Enlightenment faith in the ability of science and reason to comprehend some objective reality. It, in other words, 'denies the capacity of language, mind, or spirit to establish standards in an objective manner'.[36] It is words and ideas that construct our reality.[37]

A postmodern perspective is suspicious of metanarratives – what Lyotard calls the 'grand narrative'[38] – broad interpretations which supposedly describe truth and reality. These metanarratives, which can become 'totalizing discourses', include the aforementioned idea of progress, Marx's theory of the inevitability of class struggle and revolution, Freud's psychoanalytic theories, and Einstein's theories of relativity. Metanarratives can marginalize other perspectives. As the market system engulfs the world, other economic perspectives are submerged. As attempts to control the environment proceed, perspectives which call into question the abuse of natural resources are silenced.[39] And, as state sovereignty is accepted, and the state becomes the 'master noun of political argument',[40] other possibilities are dismissed or forgotten.[41]

This is where a postmodern (or constructivist) perspective is useful in analyzing sovereignty. The state and the concept of sovereignty are rooted in a particular historical and socio-political context, and sovereignty has been socially constructed through processes embedded within this context.[42] And, the reevaluation of sovereignty arises from a new context which is problematizing the concept. Sovereignty has become a meta-narrative or 'totalizing discourse'. Camilleri and Falk talk in terms of a 'sovereignty discourse' which is 'a way of describing and thinking about the world in which nation-states are the principal actors, the principle centres of power, and the principle objects of interest'.[43] The sovereignty discourse has marginalized other ways of thinking about social arrangements and the locus of power and authority. Sovereignty 'is more than just an idea':

> It is a way of speaking about the world, a way of acting in the world. It is central to the language of politics but also to the politics of language. It is part of a more general discourse of power whose function is not only to describe political and economic arrangements but to explain and justify them as if they belonged to the natural order of things. Sovereignty in both theory and practice is aimed at establishing order and clarity in an otherwise turbulent and incoherent world. Its historical function has been to act as 'fundamental source of truth and meaning,' to distinguish between order and anarchy, security and danger, identity and difference.

> Sovereignty, as both idea and institution, lies at the heart of the modern and therefore Western experience of space and time. It is integral to the structure of Western thought with its stress on 'dichotomies and polarities', and to a geopolitical discourse in which territory is sharply demarcated and exclusively controlled.[44]

Constructivism is a way to counter the marginalization of alternatives, a way 'to render "the invisible" visible'.[45]

The sovereign state has come to be seen as necessary and natural, and over the centuries, state sovereignty has been reified through thought and practice. As power has become centralized within state structures, it seems natural that it should be this way, although as Alexander Wendt observes, '[t]he sovereign state is an ongoing accomplishment of practice, not a once and-for-all creation of norms that somehow exist apart from practice'.[46] Those who are seeking to secede or throw off oppressive state structures are, for the most part, only trying to create their own state structures rather than some other type of social arrangement. The recently decolonized countries hold onto the concept of sovereignty, for they see this as the only way to keep out their former colonizers. And, as Walter Truett Anderson points out, the most potent form of reification is the process by which people 'invent institutions and then forget they have done so'.[47] He further notes that 'reification is often deification', which might include viewing a monarchy as being sanctified by god, as well as 'the popular reverence for the framers of the Constitution' in the United States which has become 'secular deification'.[48]

Yet, even as the state has become reified, there is a need to 'denaturalize' the state.[49] Allott observes that '[s]overeignty is not a fact of the physical world. . . . Sovereignty is not a fact but a theory.'[50] As Camilleri and Falk note:

> sovereignty may not be the last word on the subject. Given the far-reaching transformation of the social and political landscape we have witnessed this century, and especially these past several decades, there is a pressing need to rethink the concept and practice of sovereignty.[51]

Anderson ties these transformations to adopting a postmodern worldview:

> Globalizing processes require us to renegotiate our relationship with familiar cultural forms, and remind us that they are things made by people: human, fallible things, subject to revision. Globalism and a postmodern worldview come in the same package; we will not have one without the other.[52]

Investigating the postmodern condition can be disconcerting. It is a recognition of contingency and ambiguity in our social relations. Sovereignty has acted as 'a foundational source of truth and meaning',[53] thus negating any uncomfortable ambiguity. Yet, questioning this 'foundational source' is necessary to combat the reification processes which have shored up state sovereignty as an absolute institution. The following pages will discuss the contradictory centralizing and decentralizing tendencies, the clamour for autonomy from substate units, and the calls for greater control over formerly sovereign entities, all of which are now emerging in global politics. These are just some of 'the ambiguities which at every level now surround the principle of sovereignty',[54] but which also must be faced in the emerging global order.

Two other points will serve to end this analysis of the relevance of postmodernism to the changing nature of sovereignty. First, the above discussion has left out much of what many would include in postmodern/constructivist discourse; however, it is sufficient for the purposes of my argument.[55] And, there are those working within a postmodern framework who take it to such an extreme that it, itself, becomes a 'totalizing discourse'. However, it is the very nature of the postmodern condition which allows us to see postmodernism as a 'corrective' to other discourses without being caught up in epistemological contemplation to the detriment of action.[56] This brings me to my second point. Epistemology can help us understand how we think about things and how we socially construct those things we are thinking about. However, as Wendt points out, '[n]either positivism, nor scientific realism, nor poststructuralism tells us about the structure and dynamics of international life. Philosophies of science are not theories of international relations.'[57]

UNDERMINING SOVEREIGNTY

The above discussion has provided a basis for problematizing state sovereignty as a natural and absolute concept. The focus will now shift to why '[n]ot all is well with the theory of sovereignty' and why the analytic validity of sovereignty is declining.[58] We are at an 'historical breakpoint',[59] brought on by a postmodern 'axial upheaval',[60] where our traditional concepts no longer work but are, instead, being reforged on the 'crucible of history'. Much of this stems from contradictory globalizing and localizing tendencies which are challenging, and some might say ripping asunder, the fabric of state sovereignty from above and below, from inside and outside, and between states.

As the density of interactions between states increases – including diplomatic, social, and cultural activity, communications, concerns over environmental problems – states are seen as becoming increasingly interdependent. However, as Walker and Mendlovitz note: 'The very notion of a state system implies that states are already interdependent in some sense.'[61] Thus, the very moment the state system came into being states were interdependent. They also speculate that other entities besides states might also be interdependent, although it is hard to identify what these other entities might be because of the constraining way we conceive of political life, resulting from the marginalizing influence of the sovereignty discourse.[62]

Increasing interdependence is cited as a threat to state sovereignty. There are at least two different views on this matter. Keohane, in making his distinction between formal and operational sovereignty, maintains that interdependence challenges states' abilities to carry out national policy – that is operational sovereignty – but not states' formal sovereignty. Operational sovereignty is limited by international agreements, but entering into those agreements is an exercise of (formal) sovereignty. However, loss of policy effectiveness occurs without a state's agreement, leading states to willingly give up some operational sovereignty by signing an international agreement or joining an international organization.[63] States thus make sovereign choices to engage in collaborative activity.

On the other hand, one can contend that states increasingly do not have a choice regarding whether to join or leave such arrangements. Mark Zacher uses the concept of 'enmeshment' to describe this condition: '[states] are becoming increasingly *enmeshed* in a network of interdependencies and regulatory/collaborative arrangements from which exit is generally not a feasible option.'[64] This affects not only operational sovereignty but also the autonomy to make the decision, or formal sovereignty. Between 1951 and 1986, the number of IGOs increased from 123 to 337, and the number of international NGOs increased from 832 to 4,649. Around the turn of the century there were about 100 international conferences per year, and during the 1970s there were around 3,000 per year. Finally, between 1946 and 1955, 6,351 bilateral treaties entered into force, while between 1966 and 1975, 14,061 treaties did so.[65] Thus, states increasingly are realizing that there are issues that they cannot deal with by themselves and, if Zacher is right, this realization is leading them down a very slippery slope indeed towards undermining their sovereignty.

In addition, as states become enmeshed and realize that their well-being depends on others, Rosenau posits that global culture will expand and become more all encompassing:

> Global Culture – that realm of norms which are shared on a worldwide scale – may be neither fixed nor stagnant. As technology shrinks the world and as value systems within the subcultures are exposed to the dynamics of life in a post-industrial order, global culture seems likely to undergo transformation, to encompass broadened conceptions of self-interests pursued by others.[66]

An expanded sense of global culture can have an impact on the way states are perceived. It can lead to an expansion of the normative realm, including human rights: 'whatever the explanation, the expansion of human rights ideas to a worldwide scale can be traced to the fact that the world is in many respects being transformed into one society.'[67] The implications of an expanded global society for human rights will be returned to below. However, first I will briefly look at some of the other threats to state sovereignty which are becoming increasingly important in the emerging global order.

The environment is one area where the fragility of state sovereignty can be seen with great clarity. The Chernobyl disaster in 1985 rendered impotent any arguments which contended that states were not directly and immediately affected by events outside their supposed sovereign domain. Permeable borders could not prevent radioactive gases from blanketing much of Scandinavia, other parts of Europe, and various other parts of the world. The eruption of Mt Pinatubo in the Philippines spewed so much material into the atmosphere that it blocked enough sunlight to cool down the earth by an appreciable amount.

Yet, these dramatic occurrences are only the most visible reminders that borders are permeable. Ozone depletion and global warming are two processes, brought about by the modernist activity of the industrial revolution, which have enabled humankind 'to alter the environment on a planetary scale'.[68] In the course of industrial development, massive amounts of carbon dioxide have been released into the atmosphere through the use of fossil fuel and deforestation, increasing the concentration by 25 per cent. This, along with increased concentrations of other gases, has resulted in a process which, by 2030 or so, will increase the temperature of the planet by 1.5–4.5°C. Besides having an effect on agricultural production around the world, this will result in some melting of the ice caps, raising the level of the oceans by one to four feet. This, in turn, will result in flooding along many rivers and will negatively affect low lying coastal regions, possibly putting under water large portions of coastal states and a number of island nations.[69]

Increases in levels of chloroflourocarbons (CFCs) have also had negative global effects. These gases have been used in spray cans, refrigeration and microelectronics processing, and their release into the atmosphere has decreased the amount of ozone in the upper atmosphere which protects the surface from ultraviolet radiation. Without this protection, skin cancer, eye damage and possibly other effects on animal and plant life will result. CFC use is being phased out; however, the CFCs which are in the atmosphere will affect ozone levels for another 50 years.[70]

Two other examples will demonstrate transborder environmental effects. First, it has recently been discovered that topsoil from western and southern Africa is swept up by winds and carried west, some falling in the ocean and some finding its way to South America, Caribbean islands and Florida. While this process may be exacerbated by human activity, including deforestation and planting unsuitable crops which damage the soils, it has gone on for millennia independent of human activity.[71] Thus, some sovereign states are unable to control what might be considered the most basic component of a territorially defined entity – its land. Another process, this time human made, is also affecting the southern hemisphere. Fires in South America and southern Africa, set by ranchers, herders and farmers, create massive clouds of smog and low-lying ozone across the southern hemisphere which, in turn, contribute to widespread respiratory problems.[72]

These examples underscore Jessica Tuchman Mathews' contention that 'Environmental strains that transcend national borders are already beginning to break down the sacred boundaries of national sovereignty, previously rendered porous by the information and communication revolutions and the instantaneous global movement of financial capital.'[73] In other words, global processes, both natural and humanmade, are demonstrating in a most dramatic fashion the permeability of artificial, socially constructed borders between states, thus undermining the concrete expression of sovereignty.

Technological change has played a part in some of the environmental processes outlined above. However, the effects of technology go far beyond physical changes in the environment, and they, too, do not augur well for state sovereignty. As Wriston notes: 'Today the velocity of change is so great in all aspects of science, technology, economics and politics that the tectonic plates of national sovereignty and power have begun to shift.'[74] The computer revolution has made the manipulation of data and the access to vast amounts of information almost instantaneous. This has enabled governments to keep a closer watch over its citizens, and it has helped governments to spread information (whether propaganda or otherwise) among its citizens.[75]

Yet, the combination of computer technology and communications technology has also allowed citizens and corporations to evade governmental grasp in a number of important ways which seriously subvert the state. As these technologies have decentralized knowledge they have also helped to decentralize power. Ordinary citizens are now able to gain access to vast amounts of information about both their own home countries and what is happening beyond their borders because these borders are permeable to essentially unregulated communications. CNN provides instantaneous information from all around the world, whether in Tienanmen Square during the 1989 uprising or Baghdad during the Gulf War, and the Internet provides an accessible global computer network for all sorts of information. Thus, citizens find out what is going on outside the confines of their country, see that things might be different, have their expectations changed and expanded, and then start agitating for change, thus resulting in possibly destabilizing tendencies, which might, in turn, cross national boundaries. Gamani Corea notes that:

> Third World countries are one by one becoming 'ungovernable'. No matter what the complexion of the governments – right wing, left wing, military, or democratic – they are all in situations of not being able to respond adequately to the expectations of their people: expectations aroused by the media, by communications, by education . . . . turmoil and tension in the Third World will eventually spill over national boundaries and threaten and endanger the very fabric of global peace and stability.[76]

During the 1989 Tienanmen Square uprising in China, the students and other participants got information out of the country and received information about government and worldwide reaction by fax, engaging in what might be called 'revolution by fax'. A similar situation might be reported today as 'revolution via modem' as the ubiquitous Internet becomes increasingly uncontrollable. The electronic spread of information can fuel unrest almost anywhere. The widespread distribution of the videotape of the beating of Rodney King served as a catalyst for the Los Angeles and associated riots. As the use of such technology spreads, whether in authoritarian China or a more democratic United States, citizens can better keep tabs on their leaders and hold them accountable.[77] States are relatively powerless to stop this: 'The sovereign's laws and regulations have not adjusted to the new reality,'[78] nor may they be able to adjust.[79]

Communications technology also makes possible new kinds of communities, creating new centres of authority and relocating authority away from traditional authority structures (states) toward more ambiguous and fluid confluences and loci of allegiance and authority. It also means that territoriality is not nearly as important in the creation of feelings of community. That is, dispersed communities can form and remain cohesive more easily with the advent of the Internet, e-mail, and communications satellites.[80] Thierry Breton provides a fictional account of what he calls a 'logical state': 'an assemblage of individuals who already share the same interests and aspirations, who subscribe to the same values and are acting toward a common purpose, wherever they might be found on the planet.'[81] It is 'a supranational community that bears some resemblance to those nations that have been dispersed by historical forces but which have preserved their national identity . . . .'[82] The fictional example Breton uses is a Vatican plan to link up Catholics worldwide via advanced communications technology, thereby allowing direct and immediate address by the Pope. In this way, the Vatican could more easily exercise its authority, whereby citizens might shift their allegiance from their territorial state to the nonterritorially-bound Catholic logical state. Although currently only fiction,[83] there are many possible candidates for logical statehood – other religions, including Islam and Judaism; various transnational ethnic groups, such as the Kurds; or, possibly, even transnational corporations attempting to gain greater allegiance from their far-flung employees. Such attempts to relocate authority could have a destabilizing impact on states as the traditional holders of power and authority, and these territorially-bound units would be hard pressed to stop this process. The control of territory, which has been an important aspect of sovereignty, may diminish in importance: 'as the information revolution makes the assertion of territorial control more difficult in certain ways and less relevant in others, the nature and significance of sovereignty are bound to change.'[84]

Technology is not only directly undermining the authority of the state on the individual level; control over the realm of economic transactions is also slipping from the grasp of the state as its borders become increasingly permeable. Global telecommunications allows individuals and corporations to transfer massive amounts of capital across state borders without interference from states. In addition, as information becomes the most valuable commodity and the 'Information Standard' replaces the gold standard and Bretton Woods agreements, governments do not have the power to control their currencies.[85] Currency traders worldwide have instantaneous access to financial decisions made by governments and can buy and sell currency depending on their assessment of the government's actions, thus changing the value of the currency.[86] Further, '[t]he size and speed of the world financial market doom all types of central bank intervention, over time, to expensive failure . . . there is no way to resign from the Information Standard.[87] Thus, not only is operational sovereignty being undermined, the sovereign ability to decide whether or not to play the game has also disappeared, leading to what Wriston calls the 'twilight of sovereignty'.[88]

Changes in communications, transportation, and production technologies have also deterritorialized production, leading to a globalization of production and allowing TNCs to '[supersede] the traditional political jurisdictions of national scope'.[89] The control of territory is rendered problematic; it has diminished in importance (as well as in fact) as TNCs are able to cross permeable borders as they assemble their products. A particular product sold in the United States by a so-called 'US' company may have been produced partially in Japan, Taiwan, Mexico, Bangladesh, China, Canada and South Korea. With the advent of global Fordism, it is hard to claim that a product is 'Made in the USA', and even those products which have been produced mostly within the territorial boundaries of the US are likely to have been the result of foreign capital and organization, such as Japanese designed and financed cars which are assembled in the United States (and exported back to Japan).[90]

States are still important in coordinating and regulating global commerce and financial flows, although even those countries which have relied heavily on government intervention in the past (such as France and the United Kingdom) have joined more 'liberal' oriented governments (like the United States and Germany) in reducing barriers to global capital flows.[91] Yet, the results have been contradictory, and states have been forced to act in ways – including turning to international institutions –

which undermine their sovereignty. In the Third World, two other issues are particularly important. First, weak developing states are frequently at the mercy of TNCs for foreign capital and technology, which in turn allows these TNCs to have free reign of the country, in some instances plundering them and exporting the profits. At the same time, however, Robert Jackson notes that Third World states do have some control over TNCs, especially in granting initial access to the territory,[92] although this is sometimes undertaken by government elites for personal gain. Regardless, once TNCs are inside a country they frequently have been able to evade any meaningful controls. Second, indebted Third World states are frequently beholden to the World Bank and IMF for funds just to keep afloat and, in many cases, must agree to extreme austerity measures and reorganization as a *quid pro quo,* thus further externalizing control over important economic and social policies, and undermining sovereignty.

In sum, then, in order to coordinate a globalizing economy, power and authority over economic matters have been relocated partially away from states themselves to TNCs and international organizations:

> the sovereign state, though it remains a key instrument for the coordination and expansion of the productive process on a global scale, can no longer perform this function single-handedly. More importantly, the very performance of this function requires the state to act in ways that weaken its claim to sovereignty.[93]

Thus,

> In the second half of the twentieth century we are witnessing the emergence of a complex yet relatively integrated world system which encompasses, and in part operates through, the state system, but whose logic and *modus operandi* are no longer subordinate to the will or organizational priorities of sovereign jurisdictions.[94]

States are also finding themselves unable to adequately ensure security, which is perceived as one of their most important functions. Ephemeral borders have become increasingly permeable to outside threats. Technological advances in the middle decades of the century created weapons with such destructive power that they threaten the very existence of the human race, to say nothing of citizens of particular countries, and states are essentially powerless to counter these weapons. Missile-based nuclear weapons can reach their targets within thirty minutes and, 'Star Wars' notwithstanding, have little possibility of being intercepted. Such weapons could also be floated into the harbour of a major city undetected. Governments have entered into various agreements and alliances (for example

NATO, Warsaw Pact, Helsinki Accords, arms control) to help counteract and defuse such threats. These agreements might also hinder some states' policymaking abilities since states must take into account the wishes of their allies. In addition, international institutions can directly intrude on a state's sovereignty. This was the case as the UN, with little cooperation from Iraq, went through that country to find and destroy all aspects of its nuclear weapons programs, although this might be characterized as nothing more than the victor (of the Gulf War) dictating terms to the vanquished (still an intrusion on sovereignty).

Although states currently have a monopoly on nuclear weapons, they do not have a monopoly on other forms of violence. Reports of the violent activities of terrorist[95] organizations are ubiquitous. Whether it is the IRA exploding a bomb in Piccadilly Circus, Israelis and Arabs and Palestinians killing each other, Pablo Escobar ordering the assassination of public officials in Colombia (or being hounded in a similar fashion by former associates), an Islamic group planting a bomb under the World Trade Center, or a US citizen blowing up a US federal government building, it is obvious that states have lost control of their monopoly of violence. The global arms market is such that almost any weapon can be bought and transported worldwide.

One other issue related to the permeability of borders is that of human migration, and in particular refugees. There are millions of refugees outside their home countries, and an even greater number of people internally displaced within their countries. Tens of millions more are voluntarily working outside of their country of origin. Displacement, both internal and external, is the result of a number of different factors, including war, famine, economic hardship and internal oppression. These issues will be discussed in greater detail in Chapter 3. It will suffice to note here that migration can have disruptive effects in host countries, and even as borders seem increasingly porous, states are expending vast resources in what ultimately may be a losing battle to keep out unwanted migrants. One point with regard to refugee issues is worth mentioning here. Once refugees are within the territory of a country they are legally entitled, under international law, to a hearing to determine whether or not they are entitled to asylum. Thus states have certain obligations to noncitizens within their territory who they might not want to be there in the first place. This certainly can be seen as an encroachment on a state's ability – and even right – to decide who its residents are.

State borders have thus become permeable to both direct and indirect threats and capabilities, as well as by the arrangements made to respond to these threats. As Camilleri and Falk note: 'a great many bilateral and multilateral arrangements – some formal, other informal – have considerably diluted the logic and political force of territorial demarcation.'[96] That is, the way people experience and deal with the world is constrained less and less by a system of sovereign borders.

INTERNATIONAL LAW

The previous section has discussed how state borders have become permeable, especially with respect to changes in technology and humankind's increasing ability to alter the physical environment. However, what has only been mentioned in passing is the relationship of international law to sovereignty. This issue is important in general discussions of sovereignty, as well as to the specific issue of human rights considered in this book.

There are two polar views on the relationship between international law and sovereignty. On the one hand, as noted above one implication of the concept of sovereignty is that the basis of international law – law between sovereign states – is positivistic. That is, states are only bound by what they explicitly agree to. There is no other entity, idea, or force which can bind state activity, especially within territorial borders. Thus international agreements are 'acts of sovereignty', and IGOs are premised on the existence of sovereign states.[97] On the other hand, some view natural law[98] – conceived as coming from a deity or the natural order of things – as a constraint on state behaviour, as well as providing the basis for state authority. Indeed, even Bodin, who believed that a central authority should have unlimited power, conceived of this power as being limited by natural law.

Several observations can be made on this dichotomous understanding of legal constraints on state behaviour. First, identifying law with state consent is much easier than trying to identify the basis for natural law. Yet, accepting positivism means accepting that, in the end, states do not have limits on their power.[99] However, accepting natural law is problematic because its basis cannot be pointed to in any concrete way. Saying it derives from god helps little because there are so many different theological perspectives that saying something derives from god is problematic, if not impossible. Basing law on a supposed natural order of things regardless of the existence or nonexistence of a deity does not get us much further, because a postmodern perspective essentially tells us that we cannot identify an overarching natural order. This may seem to be excessively nihilistic. However, postmodernism can also help us to see that our realities, our ways of interpreting the world are socially constructed, and thus imbued with social purpose. We may thus recognize that any view of law is contingent, but the firmness or ephemeral nature of this contingency is based on the purpose of the idea, structure, or institution we are concerned about. This is as true in law as in other realms: 'State-societies do not have any inherent legal powers. . . . To claim legal power, as much for a state as for any private citizen, is to acknowledge social purpose.'[100] States are conceived of as existing for the security and well being of their inhabitants, which is a social purpose. One might conclude, therefore, that states may be restricted in their conduct at least insofar as they violate this social purpose. This point will be discussed in greater detail below; however, it is enough to note this restriction on state sovereignty.

A second point regarding various understandings of constraints on state behaviour concerns the rights and duties of states within a system of states. As Ingrid Delupis points out:

> since international law regulates the behaviour between members of the society of nations there must necessarily exist some rules, based on reciprocity, which restrain the power of a state within its own territory. A state cannot enjoy its exclusive and general rights within its territory under international law without at the same time assuming corresponding obligations.[101]

States, by virtue of their membership in the club of states, have obligations to the other members of the club and thus restraints on their sovereign power. There is thus a contradiction between sovereignty and membership in international society. Weiss and Chopra sum up this point:

> The supremacy of state sovereignty over law is untenable. Sovereignty as a transcendent source of law is supposed to operate hierarchically between ruler and ruled; it is not supposed to function horizontally, or relatively with other sovereigns. Sovereign equality supposedly prevented developing or legitimating *primus inter pares*. The flaw in the theory of sovereignty is that it was a unitary concept operating in a community: mutual respect implied not being sovereign at all. As such, it is universally recognized that in conflicts between laws of a national sovereign and international law, the latter prevails.[102]

In addition, engaging in activity between states, particularly joining international organizations, can further erode sovereignty. It is true that such institutions are based on the existence of sovereign states. Yet, these institutions are created by states because they recognize there are issues which they cannot adequately address independently, and the arrangements to deal with these issues within the context of international institutions can intrude upon sovereignty, such as majority decision making or the veto in the UN, which allows a group of states, or one state in the case of the veto, to make decisions which are binding on others.[103] In addition, with the proliferation of treaties and organizations, the world has witnessed the formation of what Stanley Hoffman has called 'polycentric steering'.[104] That is, there are now numerous loci of power and authority concerned with various aspects of international life. This is part of the enmeshment from which states no longer have the sovereign ability to leave.

International law recognizes what might be termed 'overlapping sovereignties'. For example, the UN Convention on the Law of the Sea defines who has jurisdiction over what part of the oceans. States have exclusive control over the 12 miles along their shores, except insofar as this is mitigated by a right of passage for foreign ships. In addition, they have exclusive economic control out to 200 miles, although in other respects this is international water. Beyond that lies international water; however, if states want to gain access to minerals and other resources they must petition for such access, and a portion of the proceeds go to the international community. The oceans are thus regarded as the 'common heritage of mankind'. Thus, different parts of the oceans have various and multiple jurisdictions, rather than control by any one sovereign entity.[105]

Another part of the earth which, at least at present, is not subject to sovereign state control is the Antarctic. Under the terms of the 1959 Antarctic Treaty, all territorial claims are indefinitely suspended. In addition, two of the claimant states – France and Australia – have called for the continent to be turned into international wilderness, and other states have indicated an interest in recognizing the Antarctic as the 'common heritage of mankind'.[106]

Off the earth, the use of space is regulated by the international community. The 1967 Treaty on Principles Governing the Activities of States in the Exploration and Use of Outer Space, including the Moon and Other Celestial Bodies, among other things prohibited the placement of nuclear weapons and other weapons of mass destruction in space. Further, the Agreement Governing the Activities of States on the Moon and Other Celestial Bodies prohibits appropriation of the moon by nations or individuals. Rather, it, too, is the common heritage of mankind.[107]

The most fully developed instance of both enmeshment and overlapping sovereignties is the European Union (EU). Through their pursuit of a common currency, common foreign and defence policy, and the dismantling of internal borders, the state members of the EU are creating a new entity, ambiguous in form and goal, leading to a situation where no EU member state 'will be able to reassert the prime attributes of the classic state'.[108] Indeed, Khan asserts that 'the extinction of the nation-state may occur first in Europe, the same continent that created the concept'.[109] Further, in the European Union, there are many different centres of authority, including national and subnational governments, the state-based EU Council of Ministers, and the non-state-based European Commission, the members of which do not represent any government, and which focuses on integrating social and economic policies.[110] Each of these centres or levels or entities has responsibilities which overlap both territorially and functionally with the others.

Thus we can see that there places on (and off) the earth where there is no single sovereign entity in control. There are no clearly defined jurisdictions; rather, there are multiple jurisdictions or places where the international community as a whole has jurisdiction.[111]

International law has also served to ensure the formal sovereignty of many states which have little or no operational sovereignty. Robert Jackson makes a distinction between 'positive' sovereignty and 'negative' sovereignty. Positive sovereignty is a 'substantive rather than formal condition', where states are able to take advantage of their independence, engage in international activity, defend their territory and provide for their citizens. It is a characteristic, particularly, of so-called 'developed' states.[112] Negative sovereignty, on the other hand, is characteristic of states which 'are primarily juridical' and 'far from complete'.[113]

These 'quasi-states' are primarily the result of decolonization which was carried out without regard to whether or not the newly independent states would actually be able to carry out the aforementioned functions of sovereign states. While, as Jackson notes, there have always been empirically weak states, these states are 'exempted from the power contest' between states and treated as international protectorates.[114] In addition, because they are empirically weak they need foreign aid in order to survive. In fact, Kwame Nkrumah, President of Ghana, declared during the 1960s when decolonization was at its peak that decolonized states had a right to development assistance, since colonization was social and economic as well as political.[115] This view was a precursor to the call for a New International Economic Order. Decolonization has thus been somewhat ambiguous. On the one hand, colonized peoples were able to break free from their foreign rulers. Yet, many have also become dependent on those same countries for aid. In addition, many such quasi-states 'are not valuable places for their populations' because they have major problems with human rights abuses.[116] This, in turn, has fostered dramatic increases in the number of displaced people, especially in Africa.[117] The tensions implicit in recognizing a right to self-determination and possible effects on minority populations and human rights will be discussed in Chapter 2.

The important point is that, in some cases, there is such a disjunction between formal and operational sovereignty, as evidenced in quasi-states which are held up by negative sovereignty but possess little positive sovereignty, that the concept of sovereignty itself must be called into question in these circumstances.

SUBNATIONAL AND TRANSNATIONAL ACTORS

I have thus far demonstrated how various factors and processes are eroding sovereignty from outside the state. Equally important are the threats from within, including especially social movements and calls for self-determination.

One increasing encroachment on state authority is what Ivo Duchacek calls 'paradiplomacy'. Paradiplomacy occurs when subnational governmental actors have contact with foreign actors. These contacts might include permanent trade missions, publicized trips, fact-finding missions, participation in trade shows, foreign trade zones, and participation in international conferences or international organizations.[118] Such activity can reflect the inability of national governments to deal with many of the problems of subnational units, and can reflect the 'awareness of subnational vulnerability to extranational, distant events . . . [which have] trickled beyond the borders' as a result of increasing interdependence.[119] Sometimes these contacts are coordinated with central governments and do not conflict with the goals of the governments. Other times, as in the case of Quebec, such activity is, indeed, seen as inimical to the goals of central governments.[120] All of this activity has led to a situation of 'percolated sovereign borders'.[121]

Another challenge to state authority comes from what are called 'new' or 'critical' social movements. These social movements are a response to the expanded scope of the state as it insinuates itself into more realms of personal and social activity and the accompanying breakdown of the consensus of what encompasses the political. In addition, there has been a realization that the pursuit of nonmaterial goods is no longer assured by modern material well being and economic growth, but, rather, is constrained by these developments. There is a focus, in other words, on what Kitscheld has characterized as 'life chance',[122] which encompasses the values of autonomy and identity, 'that state sovereignty can neither satisfy nor contain'.[123] These movements include the women's movement, environmental movement, and various anti-nuclear and peace movements. They are antisystemic, working outside state institutional structures, and thus directly challenge statist conceptions of decision making and, with their focus on autonomy, call into question state authority. '[T]hey are in the process of redefining the meaning and boundaries of civil society. . . . reaffirming the priority of civil society over the state, of popular sovereignty over state sovereignty', and thus perceive the state as useful 'only to the extent that it can be used as a vehicle for the realization of popular sovereignty'.[124]

The rise of such movements has been facilitated by what James Rosenau calls the 'skill revolution'. This process has come about, to a large extent, as a result of the changes in technology discussed above:

Due largely to the advent of powerful new technologies for generating, circulating, sifting, depicting, and storing information, people in every corner of the world are increasingly capable of locating themselves in the course of events, of discerning their own interests in an ever more interdependent and complex world, of tracing complex scenarios in which their micro actions can have macro collective outcomes, of appreciating that sometimes their interests are best served through collective outcomes which enhance their subgroups and that sometimes they are better served by outcomes which reinforce their whole systems, of learning that today's actions can be the source of future problems, of grasping that long-standing habits of compliance are susceptible to transformation, of perceiving the discrepancy between official interpretations and the scenes depicted on their television screens, of emotionally monitoring the moods and orientations of their fellow citizens, and of adapting to rather than denying the presence of fundamental changes.[125]

In other words, there is an increased awareness on the part of large numbers of people 'of their own leverage, of their ability, through joining in collective action, to tip the balance toward either systemic order or subsystemic autonomy'.[126]

Such social movement activity is a large part of what Richard Falk calls 'evasions of sovereignty' – 'political action by nonstate actors that addresses the agenda of global concerns.'[127] These evasions can occur within, across, or beyond boundaries. Within states various Green Parties, while working within state structures, are calling into question state efficacy on a range of issues while espousing a global rather than state-centric ethos. They may have as their goals either reform or transformation of state structures, or a mixture. These individual parties may also be seen as part of a global Green movement. Transnationally, a multitude of groups and movements operate beyond the bounds of state authority. Amnesty

International provides critiques of the human rights practices of all countries around the world. Greenpeace, as a part of the environmental and anti-nuclear movements, poses direct challenges to state practice through both information and direct action, and demonstrates that '[e]copolitcs exceeds the limits of the sovereign state ... [although] ecopolitical action cannot ignore the state'.[128] That states perceive them as threatening can be seen in the 'extraterritorial act of war' on the part of the French government when it blew up Greenpeace's boat *The Rainbow Warrior* which was used in direct action against French nuclear testing in the Pacific. Individuals are thus working increasingly within non-state collectivities which challenge state-centric conceptions of authority and which are 'evading' states' sovereign controls.[129] This, in turn, is having effects on the concept of sovereignty itself:

> The notion of sovereignty as absolute authority exercised by the state as the by-product of an actual or hypothetical social contract is undergoing a profound mutation. Increasingly it is being supplanted by the notion of autonomy, that is the right of individuals and collectivities to pursue their life chances without infringement by other individuals or collectivities, the state included.[130]

Supranational evasions – those beyond boundaries – are not directly connected to social movements and come in two types – involuntary and voluntary. The first type involves state loss of control as a result of processes related to interdependence, such as those having to do with environmental or economic concerns. This includes the transboundary effects of the Chernobyl disaster or Bangladesh's loss of low-lying coastal lands as a result of global warming and Nepalese deforestation to which it has made little contribution. Voluntary supranational evasions involve transferring authority to international institutions in order to deal with involuntary evasions.[131]

Currently, some of the most concrete and problematic threats to sovereignty come from assertions of ethnonationalism and calls for self-determination. Worldwide, many states are being torn apart by communal conflict. Yugoslavia has broken up into several independent, and not so independent, states as a result of secessionist movements and so-called 'ethnic cleansing'. In an astonishingly short period of time, the Soviet Union completely fell apart into its constituent parts; yet, ethnic fighting still threatens the new countries. The 30 year long civil war in Ethiopia recently came to an end, and as a result, Eritrea seceded and became an independent state. Civil war in Somalia has eliminated any idea of internal sovereign control. The Kurds represent a transnational ethnic group seeking self-determination from several states. In Canada, the Quebecois and First Nations, in a much less violent way, are asking for some sort of autonomy from the Canadian government. These few examples are enough to indicate that state sovereignty is under assault from within, and this trend will likely increase.

In 1992, even before the Summer Olympics were over, planners were preparing for more than 200 country delegations for the next Olympics, up from 172. One geographer has estimated that there will be more than 300 states within the next 25 to 30 years.[132] Ernest Gellner has estimated that there are around 800 'effective nationalisms' and something on the order of 8,000 'potential nationalisms' which correspond to the estimated 8,000 languages around the world.[133] At first glance, these trends might indicate nothing more than an increase in states, a reification of borders, and the further triumph of the sovereign state over other forms of political organization. However, these trends and the factors contributing to them are much more ambiguous and contradictory. They reflect, simultaneously, globalizing and localizing trends. On the one hand, we see the effects of economic and technological integration decreasing the importance of borders:

> As we're challenging the traditional ideas of state sovereignty, globalizing economies and communications, and breaking up the last empires, the geography of the world is unhooking old connections and hooking up new ones. Along with borders, the dynamics and functions of states will change too.[134]

At the same time, there have been localizing tendencies which put more focus on smaller and smaller political entities. The skill revolution has enabled individuals and social movements to question and challenge state authority. The end of the Cold War has unleashed ethnonational sentiments which were buried by decades of bipolarity. Unlike the decolonization era when self-determination was equated with the creation of states within colonial borders, current movements are challenging some of those borders as well as others, particularly within Europe and the former Soviet Union. Thus, to a certain extent, the focus has moved from the south to the north, and identity corresponds more with the nation than with the state.[135] Many people perceive that current levels of authority are too far away from their experiences and thus cannot respond to their needs, that the social and cultural identities of smaller communities are being marginalized within large states: 'People want empowerment at the local level. When they feel their lives are being run by others far away who can't identify with them, they retreat into regionalism and local identities to counter the dehumanizing effect.'[136] Further, 'these governments will be closer to people where it counts on issues of culture, education, languages'.[137]

This is leading toward a devolution of authority from large central governments to, in some cases, smaller central governments, and, in other cases, local non-central governments. In other words, while some calls for self-determination are leading to independent states, others will result in some as yet undetermined form of autonomy. Some smaller political communities may, as a result of membership in regional blocs and other more global institutions, be able to make it on their own away from their former affiliations with larger states. Others, however, will (have to) be content with various forms of autonomy within the context of larger states. With more and more authority and allegiance being associated with smaller entities, the notion of a central government possessing absolute sovereignty within its territorial boundaries becomes increasingly problematic: 'The notion of boundaries as we've known them, in terms of absolute sovereignty and legalities, will in time dwindle.'[138]

Calls for self-determination have thus begun to challenge 'unfettered state sovereignty'.[139] Even further, however, self-determination and the other trends discussed in the preceding pages are leading to changes in the functions and dynamics of the state.

CHANGING FUNCTIONS AND DYNAMICS OF THE STATE

Camilleri and Falk point to three functions of the modern state. First is the 'organization of space'. The locus of community is territorial, which is theoretically permanent. Continuity is prized over transformation. Second, the state performs an economic function, supporting property and other rights, providing a medium of exchange, and creating the infrastructure necessary for economic development. Third, the state has had a cultural function, responding to the growth of nationalism by joining culture and politics, although this has not happened evenly.[140]

Yet, these functions are increasingly problematic as states are decreasingly able to perform them. Control over territory does not mean what it used to.[141] States cannot control their borders against many outside threats, such as environmental degradation. In addition, authority which had been associated with territorially defined entities is being relocated to other, frequently transnational, entities. Economically, too, the state is becoming increasingly irrelevant. Money moves electronically across permeable borders, and production is deterritorialized. State control over the value of its currency, and along with it the value of its exports and cost of its imports, and therefore a large part of its economic well-being, is being eroded by the global market place. And, in many instances, states have failed in their cultural function. The recent outbreaks of communal assertions demonstrate that culture and politics have not been joined successfully at the state level; rather, some cultural expressions have been marginalized by political practices within states.

Although Rosenau asserts that the state is 'on the edge of collapse',[142] he also notes that the trends are somewhat more contradictory. The state is, indeed, being undermined from within by 'subgroupism' and the skill revolution. Yet, the state has insinuated itself into domestic economic life, and modern technology has allowed states to further control its citizens and keep order. At the same time, however, states have not been able to deal with many problems such as unemployment, poverty, and pollution. In addition, even as the state has become further enmeshed within its domestic economy, global enmeshment has undermined its control. This is part of what he calls 'cascading interdependence' – communities have become linked, distances have shrunk, and the line between domestic and foreign have become increasingly blurred. Thus, the state's competence is both 'widening' and 'withering,' and the processes which accompany each also contribute to the other.[143] Likewise, Camilleri notes 'on the one hand, a growing web of international interdependencies and, on the other, increased centralization of national institutions and decision making processes'. They are 'inextricably intertwined and mutually reinforcing' and, insofar as they blur the distinction between foreign and domestic, 'call into question the traditional understanding of state sovereignty'.[144]

Others also see contradictory tendencies. Richard Falk sees resilience in the state system. Technology has expanded state power, and this power has been used to shore up dominant nationalisms while it suppresses or marginalizes insurgent nationalisms. In addition, the war system – the institutionalization of war and preparations for war – has buttressed the state system by stabilizing the system of territorial-defined entities which claim sovereignty.[145] Yet, the state 'has become virtually a mirage'.[146] As a result of the (declining) bloc system, 'states have lost control of their destiny on issues of war and peace', and citizens have become nuclear hostages.[147] In addition, 'the state is losing its monopoly over law-making' and its ability to use its formal structures to gain compliance from its citizens. Externally, autonomous groups are challenging state activity, especially in the areas of security policy and human rights, and bringing to light state abuses: 'These various activities express, among other things, a loss of confidence in the existing machinery of government to address the normative failures of statism, as well as the legitimacy of spontaneous additions to "government" by societal initiative.' In addition, within domestic legal structures, individuals and groups challenge state policy, especially activity which is illegal in international law. While this may seem inconsequential, such actions do demonstrate that the state is losing legitimacy and the ability to coerce some of its citizens to acquiesce in its 'dirty work'.[148]

The above analysis leads to the conclusion that, although the state has expanded its capabilities for control and involvement in some areas, overall the trend has been toward the 'diminution of state authority'.[149] Authority has been relocated both upward to various international institutions which help states deal with various issues, and downward as individuals and groups assert themselves in myriad ways and toward multiple goals. Thus, the 'emergent global system rests on an increasingly fluid pecking order'.[150] All of this serves to undermine state sovereignty. Further, Rosenau postulates that all of this turbulence has resulted in a bifurcated global system 'in which actors in the state-centric world compete, cooperate, interact, or otherwise coexist with counterparts in a multicentric world comprised of a vast array of diverse transnational, national, and subnational actors.'[151] In this conception of global interaction 'sovereignty-free' collectivities (non-state actors) compete with 'sovereignty-bound' (state) actors.[152] This formulation is useful in identifying the ways in which the sovereignty discourse is being undermined and non state actors are challenging states in significant and meaningful ways on the global stage and reinforces the idea that state authority is being undermined and relocated and, consequently, that sovereignty is not what it used to be.

HUMAN RIGHTS

Thus far I have examined how state sovereignty is being undermined in a number of different contexts, including technological change, the permeability of borders, the creation of international institutions, and the relocation of authority and allegiance to non state actors. However, the most fundamental issue regarding sovereignty is that of the relation of individuals to sovereign entities and their rights contained in this relationship. Since the first formulations of sovereignty were put forward there have been debates regarding what limits the sovereignty entity – the state – has in its dealings with its citizens. In other words, do people have rights beyond what the state grants them? If these rights do exist who has the right to ensure that they are upheld? The latter question will be dealt with below and in even greater detail in Chapter 4. The previous question can be answered in the affirmative without much hesitation. Why this is so can be investigated from two different perspectives, corresponding to the sources of law discussed above.

First, while contending that the source of natural law is hard to identify, I argued that, instead, if we accept that our realities are socially constructed, we can examine the social purpose of our ideas and institutions for a (contingent) ground for law. In this way, by looking at the social purposes of the (denaturalized) sovereign state, we can interrogate what limits this puts on this social creation.

Theoretically, states exist for the well-being of their inhabitants. The primary function of states is that of protection. In other words, the state exists to ensure that its citizens are able to live their lives free from the fear that an outside force will interrupt their lives. A reasonable extension of this would be that the inhabitants of a state should also be as free from internal persecution as from external persecution. Thus, the social function of states is to ensure the ability of people to live.

If, then, the state exists only for the purpose of enabling the individuals who comprise the state to live their lives relatively peacefully, and for no other purpose, then one cannot say that sovereignty ultimately rests with the state. Rather, it rests with individuals within the state. They may turn over part of their sovereignty to the state as a condition for protection and to enable the state to engage in activities which will provide for various needs of the individuals, but, ultimately, this is only a loan which, theoretically, can be called in whenever the state is not fulfilling the conditions implicit in the loan.[153]

If sovereignty rests with individuals what does this actually mean? In other words, are there certain rights which go along with this sovereignty – fundamental human rights? Recognizing the state as a socially constructed institution with the social purpose of providing security for its inhabitants would be incomprehensible without at the same time linking that social purpose to each and every individual within its realm. In other words, since the social purpose of the state is to enable its citizens to live, then it makes sense to recognize that social purpose as a right for each person.

Thus, the right to live is the most basic right. In addition, one might expand the concept to include the right to live in a certain way. One part of this right would be freedom from torture and other persecution – such as unwarranted detention, discrimination, or mass movements of populations, which, while not necessarily threatening the actual life of an individual, precludes the individual from using his or her right to live. Further expanding this right would include the right to what Michael Walzer calls a 'common life' – in other words the right to self-determination, the ability to decide how you will lead your life politically, socially and culturally. There are, of course, limits to this, especially when one group's 'common life' infringes on another group's 'common life'. This probably comes closest to the true meaning of the nation-state – a group of people who have certain things in common socially, culturally, and linguistically and who have established a 'common life' together. Territorial boundaries might (contingently) be put around this group to protect the inhabitants' freely chosen, non-infringing way of life.[154] The concept of self-determination and the multiple meanings it may have will be discussed in much greater detail in Chapter 2. What is important here is that if a government violated any of these rights – and therefore was not carrying out its social function – it could be declared illegitimate and the people could call in their loan of sovereignty. Philip Allott provides a similar view:

> If you claim to have a legal power, if you seek to act on the basis of a legal power, you acknowledge the legal system which creates the power and which confers it on you, and you acknowledge that the power is in principle limited, and you acknowledge the specific limits of the power.[155]

Those who are acting within the realm of the socially constructed state must accept the purposes of that entity in order to be able to claim legitimacy for their actions.

Some might argue that the notion of 'rights' is quintessentially modern, that it derives from the Western, rationalistic, absolutist project to identify a natural order of things, including natural human rights. This may be true. However, a notion of rights can also be seen in its relation with our socially created realities. In other words, there is something prior to the state which comes into being along with the state and which, as Lefort suggests, is 'constitutive of politics'.[156] Human rights, when put in opposition to the state, is 'the enemy of power'.[157] There is thus a separation between power and right.[158] In other words, power does not define right. Instead, 'the notion of human rights now points towards a sphere that cannot be controlled; right comes to represent something which is ineffaceably external to power'.[159] Thus, the notion of rights can be upheld at least insofar as these rights are seen in opposition to socially created power. In addition, as suggested above, I want to invoke a postmodern critique as a corrective to other discourses. I do not want to make postmodernism a totalizing discourse to the exclusion of others. Rather, I want to rescue what it is useful from other discourses, including the (still somewhat undefined and problematic) notion of human rights, and use it as a basis for further discussion, rather than nihilistically erasing everything.

A constructivist reading of human rights thus tells us that these rights can be derived from the social purpose of the institution against which they are arrayed – the state. A positivist approach, on the other hand, tells us what rights people have as a result of state *practice* rather than state *purpose*. A positivist approach is useful as a complement to a constructivist approach in two regards. First, most people looking at the issue of human rights – at least most state elites – do not employ constructivist analysis. Rather, they look at what conventions have been signed, what declarations have been agreed to, and what treaties are in force when looking at the application of human rights law. Second, turning to these various sources of human rights law allows us to get a better sense of how human rights might be enumerated and how they might be carried out in practice.

A first step in examining the relationship between positive human rights law and sovereignty might be to enumerate the major conventions agreed to by states. The core around which human rights law is formed is the Universal Declaration of Human Rights (UDHR) adopted by the United Nations in 1948. It describes itself as 'a common standard of achievement for all peoples and nations' and is not binding in the same manner as formal treaties (although all members of the UN supposedly accept its contents). However, W. Michael Reisman argues that it is 'now accepted as declaratory of customary international law'.[160] Delupis notes that the UDHR is perceived as having 'considerable authority'[161] and 'lays down rules which, irrespective of whether they are embodied in a binding document or not, are binding as customary international law'.[162] There are many other agreements and declarations within and outside the UN framework which further expand the rights of people and duties of states. Within the UN, these include the International Covenant on Economic, Social, and Cultural Rights; the International Covenant on Civil and Political Rights; the International Convention on the Elimination of all Forms of Racial Discrimination; the Convention on the Elimination of All Forms of Discrimination against Women; the Convention against Torture and Other Cruel, Inhuman or Degrading Treatment or Punishment; the International Convention on the Suppression and Punishment of the Crime of *Apartheid;* and the Convention on the Prevention and Punishment of the Crime of Genocide. Regional frameworks in Europe, Africa, and the Americas also provide for the protection of human rights. Most recently, the 171 states at the 1993 World Conference on Human Rights reaffirmed, in the Vienna Declaration, the universality of human rights, and recognized that 'the promotion and protection of all human rights is a legitimate concern of the international community'.[163]

These agreements provide for various degrees of bindingness and remedies. Certain human rights have achieved the status of *jus cogens,* or principles from which there can be derogation. This includes prohibitions against genocide, torture and slavery. No state can violate these principles, regardless of whether or not they have explicitly bound themselves by these principles: 'No state can rightly believe after the Nürnberg trials that international law, in the absence of treaties, contains no rules which forbid atrocities and genocide.'[164] Thus, human rights principles – as well as other principles within international law – can be binding on states without specific assent on the part of states. As Jackson notes, '[l]egal positivism offers no escape from civilized standards'.[165]

The implications of this are clear. If states can be thus bound, part of their sovereignty has been eroded. States are restricted from engaging in certain activities within their territorial boundaries and, further, as Article 21(3) of the UDHR states, they are beholden to their populations: 'The will of the people shall be the basis of the authority of government.' In addition, Article 22 says:

> Everyone, as a member of *society,* has the right to social security and is entitled to realization, through national effort and international cooperation and in accordance with the organization and resources of each State, of the economic, social and cultural rights indispensable for his [or her] dignity and the free development of his [or her] personality. (italics added)

This article also specifically relates to the earlier argument regarding rights deriving from participation in a socially constructed entity, in this case *society,* with a social purpose. In any case, with the recognition of customary restraints within international law and *jus cogens* principles, '[i]n international law, the sovereign [has] finally been dethroned'.[166]

If the sovereign has been dethroned, who or what has taken its place, if indeed anything has? A partial answer can be provided now. As Reisman points out:

> Although the venerable term 'sovereignty' continues to be used in international legal practice, its referent in modern international law is quite different. International law still protects sovereignty, but – not surprisingly – it is the people's sovereignty rather than the sovereign's sovereignty.[167]

That is, 'the people, not governments, are sovereign'.[168] This is still problematic, and will be considered below in the context of self-determination. However, these statements help us to understand, first, that individuals are subjects of international law in a way they were not when sovereignty was first conceived, and second, that states, while still significant subjects of international law, have lost some of their standing.

In other words, international law, itself, is evolving with respect to its referents. That is, there is an expanded set of subjects of international law. This includes, international organizations, which have gained a certain amount of legal personality. Further, individuals are increasingly recognized as possessing international legal personality: 'While human rights law has not been as successfully enforced as was hoped, there is little disagreement about the principle that individuals are the repositories of international legal rights.'[169]

The last point to be made here is that, as with the other aspects of sovereignty discussed above, the dividing line between international law and domestic law is becoming increasingly blurred.[170] And, as this line erodes, the principle of non-intervention which has been the link between the internal and external dimensions of sovereignty correspondingly weakens. The international community which recognizes human rights has a right to violate this principle. As former UN Secretary-General Javier Perez de Cuellar has pointed out:

> The case for not impinging on the sovereignty, territorial integrity and political independence of States is by itself indubitably strong. But it would only be weakened if it were to carry the implication that sovereignty . . . includes the right of mass slaughter or of launching systematic campaigns of decimation or forced exodus of civilian populations in the name of controlling civil strife or insurrection.
>
> . . . It must first of all be recognized just how revolutionary an idea this is. . . . Indeed, does it not call into question one of the cardinal principles of international law, namely, the obligation of non-interference in the internal affairs of states?[171]

Further, not only is there a right to violate formerly inviolable borders, there is a responsibility, for, as Walzer points out: 'If rights don't require us to intervene . . . then it is difficult to see why they should be called rights'.[172] This will be discussed further below. The task right now is to discover what all of this means for the concept of sovereignty.

THE NEW SOVEREIGNTY

The preceeding pages have provided an overview of the ways sovereignty has been chipped away, both from the outside, as technological changes increased the permeability of borders, and from within, as human rights are recognized as trumping the right of states to engage in many activities which violate these rights. In a similar fashion, we can conceive of any reconceptualization of sovereignty as moving both downward (inward) from the state incorporating both human and 'peoples' rights and upward (outward) from the state as we look for ways to respond to the need to protect these rights within a global framework as well as respond to the increasing permeability of borders.

Such a reconceptualization also joins a debate about what kind of form sovereignty may be permitted to take. Weiss and Chopra point out that there are two ways sovereignty can be conceived. First, there is a legal interpretation: 'Under international law, there are not degrees of sovereignty; it either exists or it does not. . . . Legal sovereignty cannot be partially redefined or refined.'[173] The second is a political interpretation. Sovereignty's limits are determined subjectively and its meaning is contextual. It allow for degrees of sovereignty: 'it is possible to be *more* or *less* sovereign'.[174] The former is too confining; it is tied to an old order, rather than allowing for the changing circumstances of the emerging global order. Thus the second, more fluid, formulation of sovereignty must be used because it recognizes changing circumstances, new global and subnational actors, and new and variable contexts.

Moving downward requires looking at two different aspects: people and peoples. The first relates to individuals and their rights as humans, and the second relates to collectivities of people – ethnic groups and nationalities – and their rights as collectivities. Beginning with the first aspect, I have established that individuals have certain rights as humans and, further, these rights are beyond the state. The state may hold these rights in trust, but cannot violate these rights for *raison d'état*. In addition, individuals are not only protected from abuse and assured of some basic protections, 'the people' are seen as sovereign. This is the concept of 'popular sovereignty' – the state must be beholden to the people. As the UDHR states, the basis of authority is the will of the people. It determines a state's legitimacy: 'Political legitimacy arises from the people's will – it does not descend deductively from the Westphalian principles of state sovereignty.'[175] Of course, determining the will of the people is problematic. To a large extent this leads to various conceptions of democracy to determine this will.[176] Regardless, the state is nothing more than the sum of its parts.

So far I have identified two different building blocks of sovereignty. First, individuals have human rights, which must be upheld by any entity claiming sovereignty. Second, the authority of a state is derived from the popular sovereignty of the people. If either of these are violated we might call the legitimacy of a state into question. In other words, there are two constitutive principles of state legitimacy – human rights and popular sovereignty. A third, less identifiable, constitutive principle relates to the concept of 'peoples' and their relationship with the state. This can be thought of either in terms of a dichotomy between the 'nation-state' where 'nation' and 'state' are one and multinational states, or within a framework which recognizes the multinational character of most states. The former says there must be a one-to-one correlation between nation and state for a 'people' to have self-determination. In this regard it is too atomistic and rigid, assuming there is an identifiable endpoint for self-determination and thus for the full realization of cultural expression and human rights. The latter, on the other hand, recognizes that most states – both peaceful and democratic, and strife-torn and authoritarian – are multinational and that self-determination does not, in all cases, necessarily mean a separate independent state. Rather, it might be tied more to process and autonomy.

During the period of decolonization after World War II, nationalism was tied to state building which, in turn, was seen as a necessary component of the decolonization process. The colonies were given independence which meant sovereignty. Furthermore, such sovereignty was seen as necessary for self-determination and ensuring that the former colonial masters did not reassert their domination. In Jackson's terms they were provided with negative sovereignty. There was nothing else which the colonial populations could conceive of as ensuring their independence. Over the few decades since decolonization began, self-determination has come to be synonymous with maintaining state forms within colonial borders. Thus, ' "territorial integrity" has all but replaced "national self-determination" as the watch-word of the post-colonial era'.[177] The most illuminating example is in Africa. The 1963 Charter of the Organization of African Unity (OAU) recognizes the equal sovereignty of all of its members and requires nonintervention and respect of borders.[178] Further, in 1981 the African heads of state adopted the Banjul Charter on Human and People's Rights. As Jackson notes, "peoples" are the populations of states (or colonies) considered as a collectivity whose rights are exercised by governments'.[179] The term 'peoples' has been divorced from ethnic or cultural meanings and has come to denote the population within a state no matter how diverse in terms of ethnicity, culture, or nationality, thus perverting the concept of self-determination and, at the same time, condemning populations to human rights abuse within quasi-states.[180] In fact, the only two instances where self-determination has been seen as overriding established sovereign arrangements are in Israel, where Palestinians are just now gaining a measure of autonomy, and in South Africa, where the first nonracial elections were finally held in 1994.[181]

And yet, the governments of many of these former colonies, as well as some in the non-colonial world, have not been able to keep a handle on sub-state self-determination movements: '*Governments are losing control of the minds of their citizens.* Suppressed nationalisms, including passionate regionalisms, are asserting themselves everywhere. Suppressed religions are reasserting themselves.'[182] These movements are threats to both the temporal and spatial aspects of state sovereignty. Temporally, state sovereignty assumes, especially within the context of decolonization, that state borders, once set, will not be altered at some later point. Spatially, self-determination movements threaten both the internal and external borders of established states. These challenges from within lead to one of the main questions the international community will have to face in the years ahead: does self-determination imply a right to statehood, and if so, what criteria should be used, and if not, what other accommodations can be used to deal with such claims? This issue will be dealt with in more detail in Chapter 2, but I will provide a first take on the issue right now.

The right to self-determination is ambiguous. On the one hand, as Lapidoth notes, 'The right of peoples to self-determination seems to be generally accepted.'[183] What this actually means, however, is not clear. Many declarations and conventions have recognized this right.[184] Yet, to a large extent, this has been confined to the right for those under colonial control to be free of such control within the context of their own states defined by colonial borders, and state practice since then has reified those borders against other claims for self-determination.[185] Thus, self-determination of 'peoples' – defined as anybody living within the borders of a former colonial entity – requires the denial of ethnic self-determination as resulting in a separate state.[186]

Yet, this formulation is unduly arbitrary in that it does not recognize that current forms of ethnic and cultural domination within current states can be just as severe as those which legitimated decolonization. However, the unfettered right to self-determination as secession could wreak havoc, lead to hundreds of more states, and may also have negative consequences for many minorities. Thus, as I will argue in Chapter 2, while all people and 'peoples' have the right to self-determination, this can and should only sometimes lead to the establishment of an independent state. Other forms of self-determination must be envisioned and explored, for self-determination should be thought of more as an ongoing process rather than as a definite end result.

This process might be encapsulated within various autonomous relationships. Autonomy is what many groups are agitating for right now, and it does not necessarily mean independence: 'Rather, achieving autonomy means being free to select the ways in which interdependence with other individuals, groups, provinces, states, and international organizations is established.'[187] While there are still problems with such an approach, including preserving the rights of minorities within such arrangements, as well as how to achieve agreement by the many parties involved, it recognizes a useful way of approaching the problem which prevents the formation of an unwieldy number of independent states, many of whom would not be able sustain themselves (as some cannot do today).

Another way of dealing with some of the more extreme problems of ethnic conflict and the dissolution of sovereign authority might be some sort of international trusteeship. Independent states were supposed to be a remedy for such arrangements during decolonization.[188] However, there may be some instances where at least temporary UN trusteeship may be appropriate. Some have called for the United Nations to take over administration of Somalia – in which there is no identifiable sovereign control – for a while in order to end the fighting, deal with the severe humanitarian conditions and try to get the country to some degree of stability. Certain administrative activities were carried out by the UN in Cambodia as it prepared for elections and authority was reconstructed in that country. And the UN recently supervised elections in a number of countries, including Haiti and Nicaragua.[189]

Both of these types of arrangements – autonomy and trusteeship – are incompatible with identifying sovereignty solely with a central authority in an independent state, and thus undermine monolithic conceptions of sovereignty. Yet, the idea of autonomy and its relationship to self-determination helps us to get a handle on the third building block of sovereignty – that of the relationship between 'peoples' and sovereignty.

The next step is to determine how to move upward from the state in ensuring that the various conceptions of human and peoples' rights are upheld and how to deal with the increasing permeability of borders. In other words, what kinds of authority might be relocated to supranational organizations?

I have noted above a wide range of areas in which borders have become so permeable that states are unable to exercise sovereign control in many ways. In some instances states have turned to various international organizations to deal with the new realities. For example, the International Telecommunications Union (ITU) was formed to allocate frequencies for communications. States created the General Agreement on Tariffs and

Trade (GATT) (and recently the World Trade Organization) to deal with a multitude of issues related to increasing economic interdependence. Security organizations such as NATO and the Warsaw Pact (as well as the United Nations) were formed out of the realization that states could not ensure their own security by themselves. Global environmental concerns have prompted states to create a wide range of institutions related to the environment. The Earth Summit in Rio in 1992 demonstrated that states recognize the serious nature of transborder threats. Yet, a number of useful agreements were doomed or changed because one state – the US – wielded an effective veto over their implementation. Attempts to relocate authority upward from the state have had varying success. However, as the previous discussion of enmeshment suggested, the overall trend has been toward such relocation as states have been forced to enter into various arrangements as a result of interdependence and, over time, have been increasingly unable to leave such arrangements. The process may seem contradictory, but the overall trend seems clear.

The trend with regard to humanitarian issues is contradictory as well. However, developments over the last few decades have indicated both the need, and an increasing willingness, to deal with humanitarian issues. The need, which almost always comes before the willingness, arises both from the human rights violations themselves, as well as the increasing internationalization of humanitarian crises. I have identified two different ways to arrive at various conceptions of human rights. Overall, a wide variety of rights have been generally recognized. In addition, wars, natural disasters, oppression, and maldistribution of resources have all created situations in which grave humanitarian situations have spilled over borders. The most vivid and far-reaching instances are when war and famine induce refugees to pour across borders by the thousands and millions seeking food and protection from the violence. The problem is how to prevent this from happening in the first place, and how to deal with it when it does.

The sovereignty claimed by states and the corresponding unwillingness of the international community to infringe upon this sovereignty have been the major impediments to dealing with some of these issues in an effective manner. Chapter 4 deals with the question of humanitarian intervention, and in Chapter 5 I examine in more detail what institutional changes may be needed to respond more effectively to humanitarian crises. For the moment, however, I will discuss how we should think about such changes. Providing for a principle whereby the international community can intervene in humanitarian crises requires a conceptual shift in our thinking about the relationship between the individual and the global community. I have argued that the relationship between the individual and the national community – the state – is one where individuals are constitutive of state authority. Yet, the place of the individual in the world as a whole is still murky. The space outside national boundaries is perceived as somehow different from the space enclosed by constructed, yet ephemeral, boundaries. Is this necessarily the case? Of course not. Those in power over the centuries have created an illusion of an 'inside' and an 'outside'. Inside the state, there is a feeling of belonging (usually) and a feeling that 'we're all in it together', and there are generally limits on state action. Outside, there is not the same feeling of comradeship and the limits on state action are not the same.

Yet, this dichotomy is contingent, not natural. Benedict Anderson writes that national communities are 'imagined communities' which are 'both inherently limited and sovereign'. The nation 'is *imagined* because the members of even the smallest nation will never know most of their fellow-members, meet them, or even hear of them, yet in the minds of each lives the image of their communion'.[190] These communities, however much power they may have over their citizens, are ideas, constructed within the minds of those citizens. There is nothing 'natural' about them, although they may seem as such. And, national communities are just one of a number of communities we each recognize as having some sort of claim to our loyalties. We may say 'my country right or wrong', but we also may have similar feelings about our state or province, our region, our city, our neighbourhood, or even non-territorially-bound entities. Some of these might even be more important than our particular country. So why not also go the other way? A feeling of being European exists along with nationalist sentiment within the particular countries that comprise Europe. And Europe is just as much a creation as is France or Germany. It should not, then, be too great a step to also imagine the entire earth as an encompassing community.[191] In fact, one could make the case that this would be much more natural than, say, Kenya or Costa Rica. We still would not be familiar with most of the people within this imagined community; rather, just the scale would be different. Further, this would not be our only allegiance; we could still keep our other allegiances to our nation, our province, our city. What would change is that those who are now citizens could also be considered as humans. We would have 'dethroned the statist paradigm'[192] where people are defined in relation to their state rather than in relation to each other.

I will take one other step in this constructivist view of community. Above, human rights were tied to the social purpose of the state. Similarly, we can investigate the social purposes of international institutions. These institutions are created by states in order to deal with interdependence and permeable borders. States, as established above, have as their social purpose providing a decent environment for the individuals within the borders of the state to live. Since international institutions are created by entities with a social purpose, they must also be tied in with that social purpose. Thus, individuals can be connected to international institutions and to each other within a framework which recognizes them as humans as well as citizens. They are citizens within a global community as well as within national (and other) communities, and this means that the global community has certain responsibilities to its citizens, regardless of the (imagined) state in which they reside.

One can also examine this issue from a positivist approach, determining how state practice might also lead to the same conclusion that the global community has obligations to its citizens and thus the authority to ignore national boundaries. As a starting point, I will turn to the various declarations, agreements and conventions discussed above which enumerate a wide range of rights. They provide a positive basis for the investigation of the responsibilities and rights of the international community with regard to such human rights. State declarations on the subject are contradictory. For example, Myanmar's (a major human rights abusing state) Foreign Minister, U Ohn Gyaw, stated before the UN General Assembly that: 'A clear line must be drawn between internationally binding human rights norms and the modality of their implementation, which is the primary responsibility of the Member State.'[193] The Foreign Minister from Indonesia (another major abuser of human rights), Ali Alatas, told the General Assembly that:

> Basic human rights and fundamental freedoms are unquestionably of universal validity. . . . However, it is also commonly agreed that their implementation in the *national* context should remain the competence and responsibility of each Government, while taking into account the complex variety of problems, of diverse value systems and of different economic, social and cultural realities prevailing in each country.
>
> This national competence not only derives from the principle of sovereignty, but is also a logical consequence of the inherent right of nations to their national and cultural identity and to determine their own social an economic systems.[194]

Many other countries, including China, Uganda, and India (also violators of human rights to varying degrees) have also voiced opposition to granting the international community as a whole the right to violate state sovereignty in order to protect human rights.[195]

Other state representatives have argued the opposite. The Foreign Minister from Italy, Gianni de Michelis, told the General Assembly in 1991:

Intervention that is primarily aimed at securing protection of human rights and respect for basic principles of peaceful coexistence is a prerogative of the international community, which must have the power to suspend sovereignty whenever it is exercised in a criminal manner.[196]

Regarding the demarcation of the line between those matters which are seen as 'essentially domestic' and thus beyond the purview of the UN (usually seen as everything but military security issues) and non-domestic matters, the President of the Security Council stated in January 1992 that: 'The non-military sources of instability in the economic, social, *humanitarian* and ecological fields have become threats to peace and security.'[197]

This attitude was evident (to a certain extent) in the actions on behalf of the Kurds in Northern Iraq in 1991. Security Council Resolution 688 was the framework in which the aid and protection activities were taken out. It insisted 'that Iraq allow immediate access by international humanitarian organizations to all those in need of assistance in all parts of Iraq and to make available all necessary facilities and operations'. Supporters of the resolution stated that Resolution 688 was not a violation of sovereignty; rather it upheld sovereignty and protected human rights at the same time. As Weiss and Chopra point out: 'They [supporters of 688] did, however, link human rights with international peace and security. Failure to protect the Kurds would threaten the security and sovereignty of neighbouring countries, which in turn would similarly threaten Iraq further.'[198] Rather than identifying human rights by itself as legitimizing such activities, human rights was tied to the recognition of interdependence and permeability of borders, particularly in the form of refugee flows. Further, although it was not portrayed as a violation of sovereignty, this is, in fact, what it was. The international community engaged in activity which went against the wishes of the identifiable central authority – Saddam Hussein – within the country. Following the lines of an earlier argument, Hussein's legitimacy and claim to such authority may have also been called into question by the gross violations of human rights perpetrated by his regime. Thus, either Hussein's sovereign authority was violated or that authority was not valid in the first place. In either case, the principle of sovereignty was undermined.

Resolution 688 can also be seen as part of an expanding right to humanitarian aid. The General Assembly adopted Resolution 43–131 in December 1988 'which formally recognized the rights of civilians to international aid and the role of nongovernmental organizations in natural disasters'. It also adopted Resolution 45–100 in 1990 which 'reaffirmed these rights and provided specific access to corridors of "tranquillity" for humanitarian aid workers.'[199] In addition, France has taken the position that no permission is required to provide aid.[200]

The brief discussion above notes contradictory statements and actions with regard to the right of the international community to ignore state borders in defending human rights. Yet, activities and resolutions by the United Nations (made up of state actors) point to a trend of a right on the part of the international community to violate sovereignty in order to protect human rights. The actions have not always been put in such explicit terms, but the outcomes have, indeed, been violations of sovereignty for humanitarian purposes.

In addition, even those who maintained that the state level was more appropriate for upholding human rights (a view which essentially denies the universal applicability of human rights norms) also recognized the validity of human rights standards, creating a contradiction. This contradiction can be reconciled by recognizing that standards which are seen as valid must constrain the activity of those it is aimed at and that the body or forum in which these binding standards or norms were created must have a right to uphold these norms or they are worthless:

> Law constrains or it is a travesty to call it law. Law enters decisively into the willing of its subjects or it is a travesty to call it law. Law transcends the power of the powerful [states] and transforms the situation of the weak or it is a travesty to call it law. A legal system which does its best to make sense of murder, theft, exploitation, oppression, abuse of power, and injustice, perpetrated by public authorities in the public interest, is a perversion of a legal system.[201]

State rhetoric, along with more contradictory state practice, upholds the universal[202] applicability of human rights norms. In addition, the very purpose of these norms should render problematic *national* as opposed to *international* implementation of such norms. Further, above, individuals were placed within a global community with a social purpose of providing for the security of such individuals. The preceding analysis provides a basis for global action to protect human rights. And this, along with the preceding building blocks of sovereignty from below the state level, provides us with the foundation for a reconceptualization of sovereignty: The New Sovereignty.

At this point, one might question why, with the previous constructivist critique of sovereignty, is it necessary to keep any notion of sovereignty whatsoever? After all, since sovereignty is a social creation, can we not just get rid of sovereignty once and for all and come up with something else? What I would like to suggest is that recognizing the artificiality and contingency of our socially created realities does not mean that we cannot reappropriate the positive features of our social artefacts and put them to good use. Richard Falk notes that a postmodern outlook can be

> reconstructionist, optimistic, normative. It does not at all repudiate rationality and the benefits of modernity but seeks to supersede their negative features. A postmodern possibility implies the human capacity to transcend the violence, poverty, ecological decay, oppression, injustice, and secularism of the modern world.[203]

We can overcome modernist failures 'associated with artificial and constraining boundaries on *imagination* and *community*', and "reinvent" reality in more holistic, less hierarchical imagery'.[204] We can take sovereignty, banish the constraining boundaries within which supreme power has been formulated and practiced to the ash heap of history, and then take the remaining notions of reconstructed authority and put them back together in a concept which is less centralized and which takes seriously the needs and rights of those who create and are the objects of sovereignty – people.

Sovereignty, as both authority and capability to carry out authority, cannot be located in any one place, that is the state. A concept which attempts to recognize that there are, in fact, numerous types of community which all have a claim on the allegiances of their shared members must accept this basic point.

There are three different building blocks of sovereignty below the level of the state. These are human rights, popular sovereignty, and a more nebulous concept of self-determination and peoples' rights. Upholding human rights must be the goal of any community which seeks to lay a valid claim to authority. Further, that claim must be grounded in the will of the people – or popular sovereignty – although the means of determining the will of the people is still somewhat problematic. In addition, within any entity with a claim to authority there must be mechanisms by which various groups are able to determine their way of life within certain parameters. In other words, when necessary, there must be provided various forms of autonomy (or partial sovereignty) from a central authority. Thus, already I have identified a number of different centres of sources of sovereignty.

In addition, I have demonstrated how states have turned over some of their sovereignty (willingly and unwillingly) to levels above the state. The European Union, however contradictory its development is right now, is a case in point at the regional level. Globally, various organizations and institutions, most notably the United Nations, have, to differing degrees, authority over their constituent parts – states. Sovereignty has also been taken from states by various nonterritorial actors. For example, states, however much they try to regain it, have lost much of their control over their economies to currency traders and TNCs, as well as to other states. Finally, states no longer have the authority to deal with their citizens as they please in the eyes of the international community. In other words, the subnational building blocks of sovereignty are recognized and shored up by a still developing concept of individuals as humans rather than citizens of states, and as citizens of an emerging (and still nebulous and undefined) global community.

Thus, rather than identifying sovereignty with one level or centre – the state – it is possible point to multiple levels and centres of sovereignty. This, in and of itself, turns traditional formulations of sovereignty on their heads. But this is only the beginning. Besides levels and centres of sovereignty, we can point to multiple sovereignties. For example, while a state may possess certain types of authority over the waters along its coast, other entities may have certain rights within these same waters. In addition, as noted above, another variation on sovereignty may be particularly useful or necessary in dealing with some internal conflicts. A notion of partial sovereignty can be identified with that of autonomy. Providing minority groups within particular states the option of a framework of autonomy in certain areas can help to defuse violent and not so violent separatism. This will not always be appropriate, of course, but where it is, we find yet another encroachment on monolithic sovereignty.

I have also indicated how one form of what might be called global sovereignty could be used – that of trusteeship for a certain period of time while a country reconstructed itself after a war or other major disruption. In addition, however, the concept of global sovereignty can have a broader meaning where the global community has the authority – through the UN – to ensure that human rights norms, as well as other standards necessary for the well-being of individuals and the world as a whole, are upheld when states and other centres of authority violate human rights.

The previous discussion leads me to a couple of final observations. The state as a sovereign entity is not going to disappear anytime soon. However, it will be only one of a number of kinds of partially and multiply sovereign organization. It will not be the only entity which can lay claim to authority over its citizens. Thus, as we come to recognize that we are living in what Rosenau calls an era of 'post-international politics',[205] we must also realize that we are not, as Francis Fukuyama has postulated, at 'the end of history', where one form of economic, social and governmental form has triumphed over all others and what remains to be worked out are minor details.[206] Rather, we are likely in, for a long period of time where issues regarding the loci of power and authority will be up in the air and not amenable to any final solution or formulation, and will be under constant questioning and challenge by various sectors, particularly as human rights continues to be an arena of contestation. We are entering what might be called the Age of Ambiguity, where our postmodern, postindustrial, postinternational viewpoints lead to the conclusion that our social relations today and into the future will be characterized by a discomforting – yet full of potential – ambiguity.

2 The Quest for Community: Internal Challenges to Sovereignty

Et populi meditati sunt inania? Camille Saint-Saëns[1]

On the surface it seemed reasonable: let the
people decide. It was in fact ridiculous
because the people cannot decide until
somebody decides who are the people. Sir Ivor Jenning[2]

The tribes have returned, and the drama of
their return is greatest where their repression
is most severe. Michael Walzer[3]

Indeed, the tribes have returned, although one might question whether they ever fully left, or at least whether the tribes are the same ones which left. The previous chapter briefly discussed the role various kinds of nationalism, ethnic conflict and separatism are playing in undermining current conceptions of sovereignty and proposed a new role for substate communities in reconstructing sovereignty. This chapter will delve more deeply into what might more properly be called communal conflict or, as Kumar Rupesinghe characterizes them, 'identity struggles',[4] The questions, concepts, and misconceptions regarding communal struggles are many, while the answers are few, and usually contradictory.

Some groups are agitating or fighting for autonomy, others for their own state, still others for bare survival. All of them do this under the banner of self-determination. Yet, this concept is one of the most controversial and least understood in global politics and is a major force which threatens to undermine some of the bases of the international community, namely the sanctity of borders and the internal sovereignty of states. Communal conflict can have many other serious consequences, including genocide and the generation of massive refugee flows. Such conflict is so widespread that a comprehensive approach to dealing with ethnonationalism is needed. I will begin with an attempt to define some of the concepts which form the core of communal conflict. Then, I will present an overview of the current state of communal conflict around the world. The main question, however, is who is the 'self' which can claim self-determination? Thus, the next two sections will look at the legal and moral aspects of self-determination. Next, I will discuss how self-determination can – and must – be squared with human rights. Finally, I will integrate self-determination into my reconstructed notion of sovereignty.

I conclude that self-determination can be considered both a legal and moral right. I maintain, further, that while being a right in and of itself is necessary for the attainment of other human rights, these other human rights are also necessary for self-determination. In addition, I argue that self-determination can be attained in many different ways, most of which fall outside the bounds of the sovereignty discourse. Thus, taking self-determination seriously as an important aspect of the New Sovereignty means moving beyond the state paradigm and recognizing other types of communities and other ways of organizing power and authority.

WHOSE IDENTITY?

Ethnicity, nations, nationalism, peoples – these are the key words which are bandied about by any group wanting to redefine its position with regard to its state and, indeed, to the rest of the world. Ethnic groups, nations and peoples all claim a right to self-determination. However, before examining this claimed right, we must first plumb the murky depths of communal identification to find out who these selves are, although we must conclude that, in the end, there is vast disagreement about these terms and what, or who, they comprise.

As Donald Horowitz points out, ethnic identification has been in disrepute in the West partly because after World War II 'it was thought that the industrialized countries had outgrown political affiliation based on ethnicity, and anti-colonial movements had created an appearance of unity'[5] which may not have actually existed. In addition, such cleavages went against the grain of the Enlightenment universalism which was to manifest itself in, among other things, the Universal Declaration of Human Rights. However, not everyone seems to have absorbed this ethos, and ethnicity has become the basis for much communal conflict, but nobody seems to have a good idea of what ethnicity entails. Some base it on language, some on religion, some on culture, others on class or power, and still others on some outmoded idea of 'race'.

Hurst Hannum, for example, maintains that ethnic differences are usually rooted in majority/minority power, class, linguistic and religious differences.[6] In other words, ethnicity is found in dominant/dominated – or at least numerically superior/inferior – relationships based upon a whole smorgasbord of possible identifications. Hobsbawm, too, notes a congruence between ethnic identification and power relationships.[7] Usually, however, at least from the perspective of those identifying themselves as members of such a group, there is a focus on common ancestry and an exclusivity which precludes membership to all except those with such lineage or kinship.[8] Horowitz, while also accepting some sort of exclusivity within the group, maintains that ethnicity is a more inclusive concept which can be based on 'color, language, religion, or some other attribute of common origin'.[9] Ethnic identification is, of course, rooted in difference, and these differences can be contextual. For example, the difference defining two groups may be language, but the difference defining the first group and a third group may be religion.[10] Overall, the differences are generally connected to 'birth and blood' which give rise to 'a myth of collective ancestry, which usually carries with it traits believed to be innate'.[11] Horowitz thus provides a 'minimal definition of an ethnic unit . . . [which] is the idea of common provenance, recruitment primarily through kinship, and a notion of distinctiveness whether or not this consists of a unique inventory of cultural traits.'[12] In addition, he notes there must be some sort of 'minimal scale requirement, so that ethnic membership transcends the range of face-to-face interactions. . . .'[13] In other words, the ethnic group becomes an imagined community where nobody will ever meet everybody who is part of that community but which, nonetheless, has a certain hold within the minds of those who comprise the ethnic community.

Further, as Rupesinghe notes, '[e]thnicity is not a static concept but a dynamic one, in that ethnicity and ethnic boundaries can be continuously redefined. . . .'[14] Indeed, some ethnic groups are more elastic with regard to whether or not one can become part of the group by choice rather than birth.[15] Elise Boulding sees ethnicity as a 'cultural construct . . . [which] can be patterned in many ways'.[16] She has 'identified 6,267 significant ethnic groups in 159 countries', although, she notes, "[h]ow many groups you find obviously depends on how you count them'.[17] How to count them is, indeed, the question. In addition, what one is actually counting as a group can also be problematic. However, to sum up this brief discussion of ethnicity, I observe that, like the other concepts under discussion, it is contested, but it has something to do with some sort of common ancestry – 'real' or imagined to differing extents – and exclusivity with regard to other ethnic groups, based on one or more of language, colour, religion and power relationships.

The 'nation' is the next poorly defined concept which must be considered and is the one which seems to hold the greatest sway over people in many different conflict situations today. In fact, it is the nation which is supposedly entitled to self-determination – hence 'national self-determination'. This is why separatist and other groups call themselves a 'nation' regardless of whether or not they fit whatever criteria one might want to apply to nations.

Some equate ethnicity with nation. Daniel Patrick Moynihan writes that the 'nation is the "highest" form of the ethnic group'.[18] The nation, in other words, combines "a subjective state of mind as regards ancestry" – that is ethnicity – with 'an objective claim to forms of territorial autonomy . . .'.[19] In fact, this definition of nation corresponds to the concept of *nationalism* – group identity combined with territorial and political claims. Hobsbawm questions whether there is an essential difference between the nation and other collectivities, such as ethnic groups. Attempts to use set criteria to define the nation will be in vain because 'language, ethnicity [which might be based on language itself] or whatever . . . are themselves fuzzy, shifting and ambiguous, and as useless for purposes of the traveller's orientation as cloud-shapes are compared to landmarks.'[20]

The crux of the question in attempting to define the nation is whether one uses objective or subjective criteria, or both. 'Objective' criteria might include language, ethnicity (which, of course, is not 'objective' itself), religion, and culture – some of which are hard to distinguish from the others. The subjective aspect is the self-identified communal feeling which those within the nation feel as part of a group. In this respect, the nation is like the ethnic group. This communal feeling is, of course, imagined, and the imagining has limits, depending on historical specificities.

The answer to defining the nation is to use both subjective and objective criteria in defining the nation, although what this means for self-determination is not clear. Clearly, nations have some sort of objective criteria on which to base their claim of nationhood. They may be intimately tied to one another – for example, language is usually part of culture. In addition, there is a sense among the members of an imagined nation of a shared past and future destiny, which is distinct from the imaginings of the members of other nations. Or, a nation appears when there is a shared culture and recognition of the shared culture. That is, members of a shared culture 'recognize certain mutual rights and duties to each other in virtue of their shared membership of it'.[21] This shared imagining also has something to do with the legitimacy of the government of the nation, 'in the sense that governmental decisions which denigrate or belittle any of the focal elements in a given cultural tradition are viewed as abusive of power.'[22]

Regardless of what criteria one uses to describe nations, they are not 'natural' entities waiting to be discovered with natural inherent rights, although, as I will argue, they may have rights nonetheless arising out of other concerns. Of course, this is not how nationalists describe their nation, for how could they make the claims they do without such supposed national pedigrees? Although having a nation has come to be seen as 'an inherent attribute of humanity',[23] Gellner describes the nation as a 'myth': 'Nations as a natural, God-given way of classifying men, as an inherent though long-delayed political destiny are a myth. . . .'[24] Mayall and Simpson note that '[n]ations need myths to live by'.[25] Kellas describes the 'considerable amount of myth-making about the historical credentials of the nation'.[26] Thus, Hobsbawm argues that '[w]hat makes a nation *is* the past'.[27] In other words, nations, to differing degrees, create heroic pasts for themselves, sometimes out of more or less factual bases, and sometimes seemingly out of thin air.[28] As Ernest Renan noted in 1882: 'Forgetting history, or even getting history wrong (*l'erreur historique*) are an essential factor in the formation of a nation. . . .'[29]

Nationalism, then, is an exercise in myth-making. And, to the myth of the nation nationalists apply the principle of the so-called 'nation-state'. In other words, nationalism is a political principle where the political unit and the national unit are joined. Or, as Alexander Motyl notes, nationalism is a 'political ideal that views statehood as the optimal form of political organization for each nation.'[30] Thus, the nation becomes sovereign. In fact, nationalism 'is a concrete expression' of 'the sovereignty of the people'.[31]

However, this 'concrete expression' could not be thought of in such terms without the antecedent Enlightenment creation of popular sovereignty. From this one can see that nationalism is historically specific. The nation 'belongs exclusively to a particular, and historically recent, period'.[32] Ben-Israel notes that nationalism, at least in its Enlightenment roots, was not the particularist, frequently war-inducing principle it is today: 'Nationalism began not as collective egoism but as a universally liberating principle. . . . Holding up the cultural and ethnic nation to be the natural collective for the exercise of sovereignty, nationalism could theoretically gain wide societal support.'[33] Yet, as Gellner argues, modern nationalism arose not out of Enlightenment principles but the logic of industrial society. The production forms of industrial society required a certain level of specialization which could not be acquired with particular kin units. Rather, people would have to go outside of their particular locality. This, in turn, meant that disparate people would have to be able to communicate with each other and have certain basic cultural foundations in common. Thus cultural homogeneity is required. And this homogeneity is a crucial component of nationalism.[34]

Further, this homogeneity could not occur without the spread of standardized language. The advent of printing presses and mass schooling were crucial in the spread of such languages. Thus, one can see where language might come to be seen as a 'natural' basis for the nation. However, as Hobsbawm points out, the languages of nationalism frequently are not the antecedents to nationalism. That is, language does not necessarily form the basis for nationalist claims, but can, instead, result from such a claim.[35] He notes the imagining element of language construction:

> The political-ideological element is evident in the process of language-construction which can range from the mere 'correction' and standardisation of existing literary and cultural-languages, through the formation of such languages out of the usual complex of overlapping dialects, to the resuscitation of dead or almost extinct languages which amounts to virtual invention of new ones. For, contrary to nationalist myth, a people's language is not the basis of national consciousness but, in the phrase of Einar Haugen, a 'cultural artefact'.[36]

Nationalism, whatever its historical antecedent, is tied intimately with territory for, without the Westphalian ordering of the modern territorial state, talking about the 'nation-state', which is the goal of nationalism, would be nonsensical: the nation-state 'is a social entity only so far as it relates to a certain kind of modern territorial state, the "nation-state", and it is pointless to discuss nation and nationality except insofar as both relate to it.'[37] This is further evidence that the nation – and therefore nationalism, since it is nationalism which creates the nation – is 'a contingency . . . not a universal necessity'.[38]

The other term which I preliminarily touch upon is 'peoples'. As noted in Chapter 1, Article 1 of the two human rights covenants affirms that: 'All peoples have the right to self-determination.' Thus, this enigmatic term is accorded a standing similar to the 'nation' in discussion of self-determination. It is part of the category of 'selves' along with nations and ethnic groups. Between 1919 and 1945, Hannum notes that the term was used in five different ways in relation to self-determination:

> a people living entirely within a state ruled by another people (e.g., the Irish before 1920); peoples living as minorities in various countries without controlling a state of their own (e.g., Poles in Russia before 1919); a people living as a minority group in a state but understanding themselves as forming part of the people of a neighboring state (e.g., Hungarians in Romania); a people dispersed throughout many separate states (e.g., the German people in various European states); and a

people who constitute a majority in a territory under foreign domination (e.g., colonial regimes).[39]

After World War II and the subsequent decolonization, 'peoples' came to be identified almost exclusively with those living within the borders of the former colonial entities. While frequently there was a self-identification on the part of people within the former colonies as being part of a 'people' – which often was based on shared anti-colonialism rather than any other 'objective' criteria – this also frequently masked other underlying ethnic, national, or 'peoples' tension. Thus, after World War II, the term peoples moved from ethnic or national bases to a state-centric interpretation. While many peoples are agitating for self-determination in the form of their own homogeneous sovereign states – which, in most cases, is highly unlikely – the arbitrary redefinition of peoples, which has had dangerous consequences, must be addressed in any discussion of sovereignty and human rights. It is to these consequences, and other current developments, to which I turn next.

First, however, a final word on terminology. The above discussion of ethnic groups, nations, and peoples makes it clear that the distinction between them is unclear. They are frequently used interchangeably, and in keeping with the ambiguity identified in the last chapter, this is probably reasonable. Groups agitating for self-determination frequently call themselves nations, because of the legal consequences of being identified as such. Peoples, too, have a similar legal standing, although the term has been redefined, and the distinction between peoples, in their pre–1945 meaning, which is the only one which makes any conceptual sense if one wants to distinguish between states and certain types of non-state grouping, and nations and ethnic groups, is still fuzzy. Thus, unless it is clear to the contrary, they will be considered synonymous. Nationalism, then, refers to a particular kind of political project on the part of ethnic groups, nations, and peoples. The point – to be developed later in this chapter – is that they are communities which, insofar as they further the development and enjoyment of human rights, should be accorded a certain status as self-identified entities who have chosen to pursue a 'common life'. Of course, these common lives frequently come into conflict.

COMMUNAL CONFLICT IN THEORY AND PRACTICE

Communal conflict is one of the two contradictory tendencies one can discern in global politics today. On the one hand are the globalizing trajectories which are forcing states to work together and which are even crossing boundaries altogether, with no regard for increasingly illusory sovereignty. On the other hand are conflicts, based on units smaller than the states in which they take place, and frequently spilling over the borders of any particular state, which are focused on creating more independent states, or at least some sort of autonomous political space for the smaller ethnic and national groups or peoples.

The apparent increase in such conflict can be tied, at least partly, to the end of the Cold War. In some instances, ethnic tensions were submerged with the development of communist states in the Soviet Union and Eastern Europe. These tensions reemerged with the lifting of authoritarian rule. The conflicts run the gamut in terms of extremism and violence. On 1 January 1993, Czechoslovakia divided into Czech and Slovak states as a result of a peaceful referendum and parliamentary process, although this breakup also had a lot to do with sharply divergent economic situations in the two regions.[40] The extreme opposite of this is the break-up of Yugoslavia into several constituent parts. One of the parts, Bosnia-Herzegovina, is comprised of at least three different ethnic groups (peoples),[41] and the fighting was focused, particularly, on 'cleansing' one of the ethnic groups – exterminating and/or expelling them from particular regions in order to make these regions ethnically 'pure' – an ideal which, in addition to its essential impossibility on a large scale for any extended length of time, results in many morally repugnant outcomes, including mass-population transfers. The republics of the former Soviet Union also manifest numerous types of ethnic conflicts. Notwithstanding Khrushchev's and Brezhnev's attempt to create a 'Soviet People' – an example of a failed nationalist myth-making project – the 'national problem' persisted throughout Soviet rule.[42] The post-Soviet states are beset with problems ranging from tensions within states to conflicts between states which have ethnic minorities associated with other states. For an expanded list of communal conflicts and self-determination movements see Figure 2.1.

Rupesinghe has identified several disjunctions which have resulted in ethnic tensions, particularly in the former European colonies. The first is 'the contradiction between state building and nation building' where the state, as a result of centralization, comes into conflict with the different nations or peoples found within its borders. This is where 'official nationalism' can come into conflict with the 'imagined communities' of substate nations. Hobsbawm observes that most Third World nationalism has occurred since decolonization

not against a foreign imperialist oppressor, but against newly eman-
cipated states claiming a national homogeneity which they did not possess. In other words they protested against the 'national', i.e. ethnic, or
cultural, unreality of the territories into which the imperial era had par-
titioned the dependent world. . . .[43]

Rupesinghe also makes reference to tension between modernization and
ethnic groups, where development strategies 'have created a sense of psychological deprivation (relative deprivation) which has led to a backlash
in the form of a reawakening of fundamentalism'. To this I add, specifically, the tension between development and indigenous peoples where, for
example, the government promotes a strategy of development which en-
croaches upon the land and social patterns of indigenous peoples. Ethnic
conflict can also be heightened as a result of political liberalization. As the
political process begins to open up, various groups will become more as-
sertive. Frequently, a government will engage in repressive activity when
tensions arise, compounding problems and expanding conflict.[44] In addition, otherwise peaceful and benign ethnic differences can be exploited
and turned into divisive and violent conflicts by leaders who manipulate
these differences to gain or expand their power.

Figure 2.1 Communal Conflicts

Africa

Angola (Ovambos)
Burundi (Hutu)
Chad
Congo
Democratic Republic of Congo
Djibouti (Afar)
Egypt
Ethiopia (Somalis)
Ghana (Ewe)
Kenya
Liberia
Mauritania
Mali (Tuaregs)
Morocco (Western Sahara)
Niger (Tuaregs)
Nigeria
Rwanda (Tutsi)
Senegal (Diola)
Sierra Leone
Somalia

Cambodia
China (East Turkestan/Tibetans/
   Taiwanese)
Fiji
India (Kashmiris/Mizos/Nagas/Sikhs/
   Tamils)
Indonesia (Acheh/East Timorese/South
   Moluccans/West Papua)
Iraq (Kurds/Chaldeans/Shiites/
   Turkmen)
Iran (Kurds/Turkmen)
Israel (Palestinians)
Japan (Ainu)
Jordan (Palestinians)
Kyrgyzistan (Uzbeks)
Laos (Hmongs)
Myanmar (Karenni/Kachins/Shan)
Pakistan (Baluchis/Kashmiris/Pathans/
   Sindhis)
Papua New Guinea (Bougainville)
Phillipines (Cordillera, Moros)
Sri Lanka (Tamils)

South Africa
Sudan
Tanzania (Zanzibar)
Togo (Ewe)

Americas

Argentina (Mapuche)
Brazil (Yanomami)
Canada (Mohawks/Quebecois)
Chile (Mapuche)
Colombia (Indians)
Guatemala (Maya Indians)
Peru
United States (Native Americans/Puerto
  Ricans)

Asia

Afghanistan
Australia (Aboriginals)
Azerbaijan (Armenians/Kurds)
Bangladesh (Chittagong Hill Tracts)
Bhutan (Nepalese)

Tajikistan (Muslims)
Turkey (Armenians/Kurds)

Europe

Albania (Greeks)
Austria (Slovenes)
Bosnia and Herzegovina
Croatia (Krajina)
Cyprus (Greeks/Turks)
Finland (Karelians)
France (Bretons/Corsicans)
Georgia (Abkhazians/South Ossetia)
Germany
Italy (Tyroleans)
Moldova (Dnietser/Gagauzia)
Romania (Hungarians)
Russia (Chechnya/Ingushetia/North
  Ossetia)
Serbia (Kosovo/Vojvodina/Novi Pazar
  Sanjak)
Spain (Basques/Catalans)
Ukraine (Russians and Tatars in
  Crimea)
United Kingdom (Irish/Scots/Welsh)

Source: Most of the information for this (partial) survey of contemporary communal conflicts comes from: 'Ethnic Conflicts Worldwide', *Current History*, 92 (April 1993): pp. 167–8; Lawrence T. Farley, *Plebiscites and Sovereignty: The Crisis of Political Illegitimacy*, (Boulder, CO: Westview Press, 1986): pp. 11–12; Jeff Greenwald, 'The Unrepresented Nations and Peoples Organization: Diplomacy's Cutting Edge', *Whole Earth Review*, 77 (Winter 1992): pp. 32–36; Morton Halperin and David J. Scheffer with Patricia L. Small, *Self-Determination in the New World Order*, (Washington, DC: Carnegie Endowment for International Peace, 1992): pp. 123–60; Unrepresented Nations and Peoples Organization brochure.

Several different types of conflicts have been alluded to above, and a number of different authors have put together classificatory schemes for the bases for, and outcomes sought, for the claims.[45] Frequently, however, there is more than one type of self-determination movement in any one state or region. In fact, different factions of a particular movement may advocate different outcomes, such as the Kurds, some of whom want only autonomy within the various countries they inhabit, and others who want an independent Kurdistan. One way to classify self-determination movements is solely by their declared preferred outcomes which, in one way or another, affect the sovereignty claims of the central state. These are autonomy, secession, and irredentist. All three of these options are a triumph of particularity – that is communal identity – over universalism and pluralism.

Autonomy movements are those in which a group is agitating for some sort of self-rule within a particular territory. Frequently, the movements stem from a grievance, real or imagined, against a minority group, defined, for example, by language or religion. Groups seeking autonomy, while not making sovereignty claims against the borders of particular countries, nevertheless make claims which may undermine the supposed absolute internal sovereignty held by the central government.

In Quebec, some are pushing for outright secession for the province, although its status right now and probably in the future is a semi-autonomous province within a federal Canada. The term *souverainété-association*, which was the subject of the 1980 referendum in Quebec, 'was intended to imply political sovereignty coupled with association in areas of common interest'.[46] The claims to autonomy – as well as independence on the part of a significant minority, coming close to a majority in recent years,[47] of people in Quebec – have been based on language rights, as well as other cultural issues. Quebec was granted special language rights and passed a law which mandated that all signs must be in French, rather than in the minority English. It also passed certain laws regarding education. Recently, the UN Human Rights Commission ruled that some of these laws violated the human rights of the minority English-speakers. Certainly many English-speakers have felt like second-class citizens within Quebec. The conflict within Quebec has been nonviolent, although in the 1970s sporadic violence occurred.[48]

The Basques in Spain, who comprise one of seventeen autonomous regions, are split between those, including the ruling party, who advocate continued autonomy, and those, led by the violent Basque Homeland and Liberty Party (ETA), who advocate an independent state, comprising Spanish and French Basques. Similarly, within the United Kingdom, some Scots and Welsh seek increased autonomy. Having its own legal and education systems and local government, Scotland now has the Scottish National Party advocating independence from its three seats in the British parliament, and in September 1997, both Scotland and Wales voted to set up their own parliaments, thereby gaining more autonomy from London.[49]

Secessionist movements, rejecting association with their present states, attempt to create independent states. They thus directly challenge the sovereignty of a state as they seek to carve out a sovereign state from a portion of another sovereign state. In another sense, however, secessionist movements fall squarely within the logic of the sovereignty discourse insofar as they want their own sovereign state with all of the rights accorded to such states. Yet, they also undermine another principle of sovereignty which essentially fixes state borders once and for all. Secessionist movements also present troubling possibilities for minorities within secessionist territories.

Few secessionist movements have succeeded in recent years. With the help of Indian military intervention, East Pakistan seceded from Pakistan in 1971 to form Bangladesh.[50] Twenty years later, the Eritrean People's Liberation Front, which had been fighting for independence for 30 years, gained control of the entire territory of Eritrea at the same time that the Ethiopian People's Revolutionary Democratic Front overthrew the central government in Addis Ababa of Mengistu Haile Miriam. Two years later, in May 1993, Eritrea held a referendum, with the support of the new central government, in which almost all of the Eritreans voted to create their own independent state, which had *de facto* independence since 1991.[51] In addition, I have already mentioned the peaceful breakup of Czechoslovakia, the partially violent dissolution of the Soviet Union, and the continuing violent breakup of Yugoslavia. It is noteworthy that all but one of these secessions occurred within this decade.

Irredentism, which Naomi Chazan defines as 'any political effort to unite ethnically, historically, or geographically related segments of a population in adjacent countries within a common political framework',[52] is a more complex phenomenon than secession because, by definition, it includes trans-state political claims. As in other types of communal conflict, such as Israeli and Palestinian claims to Palestine (Judea and Samaria), there is a focus on the relationship between land and people: 'Irredentism, with its emphasis on the political unification of self-conscious communities, highlights the importance of people and the land they occupy in the determination of the frontiers of the state.'[53] Hedva Ben-Israel notes, however, 'the tension between land and people', and maintains that irredentism has more to do with

> territory demanded by a state on the ground that it had been or should have been an integral part of the national heritage. Ethnic populations often come into it, but it is, in my opinion, territory more than population that is central in irredentist movements, and this distinguishes irredentist from pan movements.[54]

Horowitz, on the other hand, notes the connection between ethnonational secessionism and irredentism, indicating the ethnic or national basis for irredentism as well as secession.[55]

Chazan notes two different types of irredentist claims which might be made within the communal context. First, and most common, is the claim by an ethnic majority government in one country to incorporate its co-nationals into its state, *or* a move by a minority population in one state to become part of an adjacent state where the majority of the population is comprised of its ethnic group. A second, less common and more ambiguous, type of irredentist claim is where an ethnic group which is a minority in two or more countries advocates either union with one of the countries or an independent country.[56] The first type of claim includes Somalis in Ethiopia. The second types encompasses Slovenians in Austria and (the former) Yugoslavia and Macedonians in Bulgaria, (the former) Yugoslavia, and Greece. In fact, the Macedonian province in what used to be Yugoslavia became an independent state during the break-up of Yugoslavia. However, because the Greek government feared that allowing it to call itself Macedonia might legitimate Macedonian irredentist claims on the Greek province of Macedonia, it was allowed into the United Nations only under the name The Former Yugoslav Republic of Macedonia, an awkward, and probably ultimately untenable, name.

The situation becomes even more complicated and ambiguous when irredentist claims overlap with autonomy and/or secession claims. For example some of the Kurds, spread among Iran, Iraq, Turkey and Syria, want greater autonomy within their respective countries. Others, however want to create an independent Kurdistan. In some cases where irredentist claims might be made, secession is chosen instead. In fact, secession is much more common than irredentism, to a large extent because the leaders prefer secession. In an independent state they will be at the apex of power, while where their territory is united with another country, they would have to compete with other elites and might be relegated to second class status. In addition, some groups which might make irredentist claims to join another state also might not join because of the multiethnic character of that state. Other ethnic groups within those states might also block such a move. Thus, a number of factors mitigate against irredentism in favour of secession.[57]

Finally, one might also mention 'representative' self-determination. This type of movement does not threaten the borders of the state or other sovereign aspects of the central government (except that it usually aims at the replacement of the central government with another): 'A claim to "representative" self-determination results when the population of an existing state seeks to change its political structure in favour of a more representative (and preferably democratic) structure.'[58] This is closer to the principle of popular sovereignty, whereby the people within a particular state get a say in how they are governed, and it has much to do with the democratization movements sweeping the globe. Examples include South Africa (which completed a process of representative self-determination with non-racial elections in 1994), Haiti, and Myanmar. However, there may be cases where the movement is not democratic or where it is simply a case of one ethnic group replacing another ethnic group in power.

Many of these various types of communal conflict have had severe humanitarian results. Horowitz estimates that more than ten million casualties resulted from ethnic violence between 1945 and 1975.[59] Rupesinghe notes another estimate of 14 million people killed in internal wars in the Third World between 1945 and 1990. This is contrasted with 100,000 in the developed world during the same period.[60]

Not all communal conflicts become extremely violent, and of those that do, not all of them involve identities which are constructed in such a way as to incite massive killing based upon complete exclusivity. However, some of the participants in some of these wars do have 'ethnic cleansing' as their goal. The goal of such 'cleansing'[61] is to create ethnically 'pure' territories through 'the expulsion of an "undesirable" population from a given territory due to religious or ethnic discrimination, political, strategic or ideological considerations, or a combination of these'.[62] The use of the word 'cleansing' indicates a feeling that the presence of a particular ethnic group makes a territory 'unclean' and thus in need of 'cleansing' in order to make the territory 'pure' again. Whatever else may factor into the calculations of any particular campaign, 'the main ingredient is the same: visceral hatred of the neighbours'.[63]

Ethnic cleansing has come to the fore of public consciousness as a result of the war in Bosnia-Herzegovina. However, '[t]he Serbian campaign to "cleanse" a territory of another ethnic group, while gruesome and tragic, is historically speaking neither new nor remarkable. Population removal and transfer have occurred in history more often than is generally acknowledged.'[64] Yet, it has only been in the 19th and 20th centuries that complete destruction of an ethnic group – that is genocide – has become state policy. For example, Turkey massacred Armenians in 1915. The actions of the Nazis demonstrate that such policies can include both mass population expulsion as well as mass extermination. After World War II, the victorious powers engaged in their own population transfers in Europe, removing nearly 12 million Germans from Czechoslovakia, Hungary, Poland, Romania and Yugoslavia.[65]

In addition to the vast numbers of people killed as a result of ethnically based wars and 'ethnic cleansing', millions of refugees are produced. Some cross state boundaries and become truly international problems. Others are internally displaced. Two years after the war began in April 1992, about two million people had been displaced in Bosnia-Herzegovina.[66] Gurr notes that more than half of the world's 30 million displaced people in 1990 were displaced as a result of communal conflict.[67] Before World War II, international refugee policy recognized the fact that many refugees were fleeing from ethnic conflict. After 1945, however, refugees were presumed to be fleeing from ideological conflict, and policy was adjusted accordingly, with repatriation the primary preferred solution.[68] Obviously, such a policy ignores the realities of today's displaced populations, and some solutions may have to be rethought.

SELF-DETERMINATION AS A LEGAL NORM

In Chapter 1, I examined the relationship between human rights and sovereignty from both normative and international legal perspectives. The same can be done for the issue of self-determination. I will begin by placing self-determination within its frequently ambiguous legal setting.

Self-determination is a norm of international law. However, what this means is not always clear. Some claim it is a principle, others a right, and some identify it as *jus cogens*. Further, the content of the norm is also contested, although most state practice has restricted it to decolonization.

The Universal Declaration of Human Rights does not explicitly make reference to self-determination. However, Article 21 does state that: 'Everyone has the right to take part in the government of his country, directly or through freely chosen representatives.... The will of the people shall be the basis of the authority of government.'[69] It is thus concerned with individuals as part of a community rather than as individuals as such, and may be construed as a reference to one of the aspects of the reconstructed sovereignty put forth in the last chapter: popular sovereignty. The 'self' is the political community in general, not a political community based upon any further considerations such as ethnicity.

The two International Covenants on Human Rights do, however, make specific reference to a right to self-determination in their common Article 1: 'All peoples have the right to self-determination. By virtue of that right they freely determine their political status and freely pursue their economic, social and cultural development.' When this article was up for discussion during the drafting process, it was objected to on the grounds that it was a collective right, and not a human right, and thus should not be included in a document dealing with individuals. However, defenders pointed out that it affected every individual and was crucial for the enjoyment of other human rights:

Although the principle of equal rights and self-determination of peoples constitutes a collective right, it nevertheless concerns each individual, since deprivation of that right would entail the loss of individual rights. The right to self-determination is a fundamental right without which other rights cannot be fully enjoyed.[70]

The Charter of the United Nations has two explicit references to self-determination. Article 1, paragraph 2 refers to one of the purposes of the United Nations: 'To develop friendly relations among nations based on respect for the principle of equal rights and self-determination of peoples, and to take other appropriate measures to strengthen universal peace.' The introductory part of Article 55 refers to 'respect for the principle of equal rights and self-determination of peoples. . . . ' Further, Article 73 of Chapter XI ('Declaration Regarding Non-Self-Governing Territories') and Article 76 of Chapter XII ('International Trusteeship System') both make reference to self-determination in terms of self-government and independence for colonial and trust territories.

Any question about whether self-government was ever more appropriate than independence for colonial peoples was put to rest in 1960 when the General Assembly adopted resolution 1514 (XV), Declaration on the Granting of Independence to Colonial Countries and Territories. The General Assembly noted 'the need for the creation of conditions of stability and friendly relations based on respect for the principles of equal rights and self-determination of all peoples. . . .' and 'that all peoples have an inalienable right to complete freedom, the exercise of their sovereignty and the integrity of their national territory'. It then declared in Article 1 that: 'The subjection of peoples to alien subjugation, domination and exploitation constitutes a denial of fundamental human rights, is contrary to the Charter of the United Nations and is an impediment to the promotion of World peace and cooperation.' Article 2 affirmed that: 'All peoples have the right to self-determination; by virtue of that right they freely determine their political status and freely pursue their economic, social and cultural development.' Article 6 provided the state-centric foundation for the aforementioned resistance to applying self-determination beyond colonial territories: 'Any attempt aimed at the partial or total disruption of the national unity and the territorial integrity of a country is incompatible with the purposes and principles of the Charter of the United Nations.'

Three days later, the General Assembly passed resolution 1541 (XV), 'Principles which should guide members in determining whether or not an obligation exists to transmit the information called for under Article 73e of the Charter.' It provided criteria on how to decide if a territory was 'non-self-governing', which included being 'geographically separate' and 'distinct ethnically and/or culturally from the country administering it'. This was known as the 'salt-water' theory of colonialism. It meant that minorities could not be classified as a non-self-governing entity and thus entitled to self-determination. However, in anticipation of an argument to be made below, one might ask why an ocean or other territorial expanse take precedence over other kinds of boundaries: 'there is no good reason why other defining characteristics, including historical boundaries or *de facto* boundaries established through the hostile action of the governments in question, might not also be relevant.'[71] Further, Resolution 1541 noted how a territory could become self-governing: '(a) Emergence as a sovereign independent state; (b) Free association with and independent state; or (c) Integration with an independent state.' Independence was the preferred option.[72]

The 1970 'Declaration on Principles of International Law Concerning Friendly Relations and Cooperation among States in Accordance with the Charter of the United Nations' makes several references to the principle of self-determination, while at the same time seeming to restrict it to colonial – 'non-self-governing' – territories. On the first point, it proclaimed that:

> By virtue of the principle of equal rights and self-determination of peoples enshrined in the Charter of the United Nations, all peoples have the right freely to determine, without external interference, their political status and to pursue their economic, social and cultural development. . . .

And, it recognized the modes of self-determination mentioned in Resolution 1541. The second point, that of restricting self-determination to colonial peoples, was also affirmed, and once a territory was decolonized the right to self-determination ends and territorial integrity reigns supreme. However, the Declaration also seems to indicate that states which do not represent all of the people might be vulnerable to further actions of self-determination from within. Some contend that since there was a specific racial reference,[73] only racist governments such as the *apartheid* regime in South Africa would be vulnerable. However, there is also a reference to creed, that is belief – religious or other – which might be construed as further opening up the non-colonial or post-decolonization aspects of self-determination. Others still cling to the decolonization-only opinion and maintain that political unity takes precedence over self-determination. At the time of the declaration, then, 'while there is no doubt that there is an international legal right of self-determination in the context of decolonization, the extension of that right to non-colonial situations was not clear . . . '.[74]

The 1981 Banjul Charter on Human and Peoples' Rights was the first regional human rights convention to make specific reference to the right to self-determination. Article 19 recognizes the equality of peoples: 'All peoples shall be equal; they shall enjoy the same respect and shall have the same rights. Nothing shall justify the domination of a people by another.' Article 20 recognizes the right to self-determination and states in part:

> All peoples shall have the right to existence. They shall have the unquestionable and inalienable right to self-determination. They shall freely determine their political status and shall pursue their economic and social development according to the policy they have freely chosen.

The Charter also makes specific reference to self-determination in the context of decolonization. However, African state practice has been to confine self-determination to that context and has regarded 'peoples' to be synonymous with states, regardless of the multi-ethnic or multi-national character of states, and territorial integrity replaces self-determination once decolonization is achieved.[75]

The waters were muddied slightly in December 1992 when the General Assembly adopted the Declaration on the Rights of Persons Belonging to National or Ethnic, Religious and Linguistic Minorities. It recognizes certain rights based on communal identities. Article 1 states in part: 'States shall protect the existence and the national or ethnic, cultural, religious and linguistic identity of minorities within their respective territories and shall encourage conditions for the promotion of that identity.' Article 2 declares further:

> persons belonging to national or ethnic, religious and linguistic minorities (hereinafter referred to as persons belonging to minorities) have the right to enjoy their own culture, to profess and practise their own religion, and to use their own language, in private and public, freely and without interference or any form of discrimination.

The Declaration also makes the requisite reference to territorial integrity.

Thus, this declaration, while affirming, yet again, the inviolability of boundaries, also recognizes that 'national or ethnic, religious and linguistic' groups have certain communal rights which they may exercise. This has relevance not only for minorities *vis-à-vis* the central government, but for minorities with respect to other minorities.[76] In addition, paragraph 5 of Article 2 states:

Persons belonging to minorities have the right to establish and maintain, without any discrimination, free and peaceful contacts with other members of their group and with persons belonging to other minorities, as well as contacts across frontiers with citizens of other States to whom they are related by national or ethnic, religious or linguistic ties.

This means that groups may have rights with regard to other states of which they are not citizens. This also directly relates to the concept of the 'logical state' mentioned in Chapter 1. It is an implicit recognition that groups have interests or loyalties beyond state borders. Insofar as these loyalties come to supplant loyalties to the particular state in which people reside, state control over the minds of their citizens is undermined.

Finally, a 1992 declaration by the Conference on Security and Cooperation in Europe (CSCE) provides a precedent for a right to self-determination. The CSCE declared that Yugoslavia could not use force to preserve its internal borders. Yugoslavia was essentially stripped of its sovereign rights to prevent the country from disintegrating, and the rights of peoples were given preference over the rights of a state. This action could have far-reaching consequences for other communal conflicts, and it certainly represents a shift away from the automatic preference given to states, at least in the context of internal conflict.[77]

The question still unanswered with this brief overview of the legal context of self-determination is exactly what is the status of self-determination? Is it a principle, a right, or *jus cogens,* and in what context can self-determination be claimed? As Shivji points out, the right to self determination is 'hotly contested terrain'.[78] However, what is not contested is that there is a right to self-determination in a colonial context. Cristescu ties the right to self-determination to international peace and security and characterizes it 'as an established principle, a universal right under contemporary international law, and a legally binding principle enjoying universality and constituting a general rule of international law.'[79] This right continues after any particular act of self-determination (that is decolonization) and is carried forth in the principles of sovereignty and non-interference.[80] This would seem to put self-determination within a state-centric context. However, as will be seen below, the situation is somewhat more ambiguous than this.

Regarding self-determination as *jus cogens,* Lapidoth notes that if it is to have binding force, self-determination must be either *jus cogens* or *jus dispostivium,* which allows derogation by consent.[81] Both the Subcommission on the Prevention of Discrimination and Protection of Minorities and the International Law Commission have characterized self-determination as *jus cogens*.[82] This right is suspended when it comes into conflict with national sovereignty: 'Where the territorial integrity of the State is involved, then self-determination does not in principle apply.'[83] However, Héctor Gros Espiell notes that

> if the national unity claimed and the territorial integrity invoked are merely legal fictions which cloak real colonial and alien domination, resulting from actual disregard of the principle of self-determination, the subject people or peoples are entitled to exercise, with all the consequences thereof, their right to self-determination.[84]

Cristescu concurs: 'non-intervention should not be used to cover up violations of self-determination. . .'[85] In other words, self-determination can, indeed, override state sovereignty when a people is under 'alien domination' or subject to oppression. This extends self-determination beyond decolonization. What this might mean is still not clear, and will be discussed in the next section. However, I will briefly touch upon the legal aspects of one of the most obvious manifestations of self-determination: secession.

Lapidoth notes that secession, at least in the post-colonial context, contradicts the principle of *uti posseditis* – the principle that new states' boundaries should follow colonial boundaries. However, I have demonstrated that self-determination, in certain instances, can apply outside of decolonization. Cristescu notes that there is a limited right to secession:

> The right of secession unquestionably exists, however, in a special, but very important case: that of peoples, territories and entities subjugated in violation of international law. In such cases, the peoples concerned have the right to regain their freedom and constitute themselves independent sovereign States.[86]

State practice has, in general, not allowed secession,[87] although the international community has accepted the secessions of Bangladesh from Pakistan, Slovakia from Czechoslovakia, and Eritrea from Ethiopia.[88] Self-determination comes into conflict with many different international norms, most notably territorial integrity in the case of secession, and 'it should be apparent that the relationship of the principle of self-determination to other crucial norms of international behavior is frighteningly obscure'.[89]

There is a large literature on secession, most of which come to the same conclusion regarding an ambiguous, limited right to secession.[90] However, secession by its very nature is state-centric in that discussion of secession only allows (or disallows) the creation of a new sovereign state. The premise of this book, however, is that there is a need to break out of state-centric analysis. Why this is so, and how this might occur, is the subject of the following sections.

SELF-DETERMINATION AS A MORAL PRINCIPLE

Woodrow Wilson has become indelibly identified with self-determination. He forcefully put forward self-determination as an overriding norm for international relations:

> No peace can last, or ought to last, which does not recognize that governments derive all their just powers from the consent of the governed and that no right anywhere exists, to hand peoples about from sovereignty to sovereignty as if they were property.
>
> Peoples and provinces are not to be bartered about from sovereignty to sovereignty as if they were mere chattels and pawns in the game. . . . Self-determination is not a mere phrase. It is an imperative principle of action, which statesmen will henceforth ignore at their peril.[91]

These lofty goals were certainly worthwhile and well-intentioned. However, one can make two damning criticisms of Wilson. First, these principles were only to apply to Europe after World War I. The United States had entered the war on the side of other colonial powers, most notably Great Britain and France, and how could he undermine his allies by expanding self-determination to the rest of the globe, most notably in Africa and Asia? Second, Wilson, while well-intentioned, was extremely naive in the way he thought European self-determination would proceed. He felt that the breakup of the European empires could occur along existing national lines.[92]

Wilson had many critics, notably Robert Lansing, his secretary of state, who, in an oft quoted passage, wrote:

> The more I think about the President's declaration as to the right of 'self-determination,' the more convinced I am of the danger of putting such ideas into the minds of certain races. It is bound to be the basis of impossible demands on the Peace Congress, and create trouble in many lands. . . .
>
> The phrase is simply loaded with dynamite. It will raise hopes which can never be realized. It will, I fear, cost thousands of lives. In the end it is bound to be discredited, to be called the dream of an idealist who failed to realize the danger until too late to check those who attempt to

put the principle into force. What a calamity that the phrase was ever uttered! What misery it will cause![93]

A large part of this calamity had to do with the fact that, as is the case almost everywhere, ethnic frontiers cannot be simply drawn, or even drawn at all for that matter. There were Germans in Poland and Czechoslovakia, Magyars in Czechoslovakia and Romania, and Jews, persecuted everywhere, throughout Eastern Europe.[94] Hobsbawm points to 'the utter impracticability of the Wilsonian principle to make state frontiers coincide with the frontiers of nationality and language'. Except for some concessions to Italy and Poland, and certain decisions about Germany's borders, the peace settlement attempted to put this principle into practice. However, '[i]t simply did not work. Inevitably, given the actual distribution of peoples, most of the new states built on the ruins of the old empires, were quite as multinational as the old "prisons of nations" they replaced.'[95]

This project of ethnic delineation perhaps laid the groundwork for some contemporary conflicts. Certainly the problems associated with the Wilsonian vision have not abated. As M.B. Ramose has noted, 'decolonisation has not ushered in self-determination',[96] either in the case of Europe after World War I, or in the post-1945 wave of decolonization. The resulting states were filled with numerous groups, each seeing themselves as distinct from the others. Strict ethnic separation was not achieved, nor could it have been, because the increased mobility of people, as well as the attempts at ethnic cleansing which push certain groups into other, equally alien territories, have irretrievably mixed up the numerous language, religious, and other groups. Many countries look not like the famed 'melting pot' of the United States (although one could question whether this is really an apt description) but rather more like 'tossed salads', where various groups have been mixed in together but still retain their identifiable characteristics. Attempts at assimilation have not reinforced the proximity which these groups have with respect to one another; indeed, forced assimilation usually heightens tensions between groups.

All of this leads to the following questions: who is the 'self' which is entitled to self-determination, what form(s) should that determination take, and how does one reconcile competing claims, not just between groups, but between group and individual rights? In other words, how is it possible to include the tensions between groups and between groups and individuals in a reconstructed notion of sovereignty? At the beginning of this chapter I attempted to provide tentative definitions of the various entities which are supposedly entitled to self-determination. The definitions and distinctions between them are not very satisfying. All of them are social constructions; none are natural entities. However, this does not mean that they are any less valuable for the members of these groups insofar as they provide a 'common life', and any less worthy as moral subjects:

> What is at stake is the value of a historical or cultural or religious community and the political liberty of its members. The liberty is not compromised, it seems to me, by the postmodern discovery that communities are sociological constructions: imagined, invented, put together. Constructed communities are the only communities there are; they can't be less real or less authentic than some other sort. Their members, then, have the rights that go with membership. *They ought to be allowed to govern themselves* – insofar as they can do that, given their local entanglements.[97]

What it does mean, however, is that no particular community or type of community has an absolute claim to determine its status without regard to other communities. Walzer points out that '[s]elf-determination has no absolute subject'.[98] In other words, each community must pursue its common life in some sort of harmony with other common lives. This is because each community is comprised of, comprises, and overlaps with other communities, which also want to pursue their own autonomous common lives.

Regarding the value of communal identity, MacCormick notes that 'a sense of nationality is for many people constitutive in part of their sense of identity and even of selfhood',[99] and it thus must be respected. Indeed, our identity is usually constituted by membership in, and identification with, a number of different communities, territorially and non-territorially based. They are part of who we are, and can provide for certain material and psychological wants and needs. However, the specific type of community is not decided in advance. And, the bases of communities can be simultaneously constructive and destructive: 'ethnicity is one of those forces that is community building in moderation, community-destroying in excess. It is both fruitless and undesirable to attempt to abolish ethnic affiliations, but not at all fruitless to attempt to limit their impact.'[100] Walzer further maintains:

> Tribalism names the commitment of individuals and groups to their own history, culture, and identity, and this commitment (though not any particular version of it) is a permanent feature of human social life. The parochialism that it breeds is similarly permanent. It can't be overcome; it has to be accommodated: *not only my parochialism but yours as well, and his and hers in their turn.*[101]

It is this last portion which is particularly relevant. The claims of all communities must be given attention. However, the outcomes may be different. The goals of these various communities frequently come into conflict. A particular group may claim a right to self-determination, usually based on oppression by some larger entity of which they are a part. They identify themselves as different from the other from which they wish to separate. This difference may be based on any of the criteria with which we define ourselves. Earlier, I pointed out that these differences are relational. That is, the difference – real or imagined – which may supposedly create an irreconcilable divide between two groups, may either provide a basis for self-perceived commonality between one of the groups and a third (although another characteristic may tear them apart) or at least not be a source of conflict – an accepted difference.

Thus the pressures pushing groups away from each other will vary by circumstance, and the defining differences will occur at various levels of aggregation. There may also be conflict between two seemingly homogeneous groups. Small differences, not discernible to an outside observer, may, in different circumstances – such as when another conflict no longer divides the groups (internally unites the individual groups) – provide grist for the communal conflict mill. This might occur, for example, when there is a change in the international environment. For many years, Czechoslovakia functioned as a unitary state, with little internal conflict, within the larger geostrategic logic of the East-West conflict. Once that conflict receded, the Slovaks, peacefully, seceded, based upon some older conflict, as well as differential economic situations. Yugoslavia was seen as a model multinational state, with different groups living together more or less peacefully. Yet, as soon as it was possible, most of the constituent republics, some more homogeneous than others, broke away, and massive atrocities have been perpetuated, based upon partially historical, and partially recently distorted, animosities and bigotries.[102]

What this indicates is that it is seemingly theoretically possible for each group, once it has attained some sort of autonomy from some larger entity, to be split apart by some other conflict *ad infinitum*. Certainly, this is part of what motivated Secretary of State Lansing's fears with regard to Wilson's plans for post-World War I European self-determination. And, it is also the basis for fear among those who see the current international system of roughly 200 sovereign states as a reasonable and workable configuration for global politics and who see communal conflict as undermining the basis of this system.

What this does not indicate, however, is what the entities which should have a right to self-determination should look like. Should subjective self-identification be the basis for self-determination? Should there be some numerical threshold which a group must attain before it has rights, for certainly there is some sort of minimum number of people and resources a community must have in order to be able to survive in the global industrial/postindustrial milieu? Or, alternatively, is the world community willing to take on even more 'charity' cases in order to provide some sort of self-determination? The answer to these questions will depend, partly, on what form of self-determination one is talking about.

Colonial peoples – those who are ruled by others outside of their communal territory – have a right under international law to break free of the state which rules them from afar. This is certainly reasonable, for if one assumes that there is value to communities, because they provide certain benefits for their members, and that the members should decide what those benefits are and how they are distributed – otherwise there would be no feeling of community – then having those decisions made by others outside of the community would destroy the very basis of community.

Beyond this, things get murkier. However, there is no reason why a community which is not subject to domination from outside its particular state should not also be free to determine the scope and outline of itself:

> One searches in vain, however, for any principled justification of why a colonial people wishing to cast off the domination of its governors has every moral and legal right to do so, but a manifestly distinguishable minority which happens to find itself, pursuant to a paragraph in some medieval territorial settlement or through a fiat of the cartographers, annexed to an independent state must forever remain without the scope of the principle of self-determination.[103]

There is no fundamental difference, in other words, between a territorial entity which, if it were not dominated by an outside state, would be considered a state and a community within a state which experiences discrimination. The former is called 'colonialism', the latter has been characterized as 'internal colonialism'.[104] Since the state is not a natural entity with attendant natural rights above and beyond other communities, there is no *a priori* justification for treating the two cases as having different moral qualities. Thus, it is possible to treat claims on the part of different kinds and sizes of communities more or less equally. In other words, there is no inherent imperative to favour and preserve the status quo. What is important is the balance between competing claims.

It is usually minority communities which make claims against the state. Except for the ten per cent of states which are more or less ethnically homogeneous, all states are heterogeneous and thus have minorities, including the 40 per cent of states in which no communal entity comprises a majority.[105] What actually constitutes a minority, and the rights that go along with such an appellation, are not clearly defined. Some make a distinction between minorities, which supposedly are not entitled to self-determination, and peoples or nations, which do possess such a right. Espiell maintains that under international law peoples have a right to self-determination, while minorities do not.[106]

Hannum notes that there is no accepted definition of what constitutes a minority,[107] although he does provide a working definition of a minority: 'a numerically smaller, non-dominant group distinguished by shared ethnic, racial, religious, or linguistic attributes'.[108] It is hard to see a distinction between this definition and that of a community which is entitled to self-determination. 'Peoples', too, are characterized by 'shared ethnic, racial, religious, or linguistic attributes'. Minorities, because of their status as distinct communities which provide certain benefits to the members of their community, have a moral right to self-determination. When the distinction is made between a minority on the one hand, and nations or peoples on the other, it is usually for political purposes. For example, as one Geg leader commented about the Serbian President Slobodan Milosevic in 1992:

It's all a tragic absurdity. In fighting for Serbs in Croatia, and now in Bosnia and Herzegovina, [he] says that all Serbs have the right to live in a single Serbian state. But here in Kosovo, where Albanians would like to claim that right for themselves, we are told that we are not a nation, we are a minority. It's simply a matter of double standards.[109]

Another type of community which can make claims on the basis of its self-identification as a distinct group is the indigenous community. They may be considered a special case of minorities who, in addition to that status, have a relationship to the territory in which they live which dates back usually centuries before the majority inhabitants of the territory – that is colonizers and others – came to the territory. In 1989, the International Labor Organization changed the language referring to indigenous communities from 'populations' to 'peoples', thus indicating a legal status with rights to self-determination.[110]

Almost all indigenous peoples have had their rights ignored and their land taken, even in cases where they are supposedly self-governing. Many states have assumed that indigenous peoples would be assimilated into the dominant culture and have been hostile to indigenous language and culture.[111] In addition, indigenous rights have crumbled in the face of development in the less developed countries.

Most states, especially those with significant indigenous populations, do not classify them in such a way as to grant them rights to self-determination. And even in cases where they are supposedly granted special autonomous status they generally do not possess equal rights within the larger state context. However, as with other minorities, indigenous communities have a moral right to self-determination on the basis of their status as distinct communities which are chosen by their members and which provide social goods to their members. As R.S. Bhalla has written:

> The granting of the right to self-determination to indigenous people by excluding others may appear intangible, ambiguous and problematic, but this does not make the principle of self-determination unnecessary nor invalid. Such an application of the right of self-determination is rational and unbiased, based on the colonial power's obligation towards those from whom the colony was seized and on a proper regard for their cultural identity. Such an application of the right of self-determination may or may not be comfortable to some, but it is certainly the most durable.[112]

The reference to colonialism brings up another point. Insofar as indigenous populations are being dominated by alien societies – that is societies which did not originate in the territory – they can be considered as colonized peoples. One might make the case that they should be entitled to decolonization. The states in which the indigenous populations live are not governed by another state, and thus are not considered colonies per se. However, the term internal colonialism certainly applies, and indigenous peoples are thus entitled to forms of self-determination which will remedy this situation.

This discussion of indigenous peoples, itself, is predicated on a certain starting point for identifying political communities. That is, the political community that is called Brazil, for instance, is called such as a result of foreign domination which began hundreds of years ago and continues today. The part of Brazil inhabited – or which used to be inhabited – by the indigenous Yanomami is not called Yanomamiland or some other similar designation, because the international community has accepted norms for identifying and reifying certain types of identities which submerge other types of identities. Thus the term 'indigenous' depends upon an international norm which recognizes the 'nonindigenous' and allows them to identify the communities within a particular territory.

Above I presented in broad strokes an outline of the types of groups which are entitled to some form of self-determination. However, claims for self-determination frequently come into conflict with each other, and self-determination by one group usually denies self-determination to another. In addition, we all are simultaneously members of several groups at one time. We might identify ourselves by nationality, by religion, or by language, depending on the situation, and sometimes these multiple selves may come into conflict. There is no inherent, singular self – or 'absolute subject' in Walzer's words – which we can identify and give self-determination: 'as is the case with minorities, selves can never be wholly eliminated'.[113] Thus, as we discuss who deserves self-determination, we must be mindful that selves are always determined in relation to other selves, which must be accommodated. In addition, frequently the way self-determination is implemented comes into conflict with other collective and individual rights, and a balance must be struck. Neither are inherently more important, for each can buttress the other.

HUMAN RIGHTS AND SELF-DETERMINATION

Recent waves of communal conflict have vividly illustrated the tensions between various 'selves' definitions of self-determination and human rights. Moynihan points to the 'question of sorting out such values [democracy and human rights] in the context of ethnic group demands in which people define whom they love by whom they hate'.[114] However, the tensions between self-determination and human rights are not only based on deep-seated hatred, but also on general disregard or dismissal of other groups. The link between self-determination and human rights raises many questions, including: is self-determination a precondition for human rights; alternatively, are human rights preconditions for self-determination? The answer to both of these questions, while seemingly mutually exclusive, is yes.

Individuals have certain rights with regard to personal autonomy. These rights are expressed within the context of relations with others – that is within a community or a number of communities simultaneously – and are tempered by these relationships. I noted above that communities partially define who we are – our 'selves'. Insofar as communities provide an environment for the fulfillment of human rights and help us to define our various 'selves', they are valuable and might be considered preconditions for human rights. And as such, communities have certain attendant rights as a collectivity: 'Self-determination is a democratic principle which extends the principle of personal autonomy to a collective level. Just as the individual is free to decide on moral beliefs and moral conduct, so are communities free and sovereign to decide how they organise themselves.'[115] Further, self-determination is 'the right of a group of individuals in association; it [is] certainly the prerogative of a community, but the community itself consist[s] of individuals and any encroachment on its collective right would be tantamount to a breach of their fundamental freedoms.'[116]

These communities have rights precisely because they provide space for the development and enjoyment of other rights:

> It is not the case that one can simply proclaim a list of rights and then look for armed men to enforce it. Rights are only enforceable within political communities where they have been collectively recognized, and the process by which they come to be recognized is a political process which requires a political arena.[117]

In other words, rights need a community in which they can be shaped, contested and enjoyed. Rights are relational, and the community provides the relationships for these rights.

However, communal assertions, while positive in some instances, can also be destructive and contrary to the enjoyment of human rights. Nationalism and similar communal manifestations can represent the antithesis of the universalism which is embodied in the concept of human rights. Insofar as nationalism becomes an absolutizing project, the particularism which it spawns leads to the direct, and usually violent, suppression of the right of self-determination – and other human rights – of other groups within the territory which one group claims as its home.[118] This is where self-determination claims come into conflict with each other as well as with human rights and the rights of minorities become operative. Two or more groups may compete for what seems like the same political space and make claims upon that space on the basis of self-determination. Insofar as minority rights are implemented they can preclude such absolutist excesses. Thus self-determination in varied and overlapping forms is necessary for the enjoyment of human rights which might otherwise be undermined by absolutist projects.

Self-determination is a collective right. As such, it is related to the role the community plays *vis-à-vis* the individual. For this collective right to be carried out, however, certain preconditions must be met. Primary among these is the ability of those within the community to determine the goals and direction of the community – that is, to participate in the self-determining process. This requires rights related to participation in government.

In other words, self-determination requires the ability of individuals to engage in the process of popular sovereignty which determines the nature, scope, and direction of the community.

Thus, while self-determination is required for the development and enjoyment of human rights, human rights are also a precondition for communal self-determination. They cannot be divorced from each other. In this sense, self-determination is a human right along with civil, political, and economic rights which, taken as a whole, describe and guarantee the rights of human existence.

SELF-DETERMINATION IN PRACTICE

While I have established that to varying degrees and in varying contexts self-determination is a right, what this means in concrete terms is still unclear. In other words, to what extent does it imply a right to independence and to what extent is self-determination tied more to other forms of self-government? I shall argue that the form of self-determination is not set in advance nor is it a once and for all event, where once an action of self-determination takes place, this sets the political arrangements for all time. Self-determination involves a number of different possibilities. These might include secession and the resulting creation of an independent state; consociationalism, where minorities are given a greater say in the overall governing of a country; federalism; and, relatedly, autonomy, where certain regions which are distinct from the rest of a territorial entity are given various measures of self-government. I will discuss these various possibilities in turn.

The form of self-determination which many groups are fighting for and which discomforts national elites more than any other is secession, the breaking away of one part of a state to form another independent state. This option, of course, is the most state-centric of all possible options. Does denying an almost unfettered right to secession privilege existing states? Alternatively, does recognizing a right to secession privilege the state as a political form? Finally, what criteria should be used in deciding secession claims?

Regarding the first question, denying an unqualified right to secession for any group within a particular state may, indeed, privilege existing states. However, this is nowhere near an absolute situation. Rather, there are still many possibilities for self-determination. Indeed, there may be very good reasons for keeping a state intact. In addition, granting an unlimited right to secession would, indeed, reify the sovereign state form above all other forms of political association. There is no absolute right to secession, nor should there be. Various types of communities are too intertwined and interdependent for any community that wants to declare itself its own state to do so. The point to be developed below is that at some level communities must, for the survival of their community as well as the individuals within communities, develop ways to live with each other within various types of political associations and interdependent relationships.

However, in some cases secession on the part of a particular community from the larger community from which it is part may be warranted, and criteria must be developed to deal with these situations. Some may fear that developing such criteria will only encourage and embolden many more groups to fight for such an outcome. Yet, even without any recognized right to secession and without any real prospects for success, many groups worldwide are agitating for secession. In addition, there are many more groups which might make some sort of claim along various lines but which are quiescent, even in the current period of communal unrest. There is no reason to believe that putting forward strict criteria for secession would mobilize large numbers of groups to join the fray.

Buchanan provides a number of different justifications for secession. The first comes under the heading of rectificatory justice, which he describes as '[t]he most obviously compelling justification for secession . . . '.[119] In this case, the state of which the seceding territory is part never had a legitimate claim on that territory, it was annexed or taken over in a drive toward territorial expansion and it never formed an integral part of the state. An example of this is the Baltic states which were forcibly incorporated into the Soviet Union during World War II. This case is 'the reapportionment, by the legitimate owners, of stolen property'.[120] Yet, one might also question whether there is some time limit − a statute of limitations − for such rectification to take place. This issue arises primarily from the assumption that over an extended period time, the population of the territory in question would change in such a fundamental manner that secession would no longer represent the majority of the people and would have severe negative consequences for the changed community. In such cases, other forms of self-determination, including autonomy or guarantees of minority rights might be more appropriate.

Another justification Buchanan mentions is reversing discriminatory redistribution, where the central government discriminates against a certain group or region by imposing higher taxes or not spending the same percentage on a particular group. While there may be some cases where such redistribution is targeted unfairly at a particular group and thus may entitle them to certain remedies, this is not always the case. There are always certain parts of a country which are richer than other parts, and, because of this, there may be a net outflow of resources from a particular territory to other parts of a country in order to provide for the social welfare of others within the country. This is a simple instance of progressive economic policies which redistribute wealth within a particular community – an entire country. Such redistribution plays a major, and generally accepted, role in welfare states and cannot provide justification for secession. In other words just because a particular population is richer and provides a larger proportion of the social goods to the country than it receives it cannot then secede to protect its wealth.[121]

A third type of justification Buchanan puts forth is cultural preservation. This plays a major role in the claims made by many ethnic groups. However, cultural identity may be preserved in a variety of ways short of secession. Indeed, in some cases, secession may not help the situation at all. For example, in the case of francophones outside of Quebec in Canada, secession by Quebec would not help their situation. Given the various concessions made by Canada toward Quebec, secession would not provide significantly more remedies for cultural self-determination, at least not without also leading to further discrimination against English-speakers within the territory, which, in turn, might provide justification for certain claims to self-determination on their behalf.[122]

He delineates five criteria which must be met in order for cultural preservation to provide adequate justification for secession:

1. the culture must be 'truly threatened' in a manner more extreme than other cultures;
2. other forms of cultural preservation must not be available;
3. the culture 'must meet minimal standards of moral decency';
4. the aim of the secession must not be to set up a state where civil and political rights are routinely violated and from which free exit is denied; and
5. 'neither the state nor any third party has a valid claim to the seceding territory'.[123]

These criteria would, indeed, limit the application of a right to secede. However, they are not completely adequate. The first criterion, that a culture face threats which no other cultures, in the normal course of things, face, can probably only be found in cases where a particular group faces extreme discrimination on the part of the state. Particular cultures do not have an unfettered right to exist when that existence is based almost solely on supports from the state in the absence of discrimination:

majorities have no obligations to guarantee the survival of minority cultures. They may well be struggling to survive themselves, caught up in a common competition against commercialism and international fashion. Borders provide only minimal protection in the modern world [and thus a culture might not be able to survive as an independent state], and minorities within borders, driven by their situation to a preternatural closeness, may do better in sustaining a way of life than the more relaxed majority population. And if they do worse, that is no reason to come to their rescue; they have a claim, indeed, to physical but not to cultural security.[124]

If a group experiences discrimination then it will be able to make valid claims for protection or, possibly, secession, although the latter option might not, in the end, help them all that much. Otherwise, we must recognize that all cultures adapt, change, meld with other cultures, and are in a general state of flux, and absolute protection for cultural purity cannot be claimed as a right. Communities have a right to self-determination, but they do not have the right to inordinate amounts of resources from larger communities of which they are part to ensure that all cultural practices will stay intact for all time.

The second criterion, that of unavailability of other remedies, will not be fulfilled in most cases. As I shall argue, there are many forms of political and cultural association which will fit the bill in a majority of cases. The third criterion obviously fits in with the New Sovereignty. However, the fourth, while related, seems to imply that a seceding group could set up a state which violated its members' human rights as long as it provided an out for those who did not wish to live in such a state. Three objections can be made. First, this would be a violation of what I have argued is the social purpose of the state – to provide for the security and well-being of its inhabitants. Second, it would violate what have become international norms for behaviour by states with regard to human rights. Third, even if the first two objections were ignored, it is very hard to imagine a situation where all members at all times were truly free to leave the state, and it would entail an initial violation of the rights of a minority within the seceding territory who did not want to live in such a state and who do not want to be expelled.

Finally, the last criterion is superfluous on two grounds. First, the state from which a territory wanted to secede would have given up its legitimate claims to the territory if the population in the territory could make a good claim for secession on the basis of discrimination or oppression, which are the only grounds – apart from rectification – which could be used in this instance. Second, a third state may have a claim on the territory, but it may not have as good a claim on the *people* within the territory. That is, secession might occur some period of time after a territory was annexed by another state. In that situation, the collective self-identification may have changed and the population may no longer want to be associated with the first state of which it was originally part, and it would seem unjust to force them to rejoin the state if they had changed to such a degree that this would violate their subjective sense of self-determination. If they had not thus changed, they could still decide to rejoin the first state.

Some of these criteria are useful, but they are not completely adequate to address the issue of secession. Several other criteria must be considered. First, the seceding population must be territorially compact. Otherwise, the act of secession itself would result in human rights abuses of a fairly large magnitude, primarily from the vast population transfers involved in the rearrangement of populations – which might be considered ethnic cleansing. Bosnia-Herzegovina clearly demonstrates the effect of population transfers. Vast refugee populations are created and other human rights abuses occur. And, the movement of large populations of people against their will is on the face of it immoral. The partition of India into India and Pakistan had such results; the Pakistani Hindu and Indian Muslim populations were 'exchanged'. However, the movement of a portion of the Muslim population out of India certainly has not eliminated tensions between the Hindu and Muslim populations in India, or, for that matter, tensions between India and Pakistan.

Closely related to this is how minorities within the seceding territory are treated. Most territories wishing to secede have minority populations, particularly in cases where a territory was incorporated into another and the annexing state moves part of its population into the new territory, as in the case of the Baltic states to which significant numbers of Russians moved. With independence they, themselves, are being discriminated against. They must not be subjected to the same kind of oppression as the majority group which wants to break away, but should, instead, be granted full cultural autonomy. If, for example, an independent Palestinian state were to be formed, the Jewish settlers now there would retain certain rights, although the Palestinians would also be justified in making sure that their state was not just a nominally independent part of Israel. This question of minorities demonstrates how self-determination claims can come into conflict and that it is usually very hard, if not impossible, to separate out all of the various selves which are intertwined in a particular territory, and thus why not all groups who want their own states can have them.

In addition, the effect of the secession on the rump state must be considered. In cases where a rich province wanted to secede and leave the rest of the country in a much poorer situation, the seceding entity would have an obligation to pay reparations. This goes along with the prohibition on secession purely for economic means. A state might be affected in other ways as well. For example, in the Eritrean secession, Eritrea agreed to allow uninhibited access to a port since Ethiopia would become landlocked. This was one of the major reasons why the new Ethiopian government agreed to the referendum which led to the secession (as well as the fact that they did not want to endure another civil war like the one which had just ended).

The potential viability of a seceding territory is also relevant. In some cases, where the territory is relatively rich and not too small, this will not be a problem. However, in other cases the potential new state may be unable to develop an economy which can adequately provide for its population.

Finally, the conduct of the group claiming self-determination must be taken into account. A movement which is extremely violent, especially insofar as it denies others the right to self-determination and violates human rights, would probably also be likely to engage in repressive measures against minorities within its own state, thus violating other criteria discussed above. However, it is hard to insist upon complete nonviolence, especially in the case of self-defence. The Unrepresented Nations and Peoples Organization (UNPO), which represents the interests of those struggling for self-determination, insists upon nonviolence as a criteria for membership. However, the group's founder, Michael van Walt, also recognizes how hard it is to insist upon strict nonviolence:

> The extent of violence used against indigenous peoples is sometimes so enormous and constant that it would be unfair to say that governments and states can use violence but that the people, in their quest for independence, cannot. An example is the West Papuans, who have been fighting for their freedom with bows and arrows and are being bombed from the air by the Indonesians. To tell the West Papuans that they can't fight back is something nobody in their right conscience could do.[125]

Yet, frequently violence is a tactic of first resort, and a clear message should be sent which says that, in general, violence is an illegitimate way to pursue self-determination.

Above are a number of criteria which must be fulfilled in order for a claim of secession on the part of a community to be valid – beyond the case of rectificatory justice which, at least within a certain time frame, is justified in and of itself: (1) the group seceding must face some sort of

discrimination and their cultural self-determination must be in jeopardy;
(2) other forms of self-determination must not be available; (3) the new
state must meet certain standards of conduct; (4) territorial compactness;
(5) just treatment of minorities within the seceding territory; (6) the effects
on the rump state; (7) viability; and (8) conduct of the seceding group. This
discussion of secession is inherently state-centric, whether in disallowing
many types of secession and thus privileging the existing state, or, con-
versely, allowing secession and reifying the state as the one form which
can be the prize at the end of a struggle for self-determination. However,
with regional integration, and various infringements on supposedly sovereign borders, statehood is not the prize some secessionists imagine. In addition, there are many other forms which self-determination can take and
which will not have the disruptive effects of secession.

A discussion of non-nation-state forms of self-determination must start
by reinforcing the point, made above, that it is impossible for every 'self'
to disentangle itself from every other 'self'. All of the ways in which we
identify ourselves are bound up together. Trying to identify one basic constituent element of a group of people will inevitably come into conflict
with the various ways in which the individuals within that group identify
themselves. Most may have one identifying characteristic in common,
such as language, but also have a multitude of other characteristics not in
common, such as religion or a shared (imagined) history. When trying to
create an absolutist nationalist project based on the one shared characteristic, these other labels come into conflict, such that finding an 'essence' of
a group of individuals is basically impossible. Thus, ways must be found
to allow expression of these various characteristics without the violent
conflicts which frequently accompany communal assertions.

A second principle which must be kept in mind is that self-determination
is not a particular action which can be taken once and then disregarded. This
is true because the 'selves' involved can change their self-identification or
the balance between various selves may change. For example, in Lebanon an
accord was struck in 1943 which divided governmental posts among the main
Christian and Muslim groups, based upon the proportion of the population in
each group. This agreement provided the foundation for several decades of
peaceful coexistence among Christians and Muslims. However, the Muslim
population grew faster than the Christian population, thus undermining the
proportional basis of the accord. The Christians refused to renegotiate because this would have taken away some of their power in the government, and
a bloody civil war ensued. If a principle of continuous self-determination,
where the various 'selves' periodically reviewed and adjusted their arrangements in accordance with changing demographics and other realities, had

been followed, perhaps some or all of the bloodshed and instability may have been avoided.

Keeping these two principles in mind, I now turn to a brief look at other possibilities for self-determination and how they affect a reconstructed concept of sovereignty. There is a wide literature on attempts to deal with communal conflict.[126] What they all have in common is the initial recognition that difference is how we define ourselves, and because of this, these differences must be accommodated. These accommodations can come in varying forms, with equally varying implications for sovereignty.

Consociationalism[127] is a form of democracy which recognizes and institutionalizes ethnic differences. Minority groups are incorporated into the national government through a grand compromise among the elites which provides disproportionate representation for minorities and minority veto. Such arrangements can, indeed, help to defuse otherwise destructive conflict and provide forms of coexistence for various communities within a larger community. The groups might also enjoy various forms of autonomy, including institutional autonomy – such as having different schools – and, in some instances, territorial autonomy. Because it relies so much on elite accommodation, however, it can, at the same time, undermine part of the democratic basis of the society.

Another form of ethnic accommodation is embodied in regional autonomy without some of the consociational aspects. In other words, groups are given autonomy within particular regions, while the federal government does not have the same kind of disproportionate minority representation and veto found in consociationalism, and it also does not have to be associated with democracy per se. Autonomy can range from separate regional educational systems to recognition of regional languages and regional self-government. Such arrangements undermine the 'internal' aspects of sovereignty of the state, devolving significant powers to substate entities. In addition, insofar as these semi-sovereign regions are able to engage in contacts across state borders, especially with those in neighbouring states who they see as like them, part of a transnational imagined community, the state's sovereignty is further weakened. Indeed, in some instances, the dividing line between autonomy and independence may not mean a whole lot, and the two may mean different things than they have in the past: 'Many would say today that nowadays, when the absolute sovereignty of small states is hardly thinkable, the difference between autonomy and independence has become academic.'[128] Further, as I will argue, the evolving relationship between substate regions and supranational organization further complicates the sovereignty equation.

In cases where the selves which claim autonomy are not territorially compact, autonomy might still be useful. In such instances, self-determination would include minority rights, such as the right to different schools, the ability to use different languages, and other rights which must be negotiated within specific instances. All the autonomy schemes recognize and institutionalize the differences we all use to identify ourselves in relation to others. They do not seek to create a homogeneous 'people' out of groups which see themselves as distinct. This recognition of difference is not bad insofar as there is no overriding social imperative to pursue such an end. What matters, instead, is that human rights, including collective rights, are promoted and all persons, individually and in communities, are able to enjoy such rights.

SELF-DETERMINATION AND SOVEREIGNTY

What, then, is the relationship between self-determination and sovereignty? I have argued that self-determination can be seen as a legal right, and is necessary for the enjoyment of other human rights. However, the form and extent of this right is ambiguous, applicable in different situations in different ways. Yet, I will begin by agreeing with James Crawford: 'Self-determination as a legal right or principle would represent a significant erosion of the principle of sovereignty. It is a dynamic principle which, if consistently applied, could bring about significant changes in the political geography of the world.'[129]

One interpretation of self-determination, used by many groups asserting communal identity, is the creation of independent states: 'Sovereignty is a dry, legal question for those nations who have acquired statehood. Sovereignty is a passionate crusade for those who do not have it.'[130] Insofar as independence is the norm, sovereignty is upheld and the state system is left more or less intact. At the same time, however, those who want their own state pose a direct challenge to already established sovereign states. Since the world is already almost completely divided up as states, any new states would have to come out of the territory of established states. Thus, even though self-determination as statehood upholds Westphalian norms and falls directly within the sovereignty discourse, it is also a direct assault on sovereignty as an established, unchangeable linking of territory and people and government.

Further, even where the aim of self-determination is not the creation of an independent state, sovereignty can still be eroded. Indeed, it 'requires a more subtle view of sovereignty',[131] and the consideration of the possibility of shared or partial or divided sovereignty. When a community gains a certain amount of autonomy or self-rule, it begins to share sovereignty with the state of which it is part. It may have the opportunity to decide how to define and pursue its 'common life', while doing so in conjunction with another, more comprehensive entity, which carries out some of the other more 'external' functions necessary in this era of dwindling distances and increased interdependence. As a substate autonomous community begins to have more contacts across permeable state borders independent of a state, it engages in a further erosion, or evasion, of sovereignty.

For those who aspire to statehood, they may be seeking a prize with decreasing salience as the twin forces of devolution and integration proceed apace. The European Union, with all of its problems and false starts is a case in point. Statehood may not mean the same thing that those who seek it hope it to be. As Bengoetxea notes: 'It is recognised that the increasingly supranational politico-legal order of the European Community may well render redundant and anachronistic the very prize of national state sovereignty before it can be achieved.'[132] However, it may be that the development of the EU will enhance the possibilities for self-determination of substate communities within its realm. In addition, some EU organs have begun to notice and channel resources to such regions, bypassing states themselves.[133] In fact, in Great Britain, the EU Commission has offices in Cardiff (Wales) and Edinburgh (Scotland) in addition to its main office in London: 'This signifies that political activity in Wales and Scotland – although integrated into UK structures – is nonetheless distinct and the problems of those countries are as discrete as their histories.... therefore, sub state nationalism has had an effect on EC political discourse....'[134] With such a combination of devolution and integration, the EU is beginning to recognize the need 'to reconcile the need for larger economic units with the growing demand for smaller political units based upon ethnic identity'.[135] All this may lead to the point where

> we may be able to allow the full expression of nationalism, self-determination and cultural diversity within the European Community yet contribute, through the maturing supranationalism of that community to the goal of a stable, consistent and coherent international legal order.[136]

It is not only by recognition of a certain status of the substate regions on the part of the EU or other organization that communities will enhance their self-determination, but also through actual representation in such organizations. Indeed, Weiner notes that 'part of the solution may lie in finding ways to provide international standing to ethnic groups short of state

sovereignty – perhaps through representation for ethnic groups within regional and international organizations.'[137] This would represent a further
erosion of sovereignty insofar as international organizations, which already impinge on state sovereignty, would not be dominated to the same
degree by states, but would, instead, be more pluralistic. Substate communities would also have a greater say in determining the forms which
self-determination could take.[138]

Some observers see nationalism and other communal assertions as part
of a bygone era, being passed by supranationalism. Hobsbawm maintains
that nationalism 'is no longer a major vector of historical development'.[139]
Instead, the world 'will see "nation-states" and "nation" or ethnic-lin-
guistic groups primarily . . . retreating before, resisting, adapting to, being
absorbed or dislocated by, the new supranational restructuring of the
globe'.[140] Yet, the widespread assertions of communal identity seem to
belie this assessment. After all, communal conflict and theorized clashes
of civilizations seem to be the new challenges in the emerging global
order.[141] Indeed, George Kennan, the individual who, a half a century ago,
identified the conflict between East and West as the defining organizing
principle for years to come, has noted that 'nationalism has developed into
the greatest emotional-political force of the age. . . .'[142] Perhaps both
views have a grain of truth in them. Communal assertions appear to be on
the increase, but so too is supranational integration expanding. They are
seemingly opposed, yet in some cases complimentary, trends. Integration
may make possible different forms of self-determination for substate entities, and it may actually fuel communal conflict:

> we should expect 'national liberation struggles' to multiply in Western
> Europe after 1992, with the creation of a unified market in a democrat-
> ically ruled 'Europe of regions.' Not only will regionally based national
> minorities assert their right to self-determination, but the dominant na-
> tions will likely experience a renewal of national pride, perhaps even
> hatred, toward these minorities, toward other nations and toward other
> states.[143]

Communal assertions will persist, and that in and of itself is not cause for
worry. All types of communities can be useful; indeed, they are necessary for
the attainment of human rights and general human existence. Thus, various
ethnic and national groups and peoples will have to be, and should be,
accommodated and allowed to express their defining diversity. However, the
forms such accommodations will take will also be varied. Most communities
will not get their own states. Indeed, I have demonstrated how hard it is for
different 'selves' to be disentangled. Hobsbawm observes that

xenophobia and racism are symptoms, not cures. Ethnic communities and groups in modern societies are fated to coexist, whatever the rhetoric which dreams of a return to an unmixed nation. Mass murder and mass expulsion ('repatriation') did indeed drastically simplify the ethnic map of Europe, and might be tried in some other regions. Yet the movement of peoples has since restored the ethnic complexity which barbarism sought to eliminate. Only today the typical 'national minority' in most countries receiving migration, is an archipelago of small islands rather than a coherent land mass.[144]

In order to achieve self-determination while also upholding other human rights and other international norms, a variety of forms of political association outside of the sovereignty discourse need to be recognized which keep communities together in one kind of association, while permitting them to pursue their 'common lives' in others. In addition, we must realize that the right to self-determination is not a one-time thing, usable once and then discarded forever, and that different types of communities may be eligible to claim self-determination at different times. As Walzer notes: 'the forms [of self-determination] are historically negotiated. . . . There is no single outcome . . . the negotiation of difference will never produce a final settlement.'[145] This is consistent with the Age of Ambiguity, where political associations and forms will be in a constant state of flux, adjusting to changing circumstances in order to ensure that a reconstructed notion of sovereignty, of which self determination is an integral part, can be realized.

3 Permeable Borders: Human Migration

> [O]ne could imagine borders being like
> permeable cell walls allowing people to move
> in and out freely until an equilibrium –
> homeostasis – is achieved.   Daniel Warner[1]

Borders are central to the theory and practice of sovereignty. They establish the categories of citizen and alien. This is seen as a fundamental element of sovereignty: 'The power to admit or exclude aliens is inherent in sovereignty and essential for any political community.'[2] This conceptual abstraction is reified by such phenomena as border patrols and passports. Border patrols attempt to keep out the undesirables and passports help to regulate the temporarily desirable. Communities which are coterminous with the state are absolutized, and individuals who are not members are forgotten.

Borders also help to define the moral and ethical spheres in which we act. Moral and ethical rights and responsibilities accrue to those within constructed borders[3] who are citizens, whereas non-citizens receive little consideration. This is especially so when doing so might entail bringing some of 'them' inside our borders, into the inner sanctum of sovereign privilege. The reasons for this are many, including basic greed, racism, or a concern with cultural purity. Whatever the reason, we define individuals in terms of citizenship instead of humanity, and this allows us to discard human rights in favour of citizen rights.

This is the way sovereignty is perceived to work: states have the right and the ability to maintain exclusive sovereign control over their borders. However, a closer look at empirical realities, as well as a commitment to human rights and a recognition that states are not natural, absolute entities and thus that borders do not circumscribe the only possibility for community and protection of rights, will provide a view of borders which are not, in fact, as impermeable as the traditional concept of sovereignty would suggest.

In Chapter 1 I demonstrated how state borders are indeed permeable to many different types of incursions – ideas, such as democratic participation and human rights; money, at least in its electronic conceptualization; and people. The first is perceived as most threatening by those states which do not live up to the standards which pour across their borders via television, fax and e-mail. Financial transactions – which amount to trillions of dollars a day –

cross state borders with impunity, and states make little effort to stop this from occurring.[4] However, it is the flow of people which seems most threatening to states and people within state borders. In the past, authoritarian countries tried to keep people in. Now, more democratically-oriented countries are attempting to keep people out, especially those who are perceived as a drain on resources or as disruptive to a community.

Yet, spontaneously, in the form of mass refugee flows, and in a more calculated manner, one, two, or ten at a time, people do cross borders. Sometimes, the receiving country accepts these people graciously as part of what they see as their global humanitarian duty. Other times, people slip unwanted across porous borders, evading the officials whose job it is to put them on a bus back to their countries of origin. This illustrates one of the greatest paradoxes about the contemporary practice of sovereignty – even as states are increasing their efforts to control their borders, they are losing ground.[5]

The second issue with regard to borders, and the flow of people across them, is their moral status. In other words, even as states step up efforts to keep out non-citizens, one must ask whether they should; insofar as states are not natural, absolute communities how can they justify the claim to make such a sharp distinction between citizen and alien, those entitled to certain rights and those not entitled? If, as I argued in Chapter 1, we recognize individuals as humans first, and members of a multitude of communities second, then the absolute claims by various communities to keep out people are undermined to the extent necessary to ensure that human rights and humanitarian principles are upheld.

In this chapter, then, I am concerned with, first, how individual, state, and international practice are contributing to a somewhat ambiguous challenge to state sovereignty. Second, I investigate how the moral force of borders may not be what many would like it to be and how this may contribute to the New Sovereignty. I demonstrate that, empirically, states are fighting a losing battle in attempting to tightly control their borders and access to membership – *de facto* and *de jure*. In addition, concern with human rights and requirements of justice lead to the conclusion that borders should be much more open than they are now. Both of these observations lead to the judgment that the movement of people across state borders is further undermining the sovereignty discourse.

CROSSING BORDERS

Humanity is on the move. People constantly cross borders – city borders, provincial borders, regional borders, state borders – and while states frequently try to stop this movement, they are having little success, and what success they are having seems out of proportion to the resources expended to stop those defined as aliens from entering the sacred territory of the state: 'physical barriers to the movement of people ... are not what they once were'.[6] People move for many different reasons, including war, environmental disaster, or to go in search of the basic necessities of life – food and adequate shelter. Many are called refugees, but the traditional framework for understanding refugees ignores more than half of those who are considered displaced persons, as well as those considered economic migrants.

In 1951, when refugees were placed within an encompassing international framework, there were 1.5 million refugees. By 1979 there were 4.6 million refugees. In 1981, 8.2 million people were recognized as refugees, and by 1993, the global refugee population reached a peak of 18.2 million, with another 24 million internally displaced within their countries of origin. That is, one out of every 130 people in the world was displaced as a result of persecution, violence or natural disaster. In the following three years the number of refugees declined somewhat to 13.2 million as refugees repatriated after a number of conflicts ended, such as those in Afghanistan, Cambodia, Ethiopia and Mozambique. At the same time, the numbers of the internally displaced rose to approximately 30 million.[7]

This does not include others who have left their home voluntarily in search of work or just basic subsistence. The UNHCR estimates that there are 25–30 million legal labour immigrants. In addition, there are probably 20–40 million illegal labour immigrants. This adds up to a total of 80–100 million people living outside their countries of origin, or perhaps $1\frac{1}{2}$ per cent of the entire population of the world.[8]

The displaced are scattered around the globe. However, a majority are located in just a few areas, to a large extent those which have experienced or are experiencing conflict and vast social upheaval. At the beginning of 1996, there were approximately 5.7 million refugees in Africa, and a total of 40 million Africans are 'on the move'. In addition, there were almost 2.1 million refugees in Europe, 4.5 million in Asia, almost 130,000 in Latin America and 790,000 in North America. After the dissolution of the Soviet Union, there were 25 million ethnic Russians outside of Russia and 72 million people living outside the borders of their republics of ethnic origin. Guinea has the highest ratio of refugees to total populations, with more than one out of every ten people of its population of 6.5 million a refugee.[9] In the former Yugoslavia, the refugee population increased from 500,000 in December 1991 to 3.6 million in June 1993, an average increase of 5,600 refugees every single day for a year and a half. Within days of the attempted coup in Burundi in 1993, 800,000 citizens of that country became refugees. The single greatest refugee exodus within a twenty-four hour period occurred between 29 and 30 April, 1994 when 250,000 fled Rwanda in the midst of the civil war that started a few weeks earlier. In July 1994 another 1,000,000 people fled into Zaire in less than five days. By the middle of January 1995 there were an estimated 2.13 million Rwandans living as refugees in neighbouring countries.[10]

The causes of displacement and migration are many. They include war and other types of violence, communal conflict, human rights abuse, forcible movement of indigenous peoples, famine, environmental disasters and economic conditions. These reasons usually do not occur in isolation from each other. For example, famine is, to a large extent, the result of human action and is usually associated with some type of violent conflict where food is used as a weapon, as in Ethiopia during the 1980s and in Bosnia-Herzegovina in the 1990s. Human rights abuses are usually related to armed conflict and struggles for power within a country, particularly between different ethnic or other groups, again as in Bosnia-Herzegovina.[11] The end of the Cold War has not meant an end to communal conflict. Indeed, many of the conflicts are independent of superpower meddling and were masked by the East-West rivalry. This means that displacement as a result of such conflict is not likely to subside.[12]

Economic factors are some of the most important reasons behind migration which is relatively more voluntary compared, for example, to moving as a result of a policy of ethnic cleansing (although when one's family is living at or below mere subsistence levels it is hard to characterize such movement as voluntary). Many victims of armed conflict stay within their region if not within their country. Similarly, many economic migrants move among the poor countries of the South, such as the more than one million Arab and Asian guest workers who were forced out of Kuwait and Iraq as a result of the Iraqi invasion and subsequent Gulf War. However, many also flow from the South to the North. This makes sense not only because of the global distribution of resources. It is also partly explained by former colonial ties, as people from North Africa flow across the Mediterranean into France. In addition, advances in communication and transportation have also affected the flow of migration. In the North, television provides images of horrendous situations in the South, 'evoking feelings of compassion and responsibility', and those in the South and elsewhere can see the disparities in wealth. Greater availability of transportation has created a class of 'jet age' refugees and other migrants who are able to travel much further to improve their life chances than those just years earlier.[13]

The above provides a brief overview of the movements of people and why they occur. Next I turn to the main focus of humanitarian interest – refugees and internally displaced persons.

THE FORCIBLY DISPLACED

A refugee is, according to the 1951 United Nations Convention Relating to the Status of Refugees:

> any person who, owing to a well-founded fear of being persecuted for reasons of race, religion, nationality, membership of a particular social group or political opinion, is outside the country of his nationality and is unable or owing to such fear, is unwilling to avail himself of the protection of that country. . . .

Refugees are thus those who have left their country because of fear of persecution. This rather narrow definition has been expanded by two regional instruments, the 1969 OAU Convention Governing the Specific Aspects of Refugee Problems in Africa and the 1984 Cartegena Declaration on Refugees approved by ten countries of Latin America. They both expand the definition to include those fleeing from conflict, and the Cartegena Declaration includes those fleeing from massive human rights violations.[14] In practice, UNHCR, which has the mandate to deal with refugees, has also helped this expanded group of people. Thus, refugees can be described most simply as those who have crossed a state border as the result of persecution or conflict.

Internally displaced persons (IDPs), on the other hand, are those who are in a refugee-like situation but who have not crossed a border. It is here where borders can make all the difference in the world. Refugees, because they have crossed a border, come under the mandate of an international body which has the right and duty to assist and protect them. The internally displaced, which have not crossed a border, fall under no one's mandate, and thus gaining access to assistance and protection 'depends on the vagaries of national and international politics'.[15] UNHCR has pointed out that 'distinguishing between refugees and internally displaced people with identical protection and assistance needs is illogical and counterproductive, to say nothing of inhumane.'[16]

Mass refugee flows can create extreme strains on the social and economic infrastructure of the receiving state. For example, while Malawi was generous and open regarding Mozambican refugees, having ten per cent of a population comprised of refugees put severe strains on the country's resources and its abilities to carry out its normal functions as a state. The rise of neo-Nazi and other hate groups in Germany must be tied at least partly to non-German and especially non-European immigrants.[17] The flow of undocumented workers across the border from Mexico to the United States, as well as refugee flows, or more precisely attempted refugee flows, from Haiti, has also resulted in xenophobic reactions against immigrants.[18]

Refugee flows can also result in significant security problems. So-called refugee warriors – refugees who are also participants in an armed conflict in the sending state – can invite retaliation from that state towards the receiving state.[19] Certain segments of a refugee population may turn to banditry to acquire basic necessities, or to just capitalize on the situation, and thus turn into a problem for local law enforcement. For example, in Kenya the presence of Somali refugees resulted in a 'brazen wave of killings, rapes, and armed robberies throughout 1992', which occurred as a result of weapons smuggled into Kenya from Somalia and used by Kenyan and Somali gangs. Both Somalis and Kenyan police were blamed for the violence.[20] In addition, partly as a result of the presence of refugee warriors, but also as a result of other foreign policy considerations of both the sending and receiving states, refugee flows can result in increased conflict between states and create security dilemmas which can also come into conflict with humanitarian concerns.[21] The very act of admitting a group of refugees may be perceived by the sending state as a hostile act. Refugee flows also demonstrate that human rights abuses are not only an internal matter when other states must bear the brunt of the repression in the form of refugees. As noted in Chapter 1, Security Council Resolution 688 recognized that the consequences of Iraq's repression – refugee flows – were a threat to international peace and security. Thus, the large-scale movement of people led to a situation where the international community took action that violated the sending country's sovereignty.

The movement of people across borders does not always have solely negative consequences. It can demonstrate a positive interdependence between countries, or at least between the border regions of countries. In Europe, even while the European Union is instituting tighter controls for entry into the EU, once inside people, and most significantly workers, have relatively few constraints on their movement.[22]

CONTROLLING BORDERS?

Yet, many states, in their quest for sovereign control over their borders and thus the ability to decide who become members of their community, have in recent years taken actions intended to prevent the entry of both undocumented workers and refugees. However, these attempts are having more ambiguous outcomes than states would like: 'Rapid changes in technology and transportation continually challenge those countries which want absolute sovereign control over who can and who cannot enter a state as a prerequisite to becoming members of those states.'[23]

Along the 2,000 mile border between the US and Mexico, an ambiguous interdependence has grown up as the result of the movement of people – mostly Mexicans – across the border. The states on both sides of the border have a combined population of 52 million people, and the movement of people from South to North across the border (and back again) has created an area with distinct cultural characteristics which, if it were a country, would rank twenty-second in population. Many of the Mexicans, as well as other Latin Americans, who cross the border are undocumented workers who work as domestic help and migrant labourers, doing jobs which many Americans would not do at pay far below the minimum wage.[24] There are also other economic aspects to the movements across the border. For example, Mexicans spend approximately 30 per cent of the $8.5 billion in retail expenditures each year in El Paso, which is right across the border from Ciudad Juarez.[25] Indeed, because of these economic, as well as cultural, factors, many border residents do not particularly like the fences and other methods of preventing people from crossing the border.[26] As Oscar Mart´nez points out: 'The pronounced interdependence that exists along the border has made it essential that interruptions in the normal flow of people and trade across the boundary be avoided or at least kept to a minimum.'[27]

Yet, interruption is exactly what has occurred in recent years, as a backlash to this interdependence, permeability, perceived drain on resources, illegal activities and other negative consequences resulting from the very nature of border regions:

> what often appears to both Americans and Mexicans as a breakdown of institutions, social systems, and legal structures at the Rio Grande is in many respects the normal functioning of the border. By nature, border zones, especially those that are far removed from the core, spawn independence, rebellion, cultural deviation, disorder and even lawlessness.[28]

That is, because of the artificiality of borders, much of the social and economic activity in border regions occurs in direct defiance of, and serves to undermine the concept of, constructed and controllable borders. What develops, as one observer has put it, is 'the institutionalized anarchy of the border'.[29]

Until recently, at the border between Ciudad Juarez and El Paso alone, 10,000 illegal aliens per day crossed into the United States. About ten per cent of these were apprehended. Many of the rest came only to work during the day and returned to their homes in Mexico every night, but the United States did not have the ability using its normal level of resources to stop 90 per cent of the influx from the south. At the border near San Diego, 250,000 illegal aliens are arrested each year, again only a fraction of the actual number that gain entry into the country.[30]

In response, the United States instituted 'Operation Blockade', the intended effect of which was exactly what the name implies. Hundreds of border agents were deployed as close as 50 feet apart along a 20 mile stretch of the border near El Paso. The effort has decreased dramatically the number of people who come from Mexico along one per cent of the US-Mexican border, at great cost for the government, retailers in El Paso, and relations between the two countries. In 1994 the INS also launched 'Operation Gatekeeper', which focused Border Patrol resources on a five mile stretch of the border near San Diego. While this may have led to fewer people crossing at San Diego, early indications were that there were more people crossing in Arizona and New Mexico. National Guard and Army personnel have also been used in border patrol efforts, leading to what some see as the militarization of the border.[31] Yet, unless the United States commits significantly more resources, it will be unable to 'stem the tide' of undocumented workers and other illegal aliens from the south.

Between 1988 and 1992, 2,065,900 people applied for asylum in ten European countries. In all of Europe there were 4,379,100 refugees by the end of 1992.[32] Most of these were not granted asylum; however, neither did most of them leave Europe. Some were allowed to stay for humanitarian reasons.[33] Some had asylum claims in several countries at the same time and just moved among them. And some just disappeared from the sight of authorities within the countries in which they sought asylum.[34] Contrary to popular thought, Europe has become a 'de facto immigration society'.[35] In other words, while Europe has been perceived as the 'Old World', it is becoming the 'New World' for quite a number of people from the Third World. This has created alarmist outcries from such people as Jean-Marie Le Pen in France. Yet, recent estimates show that European countries will actually have to increase immigration, at least for skilled labour.[36] The problem for many in Europe and elsewhere is that many immigrants, in addition to being perceived as cultural threats, are also regarded as drains on the national coffers. For example, in the United States, even though the director of the Immigration and Naturalization Service has indicated otherwise, there is a widespread perception that Mexicans come to the United States solely to reap the benefits of the welfare state and provide nothing in return.[37]

All of this movement across borders has created a feeling of crisis in many countries. As Doris Meissner, Commissioner of the US Immigration and Naturalization Service, wrote in 1992: 'unregulated and emergency migrations bespeak a loss of control. They challenge the capacity of governments to uphold basic sovereignty, in this case the choice of who resides in one's country.'[38] As a result of these real and perceived on-slaughts and the concomitant threats to sovereignty, states have used a variety of policies and tactics to stop particular groups of people from entering their countries. They attempt to 'push out' their borders as well as increase efforts to prevent admittance to refugees and non-refugee aliens alike.[39]

The United States' policy toward Haitian refugees is an example of attempting to 'push out' a state's borders. Officials and citizens in Florida and other places where Haitians typically settle have complain-ed about the drain on resources and supposed increase in crime which results from 'invasions' of Haitians into their communities. As a result, the United States, instead of offering safe refuge to people fleeing oppres-sion, imposed what amounted to a naval blockade around Haiti and for-cibly returned Haitians to their country without hearing their asylum claims.

In the European Union a kind of 'Fortress Europe' is emerging as a way of keeping out unwanted asylum seekers and others. As the EU has evolved, the relevance of borders between member countries has declined. People can now travel between several of the countries without showing passports, as a result of the implementation of the Schengen Agreement of 1985 (amended in 1990). At the same time, the EU has harmonized pol-icies and tightened its external borders, making it harder to get into the EU in the first place. The Schengen Agreement provides for the Schengen In-formation System, a police database set up to share information among the border guards in the member countries, and the draft Convention on the Crossing of External Frontiers sets out the conditions for crossing one of the external borders. The goal of the Dublin Convention, signed in 1990, is to prevent asylum seekers from making claims in more than one state. It establishes criteria to determine which state should be responsible for re-viewing an asylum application.[40]

Many other states are closing borders to one extent or another. During and after the Gulf War, 1.8 million Iraqi Kurds were displaced. Approx-imately 1.4 million took refuge either in Iran or in the border region with

Iran. The other 400,000 fled to the border region with Turkey. However, Turkey refused them admittance because it has a large minority population of Kurds itself, against which it is essentially waging a war (it has also undertaken attacks against Kurdish populations in Iraq itself).[41]

Mention has already been made of some of the massive refugee flows in Africa, which are putting severe strains on community and resources. African countries have traditionally been hospitable with regard to refugee flows; however, in recent years this has begun to change. In Malawi, the government announced plans in 1992 to fence in refugee settlements. That same year Kenya demanded (a demand later retracted) that all refugees in Kenya – mainly Somalis – be repatriated immediately.[42]

Such reactions, while still disturbing, are understandable in the face of situations where state resources are being stretched beyond their limit. What is less understandable, and even more disturbing, has been the trend in the more affluent Western states with regard to admission policies. During the Cold War, the West had relatively open admissions policies, at least with regard to those coming from East Bloc countries. One of the main tenets of Western policy towards those countries was freedom of movement. That is, people in those countries should be free to leave and come to the West if they so desired. For example, in the early 1970s United States Senate passed the Jackson-Vanik amendment which tied trade and credits to increased emigration of Soviet Jews.[43] The United States allowed in virtually all individuals coming from communist countries such as Cuba and Nicaragua, assuming that since they had lived in such a system they could automatically claim persecution status. Those coming from Vietnam and the Soviet Union also had a presumptive status whereby they were assumed to be fleeing persecution. However, with the end of the Cold War, the political exigencies which led to a certain level of open admissions faded away and the United States and other Western countries, such as Germany, which has had a very open policy of asylum admission, have begun closing their borders to people who, in the past, would have had a *prima facie* claim to asylum.[44]

The way the issue has been framed in these countries has further muddled the issue. When, for example, the United States refuses entry, access to asylum procedures, or asylum itself, to people from Haiti, El Salvador, Guatemala, and other Latin American countries in which there has been violent conflict and widespread abuses of human rights, it frequently claims that they are economic migrants and thus not entitled to entry on humanitarian grounds. The United States and other affluent Western countries have conflated the categories of economic migrant and those – as individuals and in groups – with valid claims under the definition of refugee. Such a blurring of the dividing line allows states to make blanket generalizations about all of those seeking entry and deny them that entry. James Hathaway succinctly sums up why this is happening:

> Why is *non-entrée* effectively replacing *non-refoulement* as the cornerstone of contemporary international law regarding refugees? From the perspective of states, its appeal is that it permits states to exercise *control* over refugee movements without also assuming responsibility for their welfare, as admission to that state's community would imply.[45]

That is, states, with little political incentive to carry out their international humanitarian responsibilities, particularly to the extent it means allowing people inside its borders, are now trying to finesse the issue entirely. This has opened the West up to charges of hypocrisy. In the past, the West has promoted freedom of movement as a basic human right. Yet, with Cold War exigencies gone, they have modified their stance, undermining free movement as a right.

Such a change in stance among Western countries – and others – has served to undermine two basic and interrelated principles of international refugee law: *non-refoulement* and asylum. *Non-refoulement* means that refugees cannot be forcibly repatriated to their country of origin as long as the threat continues at home. A very visible violation of this principle was the interdiction and forcible return of Haitian refugees by the United States Coast Guard in the three years before President Aristide returned to power. The Haitians were fleeing documented violence and gross violations of human rights, and claiming that they were either economic migrants or that there was no evidence that they were in danger if returned was a flagrant obfuscation of the situation.[46]

Non-refoulement is an important aspect of asylum. As UNHCR points out:

> Today, asylum remains the cornerstone of international refugee protection. It is the principal means through which states meet their obligations towards refugees on their territory. The grant of asylum removes the threat of forcible return and provides the refugee with sanctuary until a solution to his or her problem can be found.[47]

Yet, as a result of the changed nature of the international situation, including massive refugee flows and reversals in Western admission policies, asylum is being undermined in a serious and dramatic fashion. As the current United Nations High Commissioner for Refugees, Sadako Ogata, has pointed out: 'The institution of asylum is coming under pressure in countries which, ironically, have been among the most stalwart supporters of

UNHCR'.[48] In fact, the 'crisis of asylum' has been a major preoccupation at UNHCR headquarters in Geneva.[49]

The very fact that states feel they must take such actions demonstrates how important borders are for the practice of sovereignty and how much borders are not what they once were. As Sadako Ogata notes, freedom of movement, at least for many Western states, ends at the border: 'Albania and Haiti also exposed the contradiction of western liberalism which supports the principle of freedom of movement but advocates restrictive action when the movements might actually cross national frontiers.'[50] However, this hypocrisy may have important and unintended implications in the future, for, as Martin points out, 'the old standards that grew up in a more hypocritical period are not likely to go away'.[51]

The policy implications are two-fold, and seemingly contradictory. On the one hand, the distinction between economic migrants and refugees must be maintained so that policies with regard to the former do not interfere with attempts to protect the latter: 'the new phenomenon of economic migrants should not be used as an excuse to deny asylum and sanctuary to genuine refugees...'[52] On the other hand, the line between different kinds of migrants *is* becoming increasingly blurred and thus forcing us to reconsider the conceptual categories we have used in the past:

> The close link between economic, social and political factors is not only confusing the dividing line between refugees and economic migrants, but also calling into question the continued relevance of many refugee protection principles developed during the Cold War period.[53]

The international framework for these principles and how it has evolved will be discussed in the next two sections.

INTERNATIONAL LAW AND INSTITUTIONAL FRAMEWORKS

The refugee and human rights regimes define the rights of refugees and obligations of states.[54] Individuals have the right to leave their country and seek asylum – this is the right which the West so strenuously defended during the Cold War. This right is enshrined in Articles 13 and 14 of the Universal Declaration of Human Rights, as well as Article 12 of the International Covenant on Civil and Political Rights.[55]

While the 1951 Refugee Convention and 1967 Protocol do not create a right to asylum, they do help define the status of refugees and certain other rights and legal protections, most notably the principle of *non-refoulement* whereby an individual cannot be forced to return to a potentially dangerous situation in the country of origin. An individual does have the right to return to his or her country of origin. Along with this right is the attendant right to a nationality which cannot be taken away arbitrarily. This is part of the right to remain which has seen increased focus in recent years even as it has been undermined by the actions of states, as well as non-state actors such as rebel groups.

In addition to the activities of UNHCR and other humanitarian organizations, a great burden falls on receiving states who must consider and process asylum claims and expend resources to assist and protect refugees on their soil. The traditional framework for dealing with refugees has been that refugees receive at least temporary protection in the country of first asylum. Then, the search for durable solutions begins. These are: (1) repatriation, (2) permanent settlement in the country of first asylum, and (3) settlement in a third country. However, as a result of the dramatically increased numbers of refugees, as well as the changed geopolitical situation, this pattern and practice is falling apart and the institution of asylum is being undermined.

The post-World War II refugee regime was not designed to deal with the huge numbers of refugees flowing across borders at any one time.[56] Asylum procedures are being overwhelmed and state resources, especially in the Third World, are being taxed to the limit. The end of the Cold War has also meant the end of political exigencies in the West which led governments to accept asylum seekers.

One new practice, which has occurred most particularly in dealing with refugees from the former Yugoslavia in Europe, has been temporary protection.[57] In this situation, the asylum claims of refugees are not examined, but refugees are allowed to remain in the country until the war is over and the situation becomes more stable. One instance where this practice could have been used, but was not, was in the case of Haitians fleeing the conflict and persecution in Haiti.[58] However, according to one US official who argued for temporary protection, most policymakers were convinced that temporary protection would turn into permanent settlement.[59] Certainly, some would want to stay and would blend into the background,[60] as have many unsuccessful asylum seekers in Europe, thus undermining the ability of the state to decide who become members. However, by and large, people do not want to leave their homes and would like to be able to return if possible. One does not make a dangerous journey on an overflowing rickety boat and become a refugee unless the situation in one's home country is extremely severe.

Actions aimed at preventing refugee flows in the first place have received increased attention in recent years. Indirectly, peacekeeping and peacemaking activities can help to create more stable conditions that are less conducive to flight. More directly, early warning activities and human rights monitoring of IDPs can also help to prevent the movement of people across borders. Prevention activities should be targeted at root causes by

> promotion of human rights, economic development, conflict resolution, the establishment of accountable political institutions, environmental protection and so forth. It encompasses, in other words, virtually the whole of the human agenda, with particular emphasis on the responsibilities of states to care for all their people without discrimination.[61]

However, such activities are not usually carried out in any systematic way. Prevention is usually restricted to addressing immediate causes, especially with respect to provision of food and other aid to decrease the need to go elsewhere for such resources, and to attempt 'to repair relations between people and government before it is too late. . . .'[62]

Prevention activities are designed with a view to 'seeking to limit the imperative to flee'.[63] In this light, prevention activities can be seen as positive ways to alleviate the conditions which can lead to dislocation across borders. In addition, such activities can lead to small but significant humanitarian incursions on state sovereignty. As one UNHCR official put it, while there is a reluctance to talk about sovereignty as such when working within a country of origin, prevention activities can lead to greater involvement by UNHCR or other humanitarian organization than to what the state originally agreed. The distinction is between what is formally permitted by a state and what can actually be done once a presence is established, such as delivering food versus monitoring and protecting human rights.[64]

However, prevention can also be seen in a much different light. Obstructive prevention, such as intercepting Haitian refugees at sea, and deterrent prevention, such as very restrictive and punitive immigration laws, do nothing to address either the root causes or the immediate needs of refugees. There is great concern that such state actions are undermining asylum. There is also concern that international organizations such as UNHCR, responsible for ensuring asylum and protection, are complicit in this undermining. For example, when Turkey refused to allow Kurdish refugees to cross its border, UNHCR acquiesced.[65] It has also been criticized for not being as forceful as it could be in other situations where states have resisted the expansion of protection:

> In the face of all of these efforts to minimize international refugee protection, the Office of the United Nations High Commissioner for

Refugees has been either silent or a tacit co-conspirator, since its negligible funding base makes it virtually entirely dependent on the continuing goodwill of the very industrialized states it ought to be attempting to influence.[66]

It has, in the words of one UNHCR official, become a 'Migration Management Organization', helping states maintain sovereign control of their borders.[67] Some point out that UNHCR's mandate (as well as refugee law in general) is to work for states: 'refugee law as it exists today is fundamentally concerned with the protection of powerful states. It is also perceived by powerful states to perform that role inadequately.'[68] However, one UNHCR official noted that to the extent this is so, this should not alleviate governments' humanitarian responsibilities.[69] Although these criticisms may be valid, one can question how else UNHCR can respond, at least in some instances. For example, in the case of Turkey, there is disagreement about what else UNHCR actually could have done in this situation. Certainly it does not have the ability to force states to accept refugees. In addition, the Kurds would probably also have become objects of persecution in Turkey, and even though it took a while, they probably ended up with greater protection as a result of the allied protection activities after the Gulf War than they would have had in Turkey. However, there is still criticism that UNHCR and others could have done more in that situation during the initial stages of the refugee flows.[70]

I have painted two different pictures of international practice in response to refugees, especially on the part of UNHCR. On the one hand, international agencies may be able to engage in humanitarian incursions on state sovereignty once they have gained access to a country. On the other, UNHCR is, to a certain extent, working with states in helping them to control entry into their territory. Both perspectives have some truth to them.[71] Yet, with respect to the question of sovereignty, it must be pointed out that to the extent that states are relying on international organizations to maintain sovereign control of their borders, they also recognize that controlling borders is a lot harder than they would like. In other words, while states are not ready to concede defeat with respect to movement of people across their borders, such attempts may be increasingly futile.

THE INTERNALLY DISPLACED

There is one other issue with regard to displacement that, in some ways, is an even more fundamental challenge to sovereign control over borders.

This is the issue of the internally displaced. By its very nature, this problem crosses conceptual and other boundaries, and will therefore be addressed not only in this chapter, but also in Chapter 4. The issue of the internally displaced will be discussed in the broader terms of humanitarian access across borders while in this chapter, I will look at the connection between IDPs and refugees, and international responses to IDPs.

Although they have not crossed a state boundary, they are displaced for many of the same reasons as refugees, including conflict, human rights abuses and disasters, and have many of the same needs for protection and assistance. They are, in other words, those who are in refugee-like situations within the borders of their country of origin, and the distinction between the two is making increasingly less sense: 'There is a growing realization that it is senseless to insist that people in flight must cross an international border before they can be offered assistance, particularly if it is the need for assistance that is propelling them toward the border'.[72] This, in turn, also indicates a 'growing realization' that borders and the sovereign claims that usually go along with them are not of the same stature with respect to humanitarian issues as they once were. In addition, there is no international agency which has a specific mandate to deal with the internally displaced and no body of law to deal with IDPs.[73]

Yet, the international community, especially UNHCR, has responded to the plight of IDPs in a number of innovative ways and has, as a result, either confronted or finessed the issue of sovereignty. The basic issue is the fact that IDPs are still within the borders of their country of origin and thus, theoretically, still under the sovereign control of the state. Under traditional sovereign arrangements, the state would have to give consent to, or actively request, the provision of aid and protection from outside.

UNHCR has been involved with IDPs in many instances as a result of General Assembly resolutions or at the request of the Secretary-General, including Northern Iraq, the former Yugoslavia, and Somalia. In all of these instances, UNHCR has provided assistance and protection to mixed populations, including refugees, returnees and IDPs.[74]

The case of Somalia illustrates some of the most innovative activities that lead one to question the utility of borders in humanitarian crises. The civil war in Somalia created large populations of refugees and internally displaced. By the end of 1992, there were more than 400,000 Somalis in Ethiopia and almost 300,000 Somali refugees in Kenya, out of a total refugee population of 400,000 in Kenya.[75] In the middle part of that year approximately 1,000 Somalis were fleeing into Kenya each day and UNHCR, along with other agencies, decided to put into place what it called 'Prevention Zones' and engage in 'cross-mandate' and 'cross-border' operations. These activities were 'primarily designed to discourage mass movements of people within and across borders by providing assistance to vulnerable groups in or as near to their areas of origin as possible'.[76] This goal had several important operational implications. UNHCR 'crossed' its mandate by providing aid and protection to those who fell outside of the definition of refugee. It went into areas close to the Kenya/Somalia and Kenya/Ethiopia borders and assisted all those in need, including returning refugees, IDPs and others in the community who were not displaced but were still in need. The objectives were (a) to contribute to the stabilization of the area, (b) prevent further famine-induced movement, and (c) facilitate repatriation and return home. Unless all of the populations in need were provided aid, the preventive activities would have been futile, and UNHCR refugee sites within Somalia would have been overrun anyway.[77]

The other innovative part of these operations, the 'cross-border' activities, indicate the irrelevance of borders in times of humanitarian disasters and refugee crises, as well as the fact that operational agencies on the ground are increasingly willing to pay less attention to such borders. UNHCR set up zones 50–100 km on each side of the borders which were seen as coherent and contiguous areas of operation within which aid organizations would work freely irrespective of borders to aid the displaced and prevent further displacement.[78] These activities not only demonstrate the empirical irrelevance of borders but also the increasing realization on the part of those responsible for aiding various populations of the moral irrelevancy of borders. That is, various aid organizations have adapted their operations in the face of what has been in the past a restriction on their operations – sovereignty – in such a way as to undermine the relevance of that restriction.

It should also be noted that 'it is mainly because of the lack of an acknowledged government authority with which the United Nations can coordinate its relief efforts, that recourse is being had to cross border operations'.[79] That is, since there is no sovereign authority in Somalia, questions of sovereignty are irrelevant. In addition, there is a general reluctance on the part of UNHCR to confront sovereignty head-on.[80] However, the issue of sovereignty and access to those in need, especially the internally displaced, is being addressed or finessed in a number of ways. UNHCR has expanded its competence and been involved in situations of internal displacement which are outside its mandate but in which either the General Assembly or the Secretary-General have requested its involvement.

Questions of access will be discussed in much more detail in Chapter 4. However, the above discussion should serve to demonstrate how, in instances of providing aid and protection to the displaced, the international community has begun to either chip away at, or get around the problem of, sovereignty. What remains now is to examine the moral standing of borders with respect to the movement of people.

THE MORALITY OF BORDERS

Boundaries are the demarcation lines we use to separate ourselves from each other. State boundaries separate 'us' from 'them', 'citizen' from 'alien', 'member' from 'other'. Borders are crucial to the theory and practice of sovereignty. Without borders there would be no focal point for an absolutized claim to sovereignty. Borders thus have a significant moral standing within the sovereignty discourse – they demarcate the space within which lies a community beholden and responsible to no other: 'national boundaries might be regarded as the outer reaches of most people's moral sympathy . . . '[81]

What are the rights of communities within borders? What is the link between the widely acknowledged right to leave one's country and the ability to enter another? What are the claims that those outside of a particular border could make to cross a border and what are the concomitant obligations a state might have with regard to such claims? Finally, what do these questions say about sovereignty? These questions are all related and cannot be disentangled from each other in a meaningful way, so they will be addressed in parallel. Let me, first, however, consider what the real differences between citizen and alien are.

An alien is '[s]omeone who, by accident of birth, born in the wrong place or to the wrong parents, is not a citizen'.[82] Consequently, she does not have access to certain rights and resources that others do. According to Carens, aliens can be likened to feudal serfs prevented from sharing in the bounty of the baron's resources because of an accident in birth: 'Citizenship in Western liberal countries is the modern equivalent of feudal privilege – an inherited status that greatly enhances one's life chances. Like feudal birthright privileges, restrictive citizenship is hard to justify when one thinks about it closely.'[83] If this analogy is correct, it is hard to see, in Beitz's words, 'why differences in citizenship should count as morally relevant differences'.[84] What, in other words, imbues borders with such moral significance?

The response usually given is that it is the right of the community to decide who does and does not enter and to decide what to do with its resources. Previously, I discussed the role of community and the influence ideas about community have on people. Communities of different kinds can help people define who they are, and they can aid in the development of individual autonomy and the protection of human rights. For communitarians such as Michael Walzer, the protection of the community and its independence – its 'common life' – is an extremely important moral good and communities have a right and obligation to ensure this through control of borders.[85] Communities require closure: 'The distinctiveness of culture and groups depends upon closure.'[86]

However, as I argued in the last chapter, this closure cannot be determined once and for all. We are all members of various types of communities and privileging one of them – the state – above all others is not justified because it is not a natural entity which has prior claims on allegiances and resources. Giving the state absolute power to control access means that other types of communities within and across state borders are prevented from determining the status and composition of their community.

Substate territorial entities generally have no restrictions on movement across their borders. An individual can move from Montana to Massachusetts or from Quebec to British Columbia with no impediments. Thus, within and between various communal entities – the state and substate entities – there is considerable individual autonomy with regard to movement and access to resources.[87]

Further, as Carens points out, the differences between such substate communities 'are often much greater than the differences across nation-states. Seattle has more in common with Vancouver than it does with many American communities.'[88] In fact, the region including these two cities – the American Pacific Northwest and British Columbia – already has a name – Cascadia. Many members of this transnational community see a regional culture emerging along with the existing 'ecological integrity' and growing economic ties. In addition, there is a shared mistrust of federal governments 3,000 miles away. And, there are special express lanes at border crossings for commuters. The commonalities in this region are not offset, to anywhere near the same degree, by the differences which can be found alongside the cultural similarities in the US-Mexico border region. Finally, there are many in 'Cascadia' who fear migration and cultural assault from Southern California much more than from across the national border.[89]

Even though Oregon and Washington may want to restrict those from California who are in search of an environmentally-based 'Ecotopia'[90]

(but who, Cascadians believe, only bring their high-stress, high-techno-
logy, high-pollution culture with them, thus affecting the culture in mea-
surable ways) they cannot do so. Why are such territorial entities morally
different from the larger states of which they are a part? Making a distinction between these types of borders makes no sense if one is concerned
with protecting individual autonomy:

> the radical disjuncture that treats freedom of movement within the state
> as a moral imperative and freedom of movement across state borders as
> merely a matter of political discretion makes no sense from a perspect-
> ive that takes seriously the freedom and equality of all individuals.[91]

Tight control of the larger borders supposedly prevents smaller communities from becoming overwhelmed by outsiders and thus preserves their
distinctiveness. This assumes that all of the smaller communities have the
same goal at the same time – exclusion. Mark Gibney points out that this is
not necessarily the case. For example, he notes that certain communities
within the United States, particularly some religious communities, have
provided sanctuary to Central American refugees who have been denied
asylum as result of the political and ideological exclusionary proclivities
of the federal government.[92] Thus, this is 'a very good indication that ideological affinity may be a much more diffuse, and much less agreed upon
phenomenon than Walzer seems to realize'.[93] On the other hand, at least
seven states in the US which have large immigrant populations have sued
the federal government for the costs of incarcerating illegal immigrants
and providing them benefits.[94]

A second issue with regard to Walzer's communitarian construction of
borders is the idea of affinity. Perhaps the connections between people do
not stop at borders, but rather with members of a society with certain affinities – ethnic, family, ideological – which serve to make strangers –
nonmembers – members. Walzer views ethnic ties, for example, as immut-
able. Such views were responsible for the internment of many Japanese in
the United States during World War II, and they are responsible today for
the discrimination many citizens and non-citizens in the US experience.
However, as I argued in Chapter 2, these ties are, in fact, extremely mutable. Walzer feels that those who share affinities with a particular community should have special access to membership in that community.
Regardless of whether or not this proposition is reasonable, the possibility
that it could be worked out in reality is virtually nil.[95] This is because one
cannot, in general, point to one core concept or idea which all members of
a community share and would be willing to identify as *the* trait on which to
base all claims of affinity: 'it is the multiplicity of ideological affinities in

a pluralistic society like ours that makes this concept of "affinity" such an unworkable concept'.[96] These affinities include ideologies – capitalism or socialism – religious views – Christian, Jewish, Muslim – those having to do with helping the most vulnerable – such as the sanctuary movement – and literally hundreds of ethnic ties with every part of the world. Many of these affinities are either perceived to be, or are in fact, exclusive of one another or at least in severe conflict with each other. In fact, if affinity were the basis for admissions, then we would be admitting a lot of people, all of whom at least some would like to keep out. When affinities *are* identified as core communal affinities, they are usually those of the powerful or the most vocal.[97]

In addition, affinity and community come into direct conflict. If those in a community have shared experiences, such as culture, history, language, government, then 'strangers, by definition, will not be imbued with these particular traits. The admission of strangers, perhaps any one stranger, would seem to cause a severe disruption to a community, at least in terms of how Walzer characterizes a community.'[98]

A different analysis arises if one realizes that communities of all types, from cities to states, are in a continual process of construction and reconstruction. Most states have, in fact, relied on significant immigration sometime in their history (and usually in their present, too) to become what they are. Immigrants have been crucial in their construction. As noted in Chapter 1, it is the process of forgetting which can reify certain ideas or institutions. In the case of the United States, for example, forgetting how it was constructed has led to a reification of an idealized, natural country founded upon the principles and hard work of the descendants of the *Mayflower* and which sprang forth in isolation from the rest of the world. The reality, of course, is much different.

OPEN BORDERS

If communities cannot be absolutized in the way many people would like, what does this say about the moral authority of states to close borders? I would argue that there are several grounds on which to base more open borders. One is the connection between the right to leave and the right to enter. Human rights instruments, as well as statements from many countries – especially Western countries – have affirmed the right to leave one's country. The question is how to make that right meaningful. Until relatively recently, free movement across borders was the norm. The 1791 French Constitution guaranteed 'liberté d'aller, de rester, de partir'.[99]

Coming, staying, and going were considered equal. In 1889, the members of the International Emigration Conference passed a resolution stating: 'We affirm the right of the individual to come and go and dispose of his destinies as he pleases.'[100] By World War I all of this would change, and by the time of the Universal Declaration of Human Rights, immigration and emigration were considered very different issues. The UDHR confirms the right to emigrate, but the right of entry is restricted to nationals.

Does this really make sense? The right to leave is meaningless if one does not have somewhere to go: 'Logically, it is an absurdity to assert a right of emigration without a complementary right of immigration unless there exists in fact (as in the mid-19th century) a number of states which permit free entry.'[101] This is certainly not the case today.[102] Thus, countries must have more open entry policies in order to ensure the right to leave. Further, the right to leave has had its roots in liberalism and liberal states have been the most forceful in advocating this right, even as they have tightened their borders. To be consistent, it is especially incumbent upon such states to open their borders more.[103] There are some limits to this, to be discussed below, but they are much less severe than those currently placed on immigration.

The rights to exit, enter and remain which have been recognized to varying degrees are all tied in with what might be described as the right to community. The right to remain means that an individual has a right to stay and participate in her community, with all of the attendant benefits, rights and duties. Because we have a right to stay in our community, and such communities are essential in developing and maintaining identity and protecting human rights, one can talk about a right to community. If an individual has a right to community, exactly how do they claim such a right? The answer is unclear. This uncertainty may arise because 'the community itself may be mutating in such a way that it is unable or unwilling to fulfil those individual's needs that we normally associate with rights'.[104] This observation can be interpreted in two ways. First, it can refer to the fact that our notions of identity are changing in such a way as to render meaningless talk of *the one* territorially demarcated community of which we are a part and which is solely responsible for ensuring our rights. Second, one can interpret it in a more concrete way, referring to that fact that many communities – that is, states – cannot attend to the needs of their members, because of civil disturbance or some sort of humanitarian disaster, or because the idea of community within a particular state-community has 'mutated' to such a degree that it excludes from membership within that community individuals who were, at one time, members. One need only look at the former Yugoslavia to see this point clearly.

If the right to community is thus undermined, an individual can make a claim against some other community for inclusion as a way of implementing the right to community. Why this is so can be seen by referring to the social purpose of the state:

> Since the very nature and creation of the state recognized that it is the *right* of every human being to have a place to live, then any individual, and not just members of a state, have the *right* to claim a place to live within that state provided that right has not already been exercised and recognized elsewhere.[105]

That is, when an individual's right to community is not upheld in their country of origin, they can make a claim for inclusion in another community – that is, a state – because part of the social purpose of the state is to uphold the right to a place to live – that is, the right to community. This is why, although there is no defined right to asylum, there is a general feeling of obligation – although apparently receding – among states to take in those who have lost the ability to be a part of a community – refugees.

Besides making the right to leave and community meaningful, there are other bases, all having to do with the obligations of states, with which one can provide for a much greater right to enter. Two are described by Gibney – the Harm Principle and the Basic Rights Principle. The Harm Principle, which seeks to protect individual autonomy, has two basic components: (1) 'individuals have a duty not to harm others' and (2) 'those who have caused harm have a duty of restitution'.[106] Thus, if a state has harmed another in some way it has a duty to make restitution, and one way to do this might mean admitting citizens of another country.[107] An obvious example of this would be war: 'I propose not only that noncombatants be protected, but I claim that in some instances the only means of doing this is by the admission of noncombatants to the intervening nation or some other country.'[108] Thus, the United States, which intervened in various ways in Central America, had a duty, for example, to admit Nicaraguans who were fleeing the US backed war.[109] Gibney further states that those admitted under such terms should be repatriated, unless those being repatriated would suffer serious harm as a consequence.[110] Such harm might have something to do with the damage the state has done in the country of origin and how this would harm those returning. In addition, although he discounts this, the state should also take into account the kinds of communal ties one has made while being forced out of one's community of origin by the actions of the intervening state. This would have the effect of letting more people stay.

The Harm Principle might also be invoked if a government is supporting an unjust regime – that which does not respect the rights of its citizens – in another country. In this case, it is contributing to the harm which is done against the people of that country and they can make certain claims against the first country.[111] For example, the US supported an unjust regime in El Salvador. It thus had a duty of reparation towards the people that were harmed by the persecution perpetrated by that regime. One way in which it could have discharged its obligation would have been to allow in the Salvadorans who were fleeing persecution. Of course, it did not do so.

The second basis Gibney puts forward for more open admissions is the Basic Rights Principle. It 'obligates nations to play some part in meeting the basic rights of individuals in other societies even if they were not the cause of this need'.[112] The rationale for this is simple: 'Why should I defend defenseless human beings? Because they are human beings and they are defenseless.'[113] If a state can alleviate a harm without inflicting similar harm upon itself, it should do so. This obligation is not tied to any particular harm inflicted and it thus broadens the obligation to all those who are in a position to help. It is not an open-ended obligation because, as Walzer points out, a duty to care for everyone means that no one will be cared for. However, while Walzer would then, for the most part, end duties at borders, the Basic Rights Principle argues that duties do extend beyond borders, but they are spread out among all such that each can make a contribution.[114] This contribution might be to give a certain percentage of GNP to development aid. Or, more relevant to present purposes, a state could discharge its obligations through admitting those in need, including those who fit the narrow definition of refugee as well as those in search of basic subsistence.[115]

This duty is based on the idea of the 'necessitous stranger'. This encompasses asylum seekers and others who are 'necessitous', including those looking for basic subsistence. However, this also maintains a basic distinction between citizens and 'strangers'. According to Warner, the duty to provide aid falls upon the state itself, not upon any particular communities within the state – he makes a distinction between the two. Thus, '[t]he notion of necessitous stranger implies that the refugee will continue to be cut off from community'.[116] However, as I shall argue, those who are admitted should not be made second class citizens.

None of these obligations are open-ended. Following Singer's formulation, the limit is when our distributive actions sacrifice something of 'comparable moral significance' – that is, when our actions threaten our basic rights by, for example, depriving us of the minimal necessary subsistence requirements. What I am interested in is what the limits are on the obligation to allow people to cross one's borders.

ADMITTING THE OTHER

First, let me review the grounds for admission: (1) to ensure the recognized right to leave; (2) to ensure the right to community; (3) human rights protection; (4) the Harm Principle; and (5) the Basic Rights Principle. The parameters for responsibility for allowing non-citizens into a state can be framed by two principles. First, preserving basic human rights, especially subsistence, becomes a moral imperative for states which undermines their claims to prevent entry. People need access to certain resources in order to be able to live. Many of these resources, and the individuals who need access to them, are distributed morally arbitrarily within and among different types of borders. That is, by virtue of accident of birth, an individual may be situated inside the border of a state which cannot take care of her minimum needs and thus might make a claim on the resources in another state to the extent that she needs them to live. And, to the extent that these resources either are not or cannot be distributed to those who need them, those in need can cross borders in order to gain access to them.

The other defining parameter on the obligation for admission is that a community – that is a state – can restrict admission when the possibility of community is undermined. That is, when the numbers of people, partly in relation to the available resources, are so great within a particular territorial area that any idea of community, perhaps as a result of environmental or population pressures, is no longer viable. This does not mean that when an existing community is in danger of changing its character somewhat it can restrict admission. It does not privilege any particular community for communities and our identification with different communities are in a constant state of flux – no community can hope to completely isolate itself from others and preserve its character forever. Rather, it recognizes that communities do change, frequently in response to immigration, and that this is a natural part of the development of communities.[117] It is only when this process calls into question the possibility of community – and therefore prevents the fulfillment of the right to community – that limits can be placed on the flow of people across borders.

Immigration, by changing communities, can, however, have both positive and negative consequences for a wide variety of values. The United

States, for example, has been based upon immigration and is what it is today because of the movements of large numbers of people into its territory. At the same time, certain types of mass immigration can have devastating negative consequences. For example, the movement of large numbers of Brazilians into the Amazon Basin in search of new farmland (which they create by burning down the rainforest) has displaced the native inhabitants and created a situation where they are so overwhelmed that the possibility of community is denied them. Of course, the same sort of thing happened in the US when the Native Americans were pushed off their land, seriously disrupting their communities and forever altering their way of life. It is at this point that the values of self-determination and open borders come into conflict. The influx of people creates a situation where the change is so great and so instantaneous that the possibility of community is foreclosed for a certain portion of the population. That is, they are no longer able to participate in the self-determination process. At this point, the value of self-determination may outweigh the value of open borders and restrictions can be put on the movement of people into a particular territory.

In between these parameters is a wide space with a number of other principles related to admission. People must be admitted on a number of human rights grounds. The first, already mentioned, is to maintain basic subsistence rights. Second is the right to community. That is, when an individual no longer has a community which fulfills her needs, then she can make a claim to join another community. Third is an obligation to admit those fleeing persecution. Although there is no recognized right to asylum under international law, if we are to take seriously protecting human rights, such a right must be put into practice. In addition, in a reversal from international practice which recognizes persecution but not starvation as grounds for admission, if we recognize subsistence rights as grounds for a claim to admission, then it makes little sense to deny admission to those who may die in a different way without admission. The fourth principle is that in order to implement the right to leave a country, a right to enter another must be recognized.

Associated with the right to enter is what rights individuals have when they do enter. I noted above that the idea of necessitous stranger results in a situation where an individual who is admitted on the basis of need is still cut off from any real access to a community, and thus is denied the right to community. There is a recognized right to self-determination for all sorts of communities. However, this right does not include the right to discriminate among people within a community – all are entitled to equal treatment. This means that a community cannot create different classes of members. Guest workers and refugees cannot be treated differently from others within a community – they cannot be denied access to food or medical services or, for that matter, jobs which will enable them to live. Walzer, who rejects relatively open admissions policies on the basis of self-determination, nevertheless states that when individuals are admitted, the way they are treated is, as Carens puts it, 'constrained by principles of justice'.[118] This means that once an individual is admitted to a community, it must be as a *member* of that community.

It must also be recognized, however, that many migrants are temporary refugees who want to go back to their country of origin when the situation changes. In these cases, while it is still incumbent upon states to admit these people and provide refuge and aid, those whose ultimate goal is to return to their country of origin would not be included in the community in the same way – with the possibility of citizenship – as others whose intention would be to stay permanently. As Hathaway contends:

> Rather than continuing the Refugee Convention's emphasis on facilitating the permanent exile of a narrowly defined subset of refugees, I believe that the international protection system should be easily accessed by a broadly defined group of involuntary migrants, but should direct itself ultimately tothe refugee's right to be restored to membership in her own community.[119]

That is, in addition to admitting refugees, it is incumbent upon the international community to ensure that their right to return is upheld. Yet, some may never be able to go back, and those, of course, should be more fully integrated into the community of refuge.

The magnitude of the refugee problem is so huge that there are some situations where countries of refuge cannot handle the massive influx of people, at least not by themselves. Thus, countries who do not border refugee producing countries have an obligation first, to admit some number of refugees as countries of second asylum and, second, when this is not practical, to provide aid to those countries who do admit large numbers of refugees. This would fulfill obligations under the Basic Rights Principle. Further, when a situation comes to a point where the influx of people threatens the possibility of community for those within the country, that country can refuse to admit any more as members. At this point it becomes clear that a much more international focus is needed with regard to dealing with refugees, and that those who are not overwhelmed, for the most part the northern states, must be more willing to accept refugees. This will be discussed further in Chapter 5 when I look at possible institutional changes to respond to humanitarian crises.

HUMAN MIGRATION AND SOVEREIGNTY

The movement of people further calls into question the concept of sovereignty as anywhere near an absolutizing principle. Movements of individuals and groups across borders have challenged the ability of states to control their borders and decide who is allowed in and who is barred from entry. The very fact that the United States, the most powerful country in the world, was able to prevent only ten per cent of those who it considered to be undesirable from crossing certain points of its border until it engaged in extraordinary measures which will be extremely difficult, if not impossible, to sustain over an extended period of time along the entire border, illustrates that borders are much more permeable than people have thought. So, one question to be raised is, if a state does not do something which it is allowed to do within the sovereignty discourse, does it lose part of its sovereignty? If a state is not able to do something which it is allowed to do, then it would seem clear that some part of its sovereignty would be undermined. If states cannot control who enters and stays – a central right under the traditional sovereignty discourse – then it would seem that one of the building blocks of traditional conceptions of sovereignty is called into question.

Flows of refugees and other migrants are having many different effects on receiving countries which they are unable to deal with. In some countries, especially in Africa, movement of people is taxing state resources to the limit as they struggle to provide for refugees. In other countries, such as Germany which has had relatively open admissions policies, there have been attacks on immigrant populations. Further, in 1993, Germany significantly amended the 1949 Basic Law which had allowed almost anybody to enter and apply for asylum, and receive welfare benefits.[120] The following year, the German Border Guard was given new powers to operate outside of its traditional areas of operation in order to crack down on smugglers and illegal immigrants.[121] In the United States, too, a nativist backlash has resulted in calls for much tighter immigration enforcement. But, immigration has also changed the character of communities, such as the ones along the US-Mexico border, where, even though there is much hostility on the part of certain parts of the population north of the border towards the south, there is still much common cultural heritage and ceasing the movement of people across the border would have severe economic and cultural consequences.

In addition, actions by international actors, such as UNHCR, have resulted in incursions on state sovereignty and increasing recognition by those organizations that borders should not be the barrier that they have been. Most notable have been the cross-border operations in Kenya,

Ethiopia and Somalia which have set up areas of operation which essentially ignore territorial demarcations.

If states did possess absolute sovereignty, then they could decide who can and cannot become members, expel members, and prevent them from leaving.[122] States are losing the ability to decide who enters, although the trends and evidence are still somewhat contradictory. For example, in the case of the United States, attempts to prevent illegal immigrants from crossing one portion of the US-Mexico border frequently just have the effect of pushing the flowing of migrants further down the border where enforcement is not as tight. In Germany, on the other hand, the 1993 revisions in the laws regarding the rights of asylum seekers do seem to have led to a marked decrease in the numbers of asylum seekers. However, court decisions and other factors have prevented it from having the full effect that it authors intended, thus lending ambiguity to its final effects and Germany's actual ability to control the numbers of immigrants within its borders.[123] Once people enter, they can become lost within the state and become *de facto* members.[124] This is so, too, with those a state allows to enter temporarily, for example while asylum claims are being reviewed. The last two actions – expelling and preventing members from leaving – are ruled out by the recognized rights to remain and to leave.

Empirical and international law considerations as well as international practice, then, have qualified the sovereign control of borders. In addition, questions of human rights and the way communities are constructed call into question the moral authority of states to control borders to a significant degree.

The global distribution of both people and resources has resulted in a feudal distribution of access to necessary resources. Thus, obligations under the Basic Rights Principle necessitate that people who do not have access to subsistence requirements be allowed access to those resources in other countries. Other issues of human rights also lead to the conclusion that borders should not be the barriers to movement they are perceived to be. Protection for those fleeing persecution and humanitarian disasters certainly qualifies one to cross borders. But so too does the acknowledged right to leave one's country, which would be inconceivable without a corresponding right to enter another.

In addition, I have argued that the very creation of the state also meant a recognition of a right to community. States have an obligation to ensure that when one's state can no longer ensure that right, another state does. Further, while certain notions of community are used to exclude people, communities are more mutable than many members would like to believe, and many factors, including the movement of people, contribute to the constant regeneration of communal identity. It is not, then, the preservation of a particular community for all times which can lead to restrictions on migration. Rather, it is when the *possibility* of community is threatened that restrictions may be imposed.

There is another connection between migration and communal self-determination. First, more open borders might help to relieve pressures which lead to communal conflict. In other words, if there was a greater degree of freedom of movement, and people saw that their ability to move were greater, they might, on the one hand, decide to move and join some other community which might be more open to their communal identity. On the other, they might decide to stay and participate in the self-determination process, knowing that they could leave if necessary. Of course, all of this movement would have to be entirely voluntary, since to do otherwise would undermine, among other things, the right to remain. Second, an expanded view of self-determination, as argued for in Chapter 2, could create the conditions for greater inclusion in the community on the part of a number of groups, thus relieving the pressures for movement which occurs alongside communal conflict.

All of this leads to the conclusion that, although many states are vigorously reasserting their rights to control their borders with respect to the movement of people and membership – *de facto* and *de jure* – they are fighting a losing battle, although some of the trends seem to be contradictory and ambiguous in their ultimate outcome. Further, questions of human rights and justice require that states open up their borders much more than they are now. This can be seen as a significant blow to one of the most fundamental premises undergirding the concept of state sovereignty – the ability to control access to and membership within the broad community called the state.

Finally, human rights considerations may also lead to the conclusion that a new concept of citizenship is needed.[125] Citizenship has been state-centric and has reified claims by states to deny entry and membership to most people. However, I have argued that people may have much broader rights to cross borders and become members of other communities than are found in the sovereignty discourse. This is because, consistent with the New Sovereignty, individuals are recognized as humans first rather than as citizens of a particular state. Thus, it is necessary to consider people as citizens of the world who also have affiliations which entail rights and responsibilities with other communal entities. As individuals with certain rights with regard to autonomy, subsistence and other values, people have the right in many different circumstances to change those affiliations. Thus, citizenship becomes, on the one hand, more mutable, and on the other, more encompassing, as a concept of global citizenship is added to other kinds of citizenship, much like, as in Chapter 1, one can identify different, multiple and overlapping sovereignties, which encompass both the local and the global.

4 Humanitarian Access and Intervention

> At the current stage of inter-state relations,
> the issue, in my view, is not so much of
> humanitarian intervention but of humanitarian
> access.   Sadako Ogata[1]

> We were so riveted to the problem of
> sovereignty . . . but a country's sovereignty
> doesn't give it the right to do what was
> happening in the Sudan.   US Official[2]

While reviewing some of the human rights and humanitarian issues which are posing challenges to the sovereignty discourse, I have demonstrated how the rights of individuals and groups are gaining in stature with respect to state sovereignty. That is, empirical investigations of international law and state practice as well as normative and theoretical interrogations of the social purpose of the state have yielded a reconstruction of the loci of rights and authority which is much more ambiguous than the familiar constructions of state sovereignty. The state cannot claim to be the sole arbiter of proper conduct within a particular territorial expanse. Rather, it is subject to a wide array of restrictions on its conduct, particularly with regard to the treatment of individuals and groups.

In addition, I have argued that the social purpose of states – which defines the proper conduct of states – can also be tied to the social purpose of international organizations of which states are members. In other words, insofar as states are obligated to provide for a space in which the individuals and groups which comprise the state can live relatively peacefully and without fear of persecution, international governmental organizations are obligated to help carry out this mandate.

The question then becomes: what should happen if a state is not carrying out its social purpose with respect to those within the state? This might encompass a wide range of activities or acts of omission, from not aiding a portion of the population in need of disaster relief to deliberate starvation of those in rebel-held territories to ethnic cleansing. In other words, what are the rights and duties of the international community as a whole, as well as particular sectors of that community, in responding to violations of human rights and humanitarian emergencies? When a population is in temporary need of assistance and protection, can the United Nations, the ICRC, or other NGOs just step in to provide such assistance, and to what extent is the active involvement of the government necessary? Or, in the case of widespread gross violations of human rights, should more forceful action be taken, including the replacement of the government which is engaging in such atrocities? If so, who should carry out this activity?

Much has been written recently about the so-called doctrine of humanitarian intervention.[3] Most of it has stayed more or less within the sovereignty discourse. That is, the discussion has been focused on when to violate the sovereignty of the state. It has assumed that the state will remain the proper primary focus of international legal and moral thought, and that only in a very few cases where the situation has become so horrendous – and has been publicized as such by the media – should the international community act in a forceful way. At that point, the debate becomes whether individual states or only the United Nations should be empowered to engage in humanitarian intervention. That debate is important, and will be joined below. What the discussion is missing for the most part, however, is a wider recognition that the state is declining in both its ability to provide for some of the needs which result in humanitarian emergencies as well as in its primacy of international concern.

In other words, the state is decreasingly able to provide for the needs of its population, particularly in situations of internal conflict. Further, the state is no longer seen as just 'the state'. Rather, it is an amalgamation of individuals and groups, all of which have certain rights and obligations with respect to each other, the juridical entity – the state – of which they are part, and the wider international community. Thus, the question is not whether to violate the supreme authority of an absolute juridical entity, but rather, how to ensure that the rights of individuals and groups within a particular territorially demarcated space are upheld. Seen in this light, the focus of the debate changes somewhat, from justifications of violations of sovereignty – although this is still important – to obligations to do so. And, the range of possible actions is expanded, too, beyond the focus on forceful military interventions against a central government to a broader debate which ranges from humanitarian access to wider humanitarian intervention.

As in the previous chapters, I will examine the international legal setting and recent practice with respect to the questions at hand. Then, I will look at the broader normative questions with regard to aiding those in need across previously sacrosanct boundaries. Finally, the answers to the above questions will be integrated into the New Sovereignty.

ACCESS AND INTERVENTION

Intervention in the emerging global order is a multi-faceted phenomenon. At its core are forceful efforts to influence a government or the outcome of an internationally-relevant situation, regardless of whether a government is involved. It can include activities such as overthrowing a government or annexing a government by force. However, it can also involve more ambiguous forceful action which may involve government or rebel acquiescence or resistance. It is done by a state or international governmental organization, usually to address a security or humanitarian problem in a particular territory (recognizing, of course, that the two frequently cannot be separated. *Humanitarian* intervention involves a situation where the humanitarian aspects are the primary factors in the decision to intervene and are the main focus of the action, such as stopping widespread gross violations of human rights like genocide or ameliorating mass starvation.

Most discussion of humanitarian intervention is rooted firmly in the sovereignty discourse. It assumes that states are sovereign and thus, by and large, are immune to intervention. It reifies the concept of a strict dividing line between domestic jurisdiction and those issues which are of legitimate international concern. In other words, it buttresses the norm of non-intervention and the idea that, in general, states are not bound by certain responsibilities and duties toward their citizenries. Only in exceptional circumstances, which seem to coincide with a finding of a threat to international peace and security, will this norm be violated. Yet, there may be times when action may be needed but where either there is no obvious 'threat to international peace and security' or where waiting for such a threat to occur would endanger many lives and ensure a worsening of the situation. Attempting to put new ideas about intervention into old concepts may undermine the usefulness of the concept. As Anne-Marie Slaughter Burley observes:

> As the paradigm shifts, the old norm is stretched to accommodate the shift. The device used . . . is to emphasize the transboundary effects of internal conflict in order to fit situations into the old model . . . . I argue that continuing to stretch the concept of threat to the peace ultimately undermines the legitimacy and authority of the entire UN Charter. Once a threat to the peace can mean anything from famine to the invasion of a sovereign state, the concept is so broad as to be useless. We need a new concept.[4]

Further, while it is legitimate in many instances to see a potential threat to the peace in internal conflicts, this need not be the basis on which action is taken. It is important to enshrine a norm that action may be taken on humanitarian grounds to ensure a more rapid response, especially when a threat to the peace is not found. This would go far in undermining traditional state-centric views of sovereignty.

Changing the basis for action would also recognize that humanitarian action, while falling outside of the sovereignty discourse, might also fall outside the ambit of intervention. In other words, there will be times when humanitarian concerns will require action to mitigate a situation which, while not a forcible military intervention, nonetheless involves crossing state boundaries against the wishes of the state and engaging in activities which the state has forbidden. This is the concept of humanitarian access. It includes instances where the UN or aid organizations negotiate with governments to gain access to affected populations, or where humanitarian access is obtained without the consent of a government, with no forcible military component in both cases.

The distinction between the two is important. First, it is only states or international intergovernmental organizations which have the resources to undertake interventions, while a wide variety of actors can engage in humanitarian access activities. Second, the legal basis for humanitarian access is somewhat different than that for intervention. Third, the different nature of the two activities has implications for how they may conceptualized within discourses about sovereignty.

One is thus left with two concepts: intervention and access. Intervention revolves around forceful action within the territorial bounds of a state against the wishes of that state. It has the possibility of resulting in much more extensive actions than access, which is usually not forceful, by its very nature cannot threaten the territorial integrity of a state, focuses solely on the needs of individuals, and can be undertaken by a broader array of actors. Access, moreover, has the added attribute that it may be seen as more neutral and therefore less threatening to the government and other forces involved. Humanitarian intervention and access are not completely distinct, as will become obvious, especially insofar as intervention may be invoked when access – with or without the permission of the government – cannot be obtained. In addition, the exercise of both further call into question claims made by states within the sovereignty discourse to a distinct dividing line between domestic and international jurisdiction.

One significant question related to this definition discussion is the extent to which peacekeeping activities might fall under the rubric of intervention. Certainly traditional peacekeeping would not since the basic premise is that all parties to a conflict have accepted the peacekeepers' presence. Further, the military component of traditional peacekeeping has been relatively small. However, there have been instances recently where peacekeepers have found themselves in rather ambiguous situations where not all parties have accepted their presence, where they have come under attack by one or more of the parties to a conflict, or where the mandate of the peacekeeping operation has been gradually changed to include increasingly more enforcement (that is military) activities. At this point, such as in the cases of Somalia and the former Yugoslavia, the line between peacekeeping and intervention becomes significantly blurred, and the international community is drawn into interventionary activity whether it had intended it or not.

INTERVENTION: THE LEGAL FRAMEWORK

The legal status of humanitarian intervention is contested. However, intervention violates most interpretations of customary as well as codified international law. The basis of this prohibition is the recognized status of states as sovereign. That is, states are regarded as the primary unit of organization and political integrity in international affairs. International law is concerned, essentially, with interactions between states, and what happens inside a state, including the treatment of nationals within their state, is outside of the purview of international law. Yet, as I have demonstrated, individuals are also increasingly becoming subjects of international law, with a concomitant relative decline in the stature of states.

As opposed to earlier times when the use of force in international affairs was regarded as a state's right, a general presumption against the use of force has evolved. This presumption that the use of force is unacceptable was codified in the Charter of the United Nations, article 2(4) of which states: 'All members shall refrain in their international relations from the threat or use of force against the territorial integrity or political independence of any state, or in any other manner inconsistent with the Purposes of the United Nations.' Article 51 of the Charter codified another principle of international law which allowed the use of force by a state in self-defence. Article 2(7) proscribes most intervention by the United Nations:

Nothing contained in the present Charter shall authorize the United Nations to intervene in matters which are essentially within the domestic jurisdiction of any state or shall require the Members to submit such matters to settlement under the present Charter; but this principle shall not prejudice the application of enforcement measures under Chapter VII.

Within this paragraph, however, are two phrases which raise flags regarding the legality of UN action. First, there is the problem of deciding exactly what falls under the domestic jurisdiction of a state. Generally, it has been assumed that just about anything which does not go beyond a state's border is within the exclusive jurisdiction of the state. This includes form of government, economic arrangements, and the way a government treats its people. Richard Falk denies that states have actually exercised the autonomy which is generally attributed to states:

> [I]n fact, the domestic order has never enjoyed autonomy in any strict sense. It is now commonplace to accept the interdependence of economic, cultural, and military affairs. In fact, nations have always had a vital concern with what goes on elsewhere, even if elsewhere is a foreign state. Sovereignty only confers a primary competence upon a nation; it is not, and never was, an exclusive competence.[5]

This primary competence would, presumably, include whatever is essentially domestic, as opposed to what might affect another state.

In addition, certain principles have evolved in the international system which are recognized as unchanging. These fall under the term *jus cogens*, or principles from which there can be no derogation. These include, among others, prohibitions against torture, slavery and genocide. They are manifestly illegal under international law, and therefore would not fall under domestic jurisdiction. They have been codified in various treaties and conventions; however, regardless of whether or not a state has ratified these conventions, it is still bound by these principles. In fact, as Newman has observed: 'we have plenty of precedents to establish that crimes against humanity [including genocide] are not essentially within the domestic jurisdiction'.[6] Or, as Kutner has written, 'Article 2, paragraph 7 of the Charter which precludes the United Nations from interfering in matters which are "essentially within the domestic jurisdiction of any state" may not be interposed because the member states have obliged themselves to promote fundamental human rights.'[7]

Further, what is considered essentially domestic changes. As the Permanent Court of International Justice maintained in 1923: 'the question of whether a certain matter is or is not solely within the jurisdiction of a state is an essentially relevant question; it depends on the development of international relations'.[8] Therefore, as Pease and Forsythe observe, 'there may be no permanent demarcation between internal and international affairs, between domestic and international jurisdiction within which authority is exercised, but only a sliding relative difference'.[9] Thus, colonialism, which was not considered to be an international issue became one. And, the rights of individuals and groups have found their place on the international agenda. The actual role of the international community with respect to such issues may still be somewhat ambiguous and in a state of flux, but that is the nature of a system where terms of reference seem to change from time to time. In fact, as Robert Pastor correctly points out, attempting to fix a boundary between the domestic and the international is futile and misleading:

> The search for the right boundary line between domestic rights and international responsibilities is a futile one, based on an errant premise of bifurcated jurisdictions. In the contemporary world it is hard to find an issue or an interest that is either wholly domestic or completely international. Most issues or problems are domestic, with a residual component that is international. For example, the famine in Somalia has domestic origins and in the long term can be resolved only by Somalis, but the international community has a residual humanitarian responsibility to prevent massive starvation . . . .
>
> The search for a boundary between domestic and international affairs is worse than useless; it is misleading. The primary issue should be *not* the division of responsibilities between governments and IOs but how the international community should perceive and respond to collective problems.[10]

If there is a such a class of activities which are recognized as not being within the realm of domestic jurisdiction, or, more properly, if most issues have some sort of international component, how should violations of humanitarian principles should be handled? One way of looking at it is by reference to the last phrase of article 2(7) of the UN Charter which refers to Chapter VII of the Charter. Chapter VII deals with actions – military as well as nonmilitary – which can be authorized by the Security Council. Article 39 refers to a 'threat to the peace, breach of the peace, or act of aggression' which might justify UN military action. It can be argued that certain acts, while violating the principles of *jus cogens* or other principles might, nonetheless, not be a threat to the peace. Yet, when an internal war or other situation, such as a famine or massive human rights abuses, creates a situation where there is massive movement of people across state boundaries, which is a frequent outcome, this is an obvious 'threat to the peace'. Of course, having to resort to a 'threat to the peace' as the basis for humanitarian action is inherently statist and is firmly rooted in the sovereignty discourse because it is only states which can be affected by a 'threat to the peace'.

One can also imagine other action taken by the UN which is not military in nature. Indeed, there already exists a certain amount of human rights machinery in the UN, including the UN Human Rights Commission. However, past practice has shown that as presently constituted these mechanisms cannot deal effectively with massive human rights abuses. There are essentially no enforcement mechanisms which work in a timely, efficient, and consistent manner. The best that can be done is to attempt to pressure governments through UN diplomatic channels, publicize the abuses, and, possibly, call for an economic boycott of the offending country by member states. These activities would not fall under the above definition of intervention, but rather would be more properly called attempts to interfere, using means which are generally regarded as legal. In addition, the United Nations (or other bodies) could take part in other activities which come under the heading of gaining access without there necessarily being a military component.

UNILATERAL HUMANITARIAN INTERVENTION

Before further discussing UN action, an examination of non-UN unilateral action is in order. Throughout the history of states, the predominant, indeed almost exclusive, actors in any type of intervention have been states. Until very recently, anyway, this makes sense. With no kind of centralized, universal organizations such as the UN, there were no other kinds of actors to engage in intervention. Of course, most of these interventions had nothing at all to do with humanitarian motives. They were for the gain of the intervening state, whether for territorial, economic, or ideological reasons. While states were regarded as sovereign entities, the use of force was still sanctioned. However, with the development of the League of Nations and the Kellogg-Briand Pact, which attempted to outlaw aggressive war, and certainly by the time of the UN Charter, the use of force by one state against the other was deemed by the international community to be aggression and therefore illegal. Essentially the only exception to this was the use of force in response to aggression – self-defence – as is outlined in the UN Charter. The use of force for the protection of nationals was also put forth as an exception.[11]

The UN Charter and post-1945 legal practice[12] seem to uphold the doctrine of nonintervention. Yet, many legal scholars argue vociferously for the right of unilateral humanitarian intervention.[13] Hoffman sums up what he sees as the prevailing view:

> [T]here seems to be agreement ... [on] the following .... [H]uman-itarian intervention is deemed legitimate intervention by force against a state which practices genocide on a large scale or which would, for in-stance, starve its inhabitants. This is the argument that was used by some to justify the removal of such monsters as Idi Amin and Bokassa, to explain Indian intervention for the independence of Bangladesh, and to defend the elimination of Pol Pot by invasion.[14]

In addition, Shawcross declared in 1946 that 'the right of humanitarian in-tervention, in the name of the Rights of Man trampled upon by the State in a manner offensive to the feeling of Humanity, has been recognized long ago as an integral part of the Law of Nations'[15] which the UN Charter did not change. Teson has argued that:

> [F]orcible action to stop serious human rights deprivations is permitted by international law, properly construed .... [T]he *best* interpreta-tion of relevant treaty materials and state practice is that humanit-arian intervention is consistent with the present international legal order.[16]

A significant reason why these, and many other, scholars support unilat-eral humanitarian intervention is that the UN has not met the original ex-pectations of collective actions in response to 'threats to the peace' and the like. One need only look at the widespread violations of human rights worldwide and the paucity of UN response to these activities, as well as the lack of machinery to deal with these issues, to see this point.[17] Cer-tainly the lack of forceful response to the genocide in Bosnia-Herzegovina illustrates this, although, as will be discussed below, one might discern a small crack in the wall of indifference.

If one does accept the legality of unilateral humanitarian intervention, the question then becomes whether or not states should act in this manner, for, certainly, not everything which is legal can or should be done, just as things which might not be legal, or at least have disputed legality, should sometimes nevertheless be done.

States act in their own interest, and usually any action which might be in the interest of another state, group, or individual is secondary to the acting state's interests. So it is with any kind of intervention, including human-itarian intervention. It is difficult to find examples where states have acted unilaterally with little or no self-interest[18] to help foreign nationals in another state. Two recent examples which are put forth as unilateral humanitarian intervention will illustrate this point.

First is the case of India's intervention in Pakistan which resulted in the creation of the state of Bangladesh from what had been East Pakistan. The East Pakistanis were being brutally treated by West Pakistan. The West Pakistan army was slaughtering East Pakistanis on a massive scale and engaging in rape and pillage. An estimated nine million refugees flowed across the border into India, certainly enough to be identified as a threat to international peace and security under contemporary usage of the term, and also enough to create an interest in the conflict on the part of India.[19] The East Pakistanis demanded independence and, in light of what was happening, India invaded and defeated the West Pakistan army. As a result, the state of Bangladesh was created. Although the Indian ambassador to the UN stated that 'we have on this particular occasion absolutely nothing but the purest of motives and the purest of intentions: to rescue the people of East Bengal from what they are suffering',[20] this was not a selfless act on the part of India. India and Pakistan were longtime rivals, and this crisis gave India the opportunity to decrease its rival's power. Even given this motive, however, many observers credit this action as being a leading case of humanitarian intervention. Yet, in the end, India did not invoke the doctrine of humanitarian intervention when it invaded.[21] Also, as Fairley points out, 'the brunt of the effort borne in the preservation of human life and dignity was undertaken by the United Nations' relief effort, the largest entertained since the conclusion of the Second World War'.[22] One hundred and five members of the General Assembly supported a resolution declaring India's actions unlawful. Therefore, given the General Assembly vote and the fact that India did not invoke this doctrine, it would seem that this case was not a true application of the doctrine of humanitarian intervention.[23]

The second case put forth as supporting humanitarian intervention is Tanzania's invasion of Uganda in 1979. Idi Amin's regime in Uganda from 1971 to 1979 has been recognized as one of the most brutal regimes the world has seen. The government engaged in massive human rights abuses, and as many as 300,000 Ugandans may have been executed. Yet, President Julius Nyerere's decision to intervene was motivated at least in part by nonhumanitarian interests. There was very little activity on the part of the outside world in response to Amin's barbarity. The West only instituted modest economic sanctions after several years and provocations involving US and British nationals, and African and Islamic countries resisted admitting that the situation was a legitimate international concern. There was long-standing animosity between Uganda and Tanzania, and in the fall of 1978 Uganda attempted to annex 710 square miles of Tanzanian territory, although Tanzania forced out the troops by December. Tanzania invaded in 1979, overthrowing Amin. While the invasion created economic hardships for Tanzania, it seems plausible to conclude that at least the timing, and possibly the fact, of the invasion itself, can be explained by self-interest. While the invasion was limited, several thousand troops were left behind in Uganda after Amin's troops were eliminated. Further, Tanzania itself seemed reluctant to use humanitarian intervention as a justification at the July 1979 OAU summit.[24] As Martha Finnemore notes: 'In fact, Tanzania went out of her way to disclaim responsibility for the felicitous humanitarian outcomes of her actions. She claimed only that she was acting in response to Amin's invasion and that her actions just happened to coincide with a revolt against Amin inside Uganda.'[25]

Given that the legality of unilateral humanitarian intervention is contested, and given that national interest would probably play a part in these activities, what conclusion should be reached regarding such unilateral actions? Can unilateral action be severed from national interest? It seems highly doubtful that this could occur. The commitment of troops and other resources means that the intervening state must see some compelling reason for it to act. It is highly unlikely that either the elites or the public in any country would see much value in sending troops to be killed for something which did not entail some sort of gain for the intervening state. Like Falk I am not sanguine about the possibility of separating out state interests:

> I am very skeptical about the sensitivity of principal governments to the values at stake, the consistency of that sensitivity, so as not to feel comfortable about giving legal sanction to the doctrine of humanitarian intervention under contemporary conditions.[26]

Intervention, in general, is done by large states to small states; indeed, it would be foolish for a small, weak state to attempt action against a much larger state. In addition, intervention is usually even more restricted to great powers. Yet, it is difficult to point to an act of unilateral intervention which they have undertaken and label it as humanitarian, or even as having much of a humanitarian component at all. As Falk observes, great power intervention 'is inevitably going to be connected with foreign policy because that is what the decisions ultimately relate to, whether or not or under what conditions to project power in foreign societies'.[27] William Rogers points to another reason why unilateral intervention should not be sanctioned:

any time the great powers intervene unilaterally, the destabilizing effect is so substantial and the encroachment to individual national personalities in the target State (and in all of the States which have identified themselves with the target State) and the consequences in terms of values affected are so great, that a very powerful presumption, in my judgment, is created against any great power intervention.[28]

Finally, some point to the actions on the part of several countries on behalf of Kurds in Iraq after the Gulf War as an argument for unilateral intervention. The question of whether those activities were unilateral or done within the mandate of resolution 688 is debatable. However, if one accepts that they were not endorsed by the UN, this still might not be reasonable justification to accept unilateral intervention. As Payam Akhavan argues:

the consequences of the Allied actions in Iraqi Kurdistan are unquestionably positive from a human rights perspective and evince a compelling argument in favour of a permissive rule allowing for unilateral humanitarian intervention by armed force. However, the fact that 'pro-democracy' American invasion in countries such as Grenada, Nicaragua and Panama – which was actuated by very different and questionable motives – is arbitrarily equated by some jurists with 'humanitarian intervention', underscores the potential for abuse of such a doctrine.[29]

Yet, as Burns Weston argues: 'if we are to limit humanitarian intervention to global organizational intervention or its equivalent, then we are not talking about the real world'.[30] Weston is essentially correct, although this may be changing somewhat. Some support unilateral intervention because the machinery – such as the Military Staff Committee – was never adequately established in the UN, as well as the fact that it has been extremely difficult to get the members, and especially the permanent members, of the Security Council to agree and act. Thus, John Moore would allow unilateral action under very stringent criteria, including 'immediate threat to fundamental human rights, particularly a threat of widespread loss of human life'. Other values would include proportionality and the use of the minimum amount of force, and sensitivity to the relationship between the values being upheld and the force used. At the same time, self-determination must not be undercut.[31] Finally, Ellen Frey-Wouters takes a slightly different position. Acknowledging that unilateral action is not permissible, she 'admit[s] that forceful unilateral intervention may have to be practiced in certain unique and extremely genocidal situations, but international law need not authorize or encourage it'.[32] In essence, this is a call for international civil disobedience, which, presumably, would be recognized as being 'right', even if not legal. She goes on to say that 'forceful unilateral action however humanitarian in intent, cannot be condoned as legal, even when acting in lieu of the duly established mechanism, lest the abuse of that unilateralism destroy the whole basis for legally constituted process'.[33]

The arguments against unilateral intervention are compelling. The inability of states to act out of purely humanitarian motives is well established. But if humanitarian objectives are achieved does this matter? If states will not act unless they have an interest in the situation – ideological, political, strategic, economic – should they be given an excuse to pursue these motives? The last thing the world needs are self-appointed police who decide, as much as on state interests as humanitarian interests, when to intervene in other states. Throughout history, the self-appointed police have shown themselves to be singularly incapable of not abusing their position, and there is no prospect for this changing in the future. Without a legal prohibition, states might feel even more free than they do now to engage in intervention.

Finally, R.J. Vincent puts forth three reasons why the doctrine of non-intervention should be upheld: (1) there is no guarantee of impartiality, (2) the action might be unwelcome because it comes from outside, and (3) there is no common morality which transcends borders from which one could derive principles of intervention.[34] The first has already been dealt with. The second reason is especially pertinent to former colonies and other states who have had a history of foreign intervention of one type or another. Of course, this is not restricted to these states; indeed, a people with a healthy dose of nationalism, or just a feeling that it is up to them to determine their own destiny, might see such an action in this light. The third reason, to a large extent, is true, although one could make the case that the prohibition against genocide, in its position as *jus cogens*, would qualify as a transcendent moral principle, as would other human rights principles. In addition, below I will further discuss other ways to derive a compelling interest in humanitarian situations, as well as a right, and possibly even a duty, to intervene on the part of certain types of international organizations. Even if there were a common moral framework, as has already been discussed, states do not, in general, act for moral reasons. Thus, it would seem that unilateral humanitarian intervention is illegitimate, and probably should continue to be so.

REGIONAL AND GLOBAL HUMANITARIAN INTERVENTION

The UN Charter, as well as much subsequent action by the UN, while reaffirming the basic principle of nonintervention, also affirms the protection of human rights as a goal. While some may argue whether or not the protection of human rights is put in a primary or secondary position in the Charter, it is nonetheless recognized as something within the UN's competence. While establishing the legality of UN action above, a few of the problems surrounding such action were mentioned. The most basic problem is that the UN, through the Security Council, has not chosen, or been able, to act in most situations. Most conflicts and situations where there have been gross violations of human rights have, until recently, been viewed by the superpowers through the lens of Cold War rivalry, which has made it virtually impossible to get them to agree, as they must along with the other permanent members, to any kind of action.

The UN did not take action during the genocidal reign of the Khmer Rouge in Cambodia, or, as already pointed out, in Bangladesh or Uganda, and has virtually ignored the dire humanitarian situation in the Sudan. However, one can point to a few hopeful signs that the UN might be ready and able to act more forcefully on the world stage. The superpower conflict has receded, and there has been renewed interest in, and reliance on, the United Nations. There has also been more great power, and general international, cooperation in attempting to resolve conflicts, such as in Angola, Namibia and Cambodia. There has also been a renewed interest in human rights. Unfortunately, this has coincided with what appear to be increasing human rights problems, including famine, brutal regimes, refugees and other grave humanitarian situations.

Even with hopeful signs, can UN action, being the result of one big power play, be seen as more legitimate than unilateral action? The UN, and particularly the Security Council, is a reflection of state interests – especially those of powerful states – and at times has been paralyzed by these interests. This has changed somewhat in recent years, but the UN has not come anywhere near being an autonomous actor above state interest, and thus these interests will come into play whenever a response to a humanitarian situation is contemplated. Yet, the UN can come closer to expressing universal outrage at human rights abuses than any other body. Given the extreme difficulty which the UN has had in the past in engaging in any kind of collective action, it is unlikely that the ability to intervene will be abused in the future.[35] And, there have been instances where the UN has recently taken some concrete action in humanitarian situations. In fact, recent events have moved one observer to remark: 'The rapidity of change and the scope of these new collective efforts have turned on its head the long-standing question of whether the UN could do *anything* useful; to-day, the question is whether the UN can do *everything.*'[36]

UN responses have been selective and will continue to be so. To a large degree, the response to a particular crisis has depended upon the interest and will of one or more great powers, and this is likely to continue. However, this selectivity does not necessarily delegitimate all UN humanit-arian interventions. Even though there may be certain instances where action will not be taken to respond to a humanitarian crisis, the world may be in for a period of time where it must take what it can get. That is, while situations like the Sudan may be ignored by the international community, and the response to Somalia was belated, this does not mean that we should not accept that which can be done – including a rather late intervention in Somalia – while at the same time trying to make international reactions more uniform and speedy.

Several recent instances of UN involvement demonstrate the still ten-tative and ambiguous nature of forceful UN action. The first is Security Council Resolution 688 and the actions taken to protect the Kurds in North-ern Iraq after the Gulf War. Resolution 688 'insist[ed] that Iraq allow im-mediate access by international humanitarian organizations to all those in need of assistance in all parts of Iraq . . . .' The legitimacy of this resolu-tion was vigorously debated. On the one hand, France argued that massive human rights abuses, even if not accompanied by threats to international security, were worthy of intervention by the Security Council, which 'would have been remiss in its task had it stood idly by, without reacting to the massacre of entire populations, the extermination of civilians, includ-ing women and children.'[37] China, on the other hand, which abstained on the vote for 688, made reference to the 'domestic jurisdiction' clause in Article 2(7). Further, the resolution made it clear that it was not violations of human rights but the consequences of those violations – refugees as threats to peace and security – which provided the basis for Security Coun-cil action.[38]

Two different initiatives were pursued to ensure that Iraq fulfilled it duties as outlined in 688. The United Nations signed a memorandum of understanding with the Iraqi government to provide humanitarian aid to the 'affected Iraqi civilian population' and which supposedly covered all of Iraq, not just Iraqi Kurdistan, and was based on a request from Iraq. Thus, it posed no challenge to the sovereign rights of Iraq. A later agree-ment paved the way for the United Nations Guards Contingent in Iraq.[39]

In addition, the British and French, joined by an initially reluctant US, declared, first, a 'no-fly zone' in Northern Iraq (as well as in Southern

Iraq where the Shi'ite population was threatened), and second, a plan to create Kurdish enclaves, protected from Iraqi forces, and introduced forces to carry out this plan. These countries relied on Resolution 688 to legitimize their actions. Yet, Resolution 688 did not specifically authorize this use of force, and the Secretary-General did not request it, although he did, in the end, acquiesce in the intervention.[40] Thus, while the Allied powers were engaging in activity which responded to the *spirit* of Resolution 688, it did not carry out its activities with respect to the *letter* of the resolution.

This activity was, clearly, a violation of Iraqi sovereignty. This led to a curious situation where those who, just months earlier, took forceful action to uphold the sanctity of state sovereignty, were undermining that same concept.[41] Further, these actions demonstrate an increased willingness, on the part of at least some of the more powerful state actors on the international scene, to take forceful action on behalf of human rights which has the effect of undermining sovereign authority.[42]

In Somalia, the Security Council approved a plan by the United States to provide a substantial number of troops to restore order and ensure that humanitarian aid could get to where it was needed. In the months following the intervention, the country was suffering much less violence and the threat of starvation had receded dramatically. The UN subsequently took over the operations from US forces.

The case of Somalia is unique because there was no sovereign authority within Somalia which would be the focal point of either negotiations or intervention. In addition, there was an obvious 'threat to the peace' as a result of the massive flows of refugees fleeing the fighting. This means that while there is an indirect connection between human rights and UN action, the main rationale for action was still the traditional threat to the peace, although the conception of this threat has changed. Yet, the instance of Somalia also indicates, perhaps, the glimmerings of change in the reasons for a major actor on the international scene – namely the United States – to become involved in forceful action. In Somalia, there were no direct economic or strategic interests of the US[43] (the bases on which the US has traditionally acted) – as opposed to the situation in Iraq – which were threatened by the continued instability and starvation. Thus, the United States – after, it must be pointed out, a significant period of delay and soul-searching – committed troops to what, at least from the US perspective, must be seen as an essentially humanitarian mission. The fact that the US pulled out after the US public finally realized the potential costs of such a commitment only partially takes away from a dramatic change in policy.

Mention must also be made of UN action, or inaction, in the former Yugoslavia.[44] The 'ethnic cleansing' which was carried out against Muslims in Bosnia-Herzegovina surely qualifies as genocide. Yet, the response was generally muted. Several thousand UN peacekeepers were put on the ground to protect aid convoys; yet, the peacekeepers had a very circumscribed mandate with regard to the use of force. This meant that commanders on the ground had to rely almost entirely on negotiations to get aid through to where it was needed, frequently resulting in delays of weeks or months. The UN and NATO periodically made bold statements regarding the need to use force to ensure that aid could get through to where it was needed and, in a couple of instances, to end the Serbian siege of a couple of Muslim enclaves, including Sarejevo. However, even in the face of demonstrated genocide – hundreds of thousands dead, and two million refugees – the international community generally failed to take forceful action to address the situation. The only exceptions to this were a few instances where NATO forces bombed Serbian forces which violated the so called 'safe zones' around the enclaves, which turned out not to be very safe at all. Yet, until the spring and summer of 1995 – more than three years after the genocide became apparent to the world community – these were very limited and did not result in significant improvements in the situation.[45] Only then did NATO expand its air strikes, to such a degree that, along with Bosnian gains on the ground, the Serbs finally negotiated an end to the war.[46] The very late use of force seemed to have changed the tide of the conflict. This demonstrates that the course of the entire conflict may have changed dramatically if force had been used three years earlier.

Those supporting UN involvement in the conflict used three intertwined justifications for that involvement. These are that the refugee situation, the humanitarian situation resulting from the war, and the human rights violations perpetrated by the Bosnian Serbs threatened international peace and security. Certainly, the hundreds of thousands of refugees impacted neighboring states, as did the prospect of the conflict spreading to more states. Here, again, is an instance where humanitarian concerns are perceived as being important and within the mandate of the UN Security Council. At the same time, however, this is also another case where these concerns have been forced into the rubric of 'international peace and security' rather than standing on their own as justifications for UN action. The human rights situation, by itself, did seem to provide the necessary justification for Conference on Security and Cooperation in Europe (CSCE) intervention, as evidenced in the Moscow Declaration of October 1991. However, it took many months just to get human rights monitors into Serbian areas, albeit without Serbian consent.[47]

The international reaction to the Rwandan genocide of up to one million people was a significant failure. The UN had advance knowledge that a genocide was being planned,[48] but this information seems to have gotten lost in the bureaucracy.[49] Once the genocide began in the wake of the assassination of the Rwandan and Burundian presidents on 6 April 1994, the international community took little action. In fact, most of the 2,500 peacekeeping troops in Rwanda as part of the 1993 Arusha peace accords were withdrawn. On 17 May that the Security Council expanded the United Nations Mission in Rwanda (UNAMIR) to 5,500 troops, but they were not deployed at the time.[50] It was not until the French, acting under a Chapter VII mandate, intervened in one part of the country in June that any forceful action was taken to stop the genocide or protect potential victims. 'Opération Turquoise' was a limited intervention and was tied up with French interests in Rwanda,[51] but it is credited with aiding humanitarian relief efforts, and protecting 13–14,000 people who otherwise might have been killed.[52] Beyond this, the international community took no forceful action to stop the genocide.

Another recent case is that of Haiti. After the first elected President, Jean Bertrand Aristide, was overthrown in a *coup* on 30 September 1991, the UN took little action. However, it did impose mandatory sanctions on Haiti in June 1993. Security Council Resolution 841, which imposed the sanctions, made reference to threats to international peace and security, as evidenced in the refugee situation. It also took into account the wishes of the recognized government.[53] However, Damrosch maintains that Resolution 841's most important aspect was that

the Haitian sanctions resolution goes farther than any other to date in applying universal, mandatory, and severe economic sanctions to influence a domestic political crisis over democratic governance. Its cautious wording (stressing more than once the 'unique and exceptional' circumstances) cannot hide its precedential significance.[54]

The pressures for international action continued to mount, most dramatically with the waves of refugees fleeing Haiti. On 31 July 1994 at the urging of the United States, the UN Security Council passed Resolution 940 by a 12–0 vote which authorized member states to 'use all necessary means' to return Aristide to power. The US heightened its rhetoric regarding its will to intervene over the ensuing month and a half and US military ships were moved into position off of Haiti. Finally, a settlement was reached after the military leadership found out that a US invasion force was on its way. Aristide returned to Haiti on 15 October 1994.

Haiti represents a significant shift in international practice with regard to forceful action for humanitarian ends, but also demonstrates the continuing ambiguities as the international community attempts to come to agreement on when and how to intervene in humanitarian situations. This was the first time that the Security Council authorized the use of force to reinstall a democratically elected leader ousted in a *coup*. The motives of the United States, which pushed for and carried out the intervention, were mixed, but were also different than in other instances of US intervention. Certainly foremost on the minds of US leaders was the continued flow of refugees from Haiti, most of whom were trying to get to the United States. However, this demonstrates the ways humanitarian crises can become international. The threat of force was used by the international community to violate the sovereignty of a state which fit all of the traditional conditions of statehood. That the *de facto* government of Lieutenant General Raoul Cédras was *not*, however, recognized by the international community, sets a precedent that human rights matter when determining the legitimacy of a government.

The ambiguities associated with this instance are threefold. First, it was two years before the UN took its first decisive actions, and it was only after the mandatory sanctions were in place that Cédras began taking the UN or OAS seriously.[55] And, it took another year for the Security Council to authorize the measures which ultimately proved necessary to restore Aristide to power. Second, although the UN Security Council authorized the US actions, it was a completely US operation. The UN representative was not even notified before the US launched its ultimately aborted invasion. This highlights the fact that the UN does not have the necessary resources and procedures to address this kind of situation. Third, the basis for Resolution 841 was, again, a threat to 'international peace and security in the region'. While this illustrates yet again an expanding view of what kinds of situations the UN can and should be involved in, it also represents the continuing attempt to fit new situations into old categories. That is, as long as the Security Council does not make the basis of its actions humanitarian, there will still be uncertainty and ambiguity regarding when it can act. While recent actions are a positive sign with respect to humanitarian action, this concern, along with the length of time it has taken to act and the unevenness of its actions, still leave significant doubt and ambiguity regarding the course of UN action.

There is thus a mixed record with respect to forceful action on the part of the UN to deal with dire humanitarian emergencies. Such action has been cast in terms of responding to threats to the peace, enabling the international community to finesse the question of sovereignty. However, as noted at the beginning of the chapter, using this as the basis for action, first, can lead to a situation where the concept of a threat to the peace is expanded to such an extent that it is rendered meaningless. Second, waiting for a situation to evolve to a situation which might be considered to have dire international consequences under traditional meanings of a threat to the peace may lead to a worsening of the humanitarian situation. Thus, more thought should be given to legitimating forceful humanitarian action more directly through evolving notions of the relationship between sovereignty and human rights.

Even if one accepts UN intervention, such action is frequently needed much more quickly than the UN has generally been able to act. How can this situation be remedied? One possibility might be to create a standing rapid reaction capability for the UN, comprised of troops earmarked by governments which would be ready on a moment's notice to be deployed in the event of a humanitarian emergency. One such proposal has recently been put forth by the Canadian Government.[56] In addition to expediting the deployment of UN forces, it might also act a deterrent. However, there is still the problem of getting the Security Council to act in the first place. In addition, such a force might not act as a deterrent until it had been used in a couple of instances and the international community had actually demonstrated its will to use it in situations of humanitarian need. This, and other possibilities, will be discussed in Chapter 5.

Some would prefer regional collective action over UN action. A major premise is that humanitarian intervention should be the result of an expression of community standards. A regional organization may, in some instances, be able to have a more true expression of community than a global organization. There are at least three reasons for preferring regional action. First, it might be more effective. There may be greater expertise on local issues within the regional organization.[57] In addition, it may be easier to get such action without having to deal with the veto in the Security Council or some political block in the UN. Second, it may have a better chance of keeping out great power involvement, which might otherwise distort or attempt to control the action for national ends. Third, the parties to a dispute might prefer a regional forum.[58]

There are many problems associated with regional action, many of which are the same as in the case of the UN. Regional organizations have been as reluctant as the UN to act. For example, they did not act in any kind of decisive way in the cases of Uganda, Bangladesh, and Cambodia. Ambassador Akwei from Ghana, talking about the OAU during the UN debate regarding the Bangladesh intervention, stated:

The Organization of African Unity knows that once intervention in the affairs of a Members State is permitted, once one permits oneself the higher wisdom of telling another Member State what it should do with regard to arranging its own political affairs, one opens a Pandora's box. And no continent can suffer more than Africa when such a principle [of nonintervention] is thwarted.[59]

While atrocities such as genocide cannot be regarded internal political affairs, Akwei expresses legitimate concerns coming from a history of hundreds of years of colonial domination and interference in Africa. The same attitude would apply to Latin America, where, for several hundred years at the mercy of the European powers, it is now still perceived by the dominant power in the region – the US – as its backyard. While these concerns might be justified, they cannot be used as a shield by states to prevent legitimate action by the international community on behalf of human rights.

There are other impediments to regional action. First, most regional organizations do not have the institutional capacity to take effective action. The one exception to this – NATO – has shown itself to be extremely reluctant to act, particularly in the former Yugoslavia. In addition, frequently regional organizations may have a particular stake in a conflict, or one or more of the main members of an organization may also be parties to a conflict or other humanitarian emergency. Further, the members of an organization may be so deeply divided as to preclude agreement on a course of action. Finally, leaders may be reluctant to approve of any action which could provide a precedent which might be used against them in the future.[60]

However, a few recent examples illustrate at least a partial shift on the part of some of the governments in these regions. First, a number of Latin American countries did support forceful action to return Aristide to power. These included Argentina and the 13 member Caribbean Community, several of whom offered a token contribution to the US force. Many of the larger Latin American countries did not support an invasion – Brazil and Venezuela abstained on Resolution 940 – but did support the outcome of the threatened action.[61] Although support for an invasion was by no means unanimous, the very fact that some Latin American countries did express support for intervention signals a dramatic shift away from the previous total non-intervention stance, and may help set a precedent.[62] Second, in the case of Rwanda, the head of the OAU supported a UN force – as opposed to an African force – to help restore order and end the genocidal killings.[63]

A third example is the intervention in Liberia by the Economic Community of West African States (ECOWAS). A civil war begun at the end of
1989 plunged Liberia into total chaos, resulting in near genocide, refugees, and very clear threats to international peace and security as a result
of the refugees flows as well as the spread of fighting to neighbouring
states. Even though called on by many Liberians to do so, the United
States did not intervene, seeing no strategic interest and claiming that it
was an African problem, to be solved by Africans. The UN Security Council, too, failed to take action. Indeed, the two African states serving on the
Security Council at the time rejected Security Council involvement,
not wanting to set a precedent. About eight months after the civil war
began, ECOWAS established the ECOWAS Cease-fire Monitoring Group
(ECOMOG) to monitor a cease-fire, although it clearly had to impose
a cease-fire first. While it has been partially successful, including imposing a two year cease-fire, fighting has continued, and at times,
ECOMOG has found itself taking sides against one of the parties to the
conflict.[64]

The international reaction to the ECOWAS intervention, and the
grounds put forth for the intervention, both demonstrate a gradual shift in
thinking regarding intervention. Many states and international organizations, such as the Organization of African Unity (OAU), European Community, and the Security Council supported ECOWAS' various initiatives
with 'guarded approval', and the Security Council passed Resolution 788,
imposing an arms embargo on Liberia. The overall response to the actual intervention has been very muted, with little condemnation, and
ECOMOG has been generally supported by the people within Liberia. The
main basis put forward for the intervention was humanitarian, and this was
generally accepted by the international community, at least by acquiescence. In fact, the OAU, Security Council and European Community all
supported the humanitarian outcomes of the intervention while at the same
time downplaying the fact that force was used.[65] Perhaps one of the most
significant statements came from the Secretary-General of the OAU,
Salim A. Salim:

. . . for an African government to have the right to kill its citizens or let
its citizens be killed, I believe there is no clause in the charter [of the
OAU] that allows this.

To tell the truth, the charter was created to preserve the humanity,
dignity, and the rights of the African. You cannot use a clause of
the charter to oppress the African and say that you are implementing the
OAU charter. What has happened is that people have interpreted the

charter as if to mean that what happens in the next house is not one's concern. This does not accord with the reality of the world.[66]

A few other African leaders supported this view, although most probably would not. However, the fact that the head of the OAU would make a statement like that and that these views would be considered legitimate for debate demonstrates change in thinking about what sovereignty entails and what kind of intervention may be legitimate.

Both the United Nations and regional organizations have been reluctant to act in a variety of situations, and have demonstrated ambiguity regarding when and on what basis humanitarian intervention should occur. Yet, the UN has acted forcefully in a few situations of humanitarian crises, if somewhat belatedly. This ambiguity will probably continue to be operative for the near future as the international community struggles to resolve the serious issues raised by humanitarian emergencies and examines how they relate to both international peace and security and sovereignty.

HUMANITARIAN ACCESS

At the beginning of this chapter I made a distinction between humanitarian access and humanitarian intervention. Humanitarian intervention is premised, for the most part, on the use of force for humanitarian ends. Humanitarian access, on the other hand, does not necessarily entail the use of force and is focused on ameliorating the immediate humanitarian situation, rather than addressing the broader political and military aspects. In addition, it has as its focus the rights of individuals, developed to the greatest extent in times of war, to receive humanitarian assistance, and the rights and duties of the international community to provide it. In addition, a much wider array of actors is involved in gaining and maintaining access than is the case in intervention.

The problems and questions posed with respect to humanitarian access and sovereignty are numerous. First, to what extent has the recognition of a right to assistance contributed to a reconstructed notion of sovereignty such that access may no longer be considered a violation of sovereignty? Second, to what extent is there a *duty* as opposed to a *right* on the part of the international community to provide humanitarian assistance? Third, since the focus of international law has been states, can NGOs which have little to no international personality actually violate sovereignty when they provide unauthorized humanitarian aid?

Recent years have provided a number of instances where humanitarian access has been needed and has been gained, with or without the permission of the state. Sometimes such actions have been put in terms of challenges to state sovereignty. In other cases, while the question of sovereignty has not been directly raised, the actions have undermined sovereignty nonetheless.

The main body of law on which the International Committee of the Red Cross (ICRC) and others base their activities and their claim that there is a right to assistance is the 1949 Geneva Conventions and the two Additional Protocols of 1977. The original conventions related solely to international armed conflict, whereas Protocol II broadened the realm of action somewhat to included non-international armed conflict. Article 59 of the Fourth Geneva Convention provides for a right on the part of civilians to receive humanitarian assistance during wartime.[67] Under Article 9 common to the First, Second, and Third Geneva Conventions, and Article 81 of Additional Protocol I, the ICRC has the right of initiative during international armed conflicts. In addition, Article 3 of the four Geneva Conventions provides for that same right. This means that the ICRC (and other humanitarian organizations) can offer humanitarian assistance to those in need during war.[68] Further, according to Article 70 of Protocol I such offers, made impartially, should not be considered an unfriendly act;[69] that is, offering aid is not a threat to the sovereignty of the state. As one observer has put it: 'As this right of initiative has been legally accepted by States, it cannot be denounced as undue interference when exercised. By recognizing this right, States have simply expressed their sovereignty.'[70] However, if it can be thought of as an act of sovereignty, then perhaps it is an act within a broadened concept of sovereignty which includes more responsibilities with respect to humanitarian issues and human rights.

Regarding internal conflict, Article 18 of Protocol II provides for impartial, humanitarian relief activities, 'undertaken subject to the consent of the High Contracting Party concerned'. While this makes reference to consent, as Denise Plattner points out, 'when correctly interpreted, it means that such agreement *must* be given if the necessary conditions are fulfilled [impartiality and neutrality], and for as long as the relief operation is taking place on the territory controlled by the legal government'.[71] Or, as she maintains with respect to Article 70 of Protocol I: 'The agreement of the State is needed, but this is in no way a matter of discretion ... '.[72] Further, Articles 54 of Protocol I and 14 of Protocol II outlaw attempts to starve a civilian population.[73]

Thus, a right to receive humanitarian assistance exists, and the ICRC and other organizations have a right to offer such assistance. And, the state in question has an obligation to accept such offers of humanitarian assistance. Even if a state does not provide consent, perhaps maintaining that an armed conflict, as such, was not occurring, Michael Bothe has argued that the ICRC can lawfully act unilaterally in undertaking humanitarian relief action.[74] Further, the right to act is also recognized in the case of rebel-held territory. Torelli makes the observation that:

> Article 3 common to the four Conventions constituted a veritable legal revolution because it meant that each State agreed, in the humiliating situation in which its authority was flouted, that its relations with the sector of the population rebelling against it would thenceforth be governed by international law.[75]

That is, the government of a state cannot stop humanitarian action in a part of its territory which it does not actually control. An aid organization need only obtain the permission of the rebel authorities on the ground. Yves Sandoz has argued that Article 3 'in practical terms authorizes the ICRC (or any other impartial humanitarian body) to enter a territory without the agreement of the government that still represents the entire State internationally.'[76] In addition, even when a government denies that an armed conflict is occurring, Sandoz writes that the ICRC 'could not forswear its action in a large area of the territory of a state over which the government has lost control simply because that government denied the obvious'.[77]

The ICRC has taken great pains to make clear that its activities are neutral and impartial and are not aimed at undermining the sovereignty of the state in which it is operating. Because of this, there is a great reluctance on the part of the ICRC to be involved in any operation which uses outside military forces as escorts for aid convoys which could (perhaps correctly in some cases) be interpreted as favouring one side or the other. Thus, the concept of humanitarian access is useful because it divorces humanitarian aid from larger political and military considerations. However, some within the ICRC argue that, perhaps, maintaining a right to assistance and access calls into question traditional concepts of sovereignty. Certainly, insofar as a state is obliged to accept assistance in situations where it cannot provide for the needs of its populations itself, certain *responsibilities* with respect to individuals within the state are added to the *rights* normally associated with state sovereignty. As one official maintains, ICRC action is not a threat to state sovereignty because the evolving concept of sovereignty includes such activities.[78]

International humanitarian law provides for a right to receive humanitarian assistance, a right to offer such assistance, and, according to some interpretations, right to provide such assistance regardless of the wishes of a government. One can see this as a threat to sovereignty, because it is a violation of supposed sovereign authority. Or, such activities and interpretations can be viewed as consistent with sovereignty because sovereignty includes *responsibilities* as well as rights. Either way, however, such views undermine the sovereignty paradigm.

UNHCR, which plays a major role in providing humanitarian relief, is also reluctant to portray its activities within countries of origin as any kind of intervention or invasion of sovereignty. One UNHCR official rightly points out that UNHCR cannot 'intervene' in a country, and this is certainly correct insofar as I have characterized intervention as involving forcible action. Others note that while some of its activities may be characterized as 'intrusions', they are not identified as coming into conflict with sovereignty by UNHCR. Part of this has to do, as noted in Chapter 3, with the fact that UNHCR is dependent upon the international community for financial support. Further, however, one official expresses concern that the state not be undermined as the basis of international society. That is, while he recognizes an expanded notion of sovereignty which includes responsibilities toward citizens, and while also recognizing that individuals are part of an international community outside of one's state borders, he also noted that undermining the state would undermine international stability.[79] One can thus see how far the sovereignty discourse reaches. Even some who see significant problems with the sovereignty paradigm reify one of the main tenets of the discourse – the centrality and necessity of the state – in order to create a particular kind of system in which human rights and humanitarian action can be ordered. Yet, this reification, even when it includes humanitarian aspects, still reinforces the idea of an international community with rigid loci of power and authority which, as I argued in earlier chapters, corresponds less and less to the way more and more people are experiencing the world.

Yet, even though UNHCR and other organizations do not publicly portray their work as challenging sovereignty, this is, indeed, what they are doing in some instances. In fact, as one UNHCR official has suggested, we may be at a point where 'the UN continues to do lip service to national sovereignty while acting as if national sovereignty were not really a concern'.[80] One type of situation where this analysis might apply is assisting the internally displaced. The instances when UNHCR has been involved with aiding the internally displaced have been in the context of an agreement with the government. Sometimes, however, this agreement may be not completely voluntary. For example, in the case of the Iraqi Kurds, the situation which produced the agreement to allow UN aid and protection to Iraqi Kurds (and others) was not particularly auspicious for a purely voluntary decision. Iraq had just been soundly defeated in a war, and the countries which defeated Iraq had announced their intention to create a safe haven for the displaced. As Howard Adelman observes: 'One possible inference is that the Iraqis were compelled, if not induced, to sign the UN agreement lest the de facto infringements on Iraqi sovereignty otherwise be legitimized.'[81] That is, Iraq engaged in an act of sovereignty – allowing foreign troops onto its soil – to maintain a fiction that its sovereignty was not being violated.

Perhaps this kind of situation is what led one individual at UNHCR to argue that sovereignty and problems of consent are 'mirage questions'.[82] That is, consent to gain access on the part of UNHCR and other governmental bodies to IDPs and others in need may not be as hard as some might think. In addition, NGOs are usually already on the ground in situations where UNHCR wants to gain access. One instance where NGOs had more success than agencies tied to inter-governmental organizations was in Ethiopia. In this instance, a wide variety of NGOs, in cooperation with the aid wings of two rebel organizations, provided aid to millions of starving Ethiopians against the will of the Ethiopian government. In fact, the government did all that it could, including bombing aid convoys, to prevent this aid from getting through. Much of this aid was provided at least somewhat covertly by governments, but it was NGOs which carried out operations, crossing into Ethiopia from the Sudan. States were thus silent co-conspirators in undermining the sovereignty of a government which was deemed to have violated its duties toward its people.[83] Thus, as the Refugee Policy Group has observed, 'innovative individuals and organizations, inside and outside of the UN system, have found ways around the constraints of sovereignty'.[84]

One organization which has argued for a right of humanitarian access and which has acted on that perceived right is *Médecins du Monde*. It has carried out clandestine, unsanctioned humanitarian activities in such places as Afghanistan, El Salvador, South Africa and Ethiopia.[85] Another French medical group, *Médecins sans Frontiérs*, has been engaged in similar activities. Both of these groups, as well as the French humanitarian movement in general, have been spurred on by the involvement of Bernard Kouchner, formerly the French Minister for Humanitarian Affairs, who has argued that providing humanitarian assistance is both a right and a duty.[86] France had been at the forefront on this issue even before Kouchner became part of the French government. For example, in October 1987 the French President stated:

As suffering can be experienced by any individual, it is universal. The right of victims to be succoured when they call for help, and to be succoured by volunteers who see themselves as professionally neutral in fulfilling what has come to be known as 'the duty of humanitarian intervention' in situations of extreme emergency, will certainly be included one day in the Universal Declaration of Human Rights. For no State can be considered sole proprietor of the suffering it causes or harbours.[87]

The General Assembly has recently passed several resolutions regarding humanitarian assistance. At the urging of France, which presented it to the UN at the request of Kouchner and others, the General Assembly adopted Resolution 43–131, entitled 'Humanitarian assistance to victims of natural disasters and similar emergency situations.' While, trying to reinforce the marriage of responsibility and rights in sovereignty, it nevertheless also reaffirmed the primacy of state sovereignty and territorial integrity. In 1990, it passed Resolution 45–100 which discussed the need to create humanitarian corridors for relief assistance. While not focusing specifically on the issue of consent, it nevertheless pointed to one way in which issues of access might be worked out.[88] One instance where such negotiated access was successful, at least for a while, was Operation Lifeline Sudan. In 1989, after having expelled aid workers, Sudan invited them back in. It allowed aid agencies to enter parts of Sudan controlled by rebel forces. Although the operation only lasted about six months, and aid workers were expelled again, it led to a situation which prompted the Sudanese Minister of Social Welfare to remark: 'We have, in effect, conceded sovereignty over a large part of our territory to the United Nations.'[89]

Numerous individuals involved with carrying out humanitarian activities have noted that while the developing countries have seen humanitarian access as a challenge to their sovereignty, many of them (as well as the international community in general) are becoming less adamant with regard to preventing such access. This is especially the case in Africa, where more states are willing to accept such interference on humanitarian grounds. The issue of sovereignty does not arise to the same extent that it used to only a few years ago.[90] Perhaps this is because aid agencies do not frame the issue in terms of incursions on sovereignty, and thus some countries are more willing to provide access. This does not mean, however, that such activities do not pose challenges to the theory and practice of sovereignty. Indeed, they do raise questions regarding the content and extent of sovereignty such that sovereignty is in a state of 'permanent evolution' according to one official at the ICRC (which has *not* been confrontational on the issue of sovereignty).[91]

In 1991 the General Assembly passed Resolution 46–182, which says that 'humanitarian assistance should be provided with the consent of the affected country. . . .' Consent is weaker than an active request from a government. In the case of Iraq, while the agreement stated that UN activity was on the basis of a *request* from Iraq, in reality Iraq just provided pro forma *consent*. In addition, one could make the argument that as long as a government did not actively object to humanitarian action it has provided consent. Further, that passage made a reference to 'the consent of the affected country' rather than to the consent of the government. This raises the possibility that the people of a country, through some other representative than the government, could request humanitarian assistance and that the UN could respond based on that request, regardless of what the government wanted. That is, the sovereignty of the people could override the sovereignty of the state.

With respect to international and state practice, then, one can identify several different contradictory trends with respect to humanitarian access and intervention. There is increasing agreement that the UN has a right to intervene on humanitarian grounds. And it has, indeed, intervened in a few situations which have had significant humanitarian components, although the foundation for such activity has been threats to international peace and security, not human rights. However, it is obvious that humanitarian concerns *have* taken precedent over state sovereignty. With regard to humanitarian access, international humanitarian law recognizes the right of individuals to receive humanitarian aid and requires that governments accept that aid. And, there has been some shift on the part of those most resistant to claims of access toward more acceptance of responsibilities in this regard.

Situations which may require humanitarian response will not disappear anytime soon. What is thus needed is a succinct statement of the conditions under which humanitarian intervention and access should take place. First, however, we must consider a few of the other moral issues with regard to humanitarian intervention.

MORAL ISSUES

The debate concerning intervention is state-centric. It is premised on the existence of state sovereignty which should only be violated in the most extreme circumstances, if even then. Yet, putting aside international law and state practice (which lend less credence to this view than is usually acknowledged), there is one other relevant and fundamental issue which I discussed in the first chapter – the social purpose of the state. According to this perspective, the state exists for the well-being of its inhabitants. That is, the social purpose of the state is to ensure the ability of people to live. I argued that there are three pillars to sovereignty – human rights, popular sovereignty and self-determination. Each of these will be discussed in turn with regard to the questions of what rights and obligations the international community may have with respect to intervention.

Regarding self-determination, Walzer argues that it is incumbent upon the people themselves to act on their own behalf. This might include non-violent action, such as what happened in Gandhi's India, or, possibly, the resort to force to topple a dictatorial regime. According to Walzer, self-determination is 'the right of people "to become free by their own efforts" if they can, and non-intervention is the principle guaranteeing that their success will not be impeded or their failure prevented by the intrusion of an alien power'.[92] In other words, a people – however defined – must create their own 'common life'. Nobody can do it for them. Outside intervention would interfere with, and distort, the ability of the community to decide for itself how it wanted to live. If the people do not act on their own behalf, then do they deserve outside help? Walzer would say probably not; if they are not willing to take action to change their situation to one they want, then why should anybody want to do it for them? The outcome of any kind of outside action certainly could not be called self-determination, and the people would not deserve any outside assistance unless they were well on their way to success.[93]

Yet, why must a community have to engage in violence (widespread violence according to Walzer) in order to be recognized as a community worthy of self-determination and thus able to receive outside assistance? As Juha Räikkä asks, 'why exactly is it a morally relevant feature that an entity struggles? Surely it is an implausible viewpoint that war and political antagonism enjoy crucial moral value.'[94] Fighting is not necessary to demonstrate that a community exists, otherwise those which did not fight would lose their right to self-determination. Further, this criteria could actually encourage even more groups to take up arms in support of their right to self-determination.[95] In fact, such actions violate the criteria developed in Chapter 2 with regard to deciding claims of self-determination, which discussed violence only in terms of a defensive last resort. Walzer's view would stand this on its head. Yet, one cannot insist on an outright ban on the use of force by groups striving toward self-determination when it is used for defensive purposes.

Thus, when thinking about engaging in intervention for purposes of ensuring self-determination, one should be content to identify a group which is entitled to self-determination as such, rather than insisting on extreme activities on the part of that group (which might, in certain cases, actually *undermine* their claims to self-determination). Further, it must be clear that other avenues within a national structure, such as autonomy, are closed to them. This criteria will not be fulfilled in most cases. When it is fulfilled, it will probably be accompanied by other human rights abuses, such as in the case of the Kurds, East Pakistanis and Eritreans.

Discussion of the extent of the activities which might be undertaken by the international community to support self-determination usually focuses on direct military intervention. This might include, as was the case with Bangladesh, carving out a piece of the territory of state for the oppressed group to use. Usually, however, groups are not in such a compact form, able to be disentangled from wider society. Thus, the intervention might involve dictating a new governmental structure such that all groups have certain rights guaranteed. This is an extreme undertaking, not to be engaged in lightly. Further, such action might, paradoxically, be viewed as undermining self-determination. This is because part of self-determination involves the 'self' – the group in question – deciding and implementing its 'common life'. Imposition from outside interferes with part of this process. Yet, when the implementation stage of self-determination is impeded to an excessive extent, intervention might still be warranted.

Further, actions other than changing a government might be warranted. For example, in the case of the Kurds, the humanitarian activities undertaken on their behalf have not resulted in a recognized Kurdish state or a different regime in Baghdad. Yet, as Akhavan points out:

> the intervention of the Allied forces has not only made possible the realization of minority rights or 'cultural autonomy' by the Kurds, but also their right to self-determination as a 'people'. It is increasingly evident that the 'safe haven' in northern Iraq is in reality a form of 'surreptitious independence' with all the attributes of Statehood except positive recognition by the international community.[96]

However, the situation is not tenable on a long-term basis and without a permanent international presence (in violation of Iraq's sovereignty) protecting the Kurds, eventually, Kurdish rights will have to be guaranteed either within Iraq itself or within a new Kurdish state.[97]

Other criteria for intervening on grounds of self-determination (as well as other grounds) might include likelihood of success, proportionality, and the likelihood that the resulting situation is 'better', and not just as repressive.[98] Finally, as should be obvious, the intervener must truly, as Walzer states, enter 'into the purposes of those people':

Humanitarian intervention involves military action on behalf of oppressed peoples, and it requires that the intervening state [or other en-
tity] enter, to some degree, into the purposes of those people. It need not
set itself to achieve those purposes, but it also cannot stand in the way of
their achievement.[99]

In the case of gross violations of human rights, especially with respect
to genocide, rather than entering into the purposes of the people as a
'people', the intervention is aimed at protecting the people as individuals,
even though they may, at the same time, be persecuted as a result of constituting a 'people'. In this instance, Walzer does not require sustained action
on the part of the people (which, however, I have already argued is not necessary): 'When a people are being massacred, we don't require that they
pass the test of self-help before coming to their aid. It is their very incapa-
city that brings us in.'[100]

Is there a right or a duty on the part of some outside entity to intervene to
stop the atrocity? I have already argued that there is a right to intervene, at
least on the part of the United Nations. Genocide and other human rights
abuses violate the social purpose of the state. When this happens, the government becomes illegitimate because it cannot claim that it is working
within the social framework which provides it with its rights and duties in
the first place. But what about an actual duty or responsibility to intervene? In addition to the individual's relationship to the state, I have argued
that the individual is connected to the larger global community. There are
many types of international organizations created by states. Because they
are created by entities with a social purpose (states) they must also be tied
in with that social purpose. They thus have an obligation to ensure that social purpose is carried out. When the social purpose is violated within a
particular state, the international community, which has been developed
along the lines of states and thus must support the social purpose of those
entities, *must* respond to the violations. The nature of the response will
depend upon the nature of the sector of the international community. Thus,
the United Nations, which has both a recognized interest in human rights,
as well as the ability to undertake the forceful actions under discussion,
has an *obligation* to take these actions.
Walzer identifies the nature of this intervention:

Governments and armies engaged in massacres are readily identified as
criminal governments and armies (they are guilty, under the Nuremberg
code of 'crimes against humanity'). Hence, humanitarian intervention
comes much closer than any other kind of intervention to what we

commonly regard, in domestic society, as law enforcement and police work.[101]

This is, indeed, how any kind of humanitarian intervention must be viewed – as a police action. The domestic analogy can be overdrawn, but here it is appropriate. Domestic police enforce the laws and, theoretically, the common moral code of society. While it is next to impossible to find a transcendent global morality, I *have* identified a way to provide for a certain minimum level of moral conduct on the part of states. Therefore, the intervening entity would be enforcing the common morality of the world with regard to the social purpose of states (as well as international law, especially with respect to genocide). Police action differs from military action in this regard. It is not for the expansion of state power or for economic or ideological reasons, but to enforce international civility.

There may also be instances where action other than wholesale military intervention, but which will still be seen as a significant violation of sovereignty, may be appropriate. One common example is a case where a population of a country, or rather a portion of the population, is being faced with starvation because of the actions of the central government. Usually, the population in need of humanitarian assistance is caught in the middle of an internal conflict situation. In such cases wholesale military intervention which might be directed at the government may not be the best option for delivering humanitarian aid.

Gaining access to the affected population is the immediate and overriding goal. While addressing the situation in which the humanitarian situation has developed is also necessary for a long-term solution and to ensure that the situation does not arise again, sometimes the immediate need might be addressed by claiming and acting upon a right to gain humanitarian access. In addition, without engaging the forces of the government attempting to address the overall situation, it may be easier for those providing aid to portray themselves as neutral and thus more accepted. Further, working within the framework of access rather than intervention may help to minimize the overall loss of life. Any military forces involved would be there specifically to ensure that aid got through and not to engage in a wider offensive against the combatants. To the extent that such engagements were avoided, less people would be killed or wounded as a result of what is supposed to be a humanitarian operation.

The role of NGOs in gaining access and providing humanitarian aid also raises interesting questions about whether and how they violate or undermine sovereignty. Discussions of humanitarian intervention usually focuses on state or UN intervention. This is because, first, it is these actors which have the necessary power to intervene, and second, they are the holders of international legal personality. However, given that it is NGOs which engage in much humanitarian access, and which are frequently the first on the ground in an humanitarian emergency, more thought should be given to the consequences of their activities. When these groups operate surreptitiously or without government permission, certainly they are undermining the ability of states to control their borders and what goes on within them. Further, their activities demonstrate that certain aspects of power and the ability to respond to the needs of people are moving away from states.

Finally, one must address the issue of what kind of action should be taken in cases where the final pillar of the New Sovereignty – popular sovereignty – is being violated. A state must involve its citizenry in governance in some fashion. Thus, one might conclude that where a government ruled without meaningful participation by members of society that it is illegitimate and therefore open to outside intervention. This is usually portrayed as democratic intervention. Yet there at least two problems with humanitarian intervention on such grounds. First, when such a right has been claimed in the past, particularly by the United States with respect to its various interventions in Latin America, such activities have had little to do with democracy or ensuring popular sovereignty. In fact, usually the regime which is installed (in violation of self-determination) has been no more democratic or respectful of popular sovereignty. This demonstrates the abuse which has been associated with such justifications.

Second, while violating popular sovereignty and the various political rights which go along with it is a violation of human rights, engaging in humanitarian intervention as discussed above may not be the best way to ensure that the situation is remedied. Such intervention quite likely will involve loss of life and destruction of property. Violations of political rights would probably not justify such a response. In other words, the response would not be proportional to the harm being caused. It is only in cases where massive loss of life is either threatened or taking place that the violence associated with military action can ever be justified. There may be other ways to ensure that popular sovereignty is ensured. However, frequently such violations do go hand in hand with other human rights violations which might justify such extreme action. In this case, addressing the other violations might be combined with action which also addressed the root causes of the violations, such as replacing an authoritarian regime which holds power by terror.

The main justification for humanitarian intervention, then, is responding to gross violations of human rights (such as genocide). Violations of self-determination and popular sovereignty may occur alongside such human rights abuses, but generally will not form the basis for intervention alone. What is now required is a clear delineation of the principles and conditions of humanitarian access and intervention.

CRITERIA FOR HUMANITARIAN ACCESS AND INTERVENTION

Humanitarian access has a focus on providing humanitarian aid to a needy population by a wide array of agencies and organizations. Humanitarian intervention, on the other hand, has a wider focus which may go beyond aiding purely needy populations and may involve broader political and military issues. Thus, while there is overlap between the two, they are still somewhat conceptually distinct, and thus the situations which they may be engaged in may be somewhat different.

The conditions under which humanitarian organizations may provide aid are straightforward. The primary condition is, of course, that there must be a needy population, such as one facing mass starvation. This, after all, is the conceptual focus of humanitarian access. This usually occurs in times of civil conflict, although other instances of humanitarian disasters may also provide this condition. In addition, the government must be either unable or unwilling to provide for the needy population. It is at this point that a right to ignore the wishes of the government is legitimate because it is not fulfilling its obligations to its citizens. If, however, a government is truly willing but unable to aid its citizens, then relief may be negotiated with the government without resorting to a claim of a right to humanitarian access.

Finally, those providing aid must observe neutrality. The organization providing aid must not side with or against the government or other parties involved in a conflict. This is a primary component of International Humanitarian Law which provides for a right to receive and provide assistance. Yet, sometimes a situation becomes so grave that an organization cannot remain silent about the situation. This will be especially so in cases where providing aid has become a long-term response and the situation requires some other sort of action. The question becomes whether providing aid actually helps to support the conditions underlying the humanitarian crisis or whether publicizing the situation, while possibly inducing stronger action – intervention – would undermine those in need. This becomes an issue because to the extent that gaining humanitarian access is an operational problem rather than one of sovereignty, the actual operational ability to provide aid may be undermined or disrupted by various parties if they are criticized.

Many organizations maintain that they would not be able to operate without strict neutrality. Yet, others maintain the opposite, that they shoulder a responsibility to criticize human rights abuses everywhere. Doing so, however, may also severely circumscribe their ability to provide humanitarian aid. So an exception results when organizations must violate neutrality – essentially those circumstances requiring intervention.

Stricter conditions and more precise criteria for humanitarian intervention apply because its possible consequences are much more severe than in the case of humanitarian access:[102]

1) *Widespread Gross Violations of Human Rights.* The primary criterion for contemplating humanitarian intervention is the presence of massive atrocities, either imminent or actually carried out by a government. This would include mass killings, deprivation of food, or other activities which result in massive loss of life. No precise number can be put forth,[103] but once a situation reached the point where many thousands or millions of lives are being lost or at risk of being lost, this criteria would probably be met. In addition, a situation where a significant portion of a specific ethnic or religious group were threatened – falling under the definition of 'genocide' in the Genocide Convention – would qualify for humanitarian intervention.[104]

2) *Multilateral Action.* As discussed above, unilateral action is illegitimate for a number of reasons. Any action should be taken by either the UN or a regional organization. Depending on the situation, one might be more preferable than the other. Both the UN and regional organizations have been essentially unable to carry out this type of action, and even with some hopeful signs, this places significant restrictions on any type of humanitarian intervention. When the UN has taken forceful action in the past, it has authorized member states or regional organizations to act on its behalf. If the UN became truly serious about forceful action in defense of human rights, the most expedient arrangement would be to have a stand-by force – possibly individually recruited by the UN and under the direct command of the UN – already assembled and available to be deployed in short order. In fact, there have been a number of proposals for the creation of such a force. However, this is unlikely to occur in the foreseeable future. Thus, any action is likely to take the form of a coalition, such as in the Gulf War. However, unlike the Gulf War, the participant states in a coalition should have an overriding humanitarian motive, rather than being in the position of acting as mercenary forces for the UN, fulfilling their particular agendas in the process. Otherwise, the decision to

take action, as well as the way in which it is carried out, can be corrupted.

3) *Overriding Humanitarian Motive.* The motives for intervening must be humanitarian in nature. If individual states were permitted to engage in this action it might be very difficult to satisfy this condition. However, considering that any action will be more like a police action enforcing the laws and morality of a universal or regional organization at the behest of such an organization, made up of many different states with different interests, this will not be as much of a problem. There may be cases where concrete humanitarian issues are combined with security issues. In fact, this may be the most likely scenario for intervention. In this case, as long as the humanitarian motives are still primary and not ancillary or used as a pretext for intervention, security interests, such as regional stability, may be present

4) *Limited Action and Proportionality.* The use of violence to stop violence is of dubious moral quality at best, and great care must be taken that the force used is proportional to the situation. Since humanitarian intervention is being sanctioned only in response to mass violence and killing, the question of using violence for situations which are not violent, or relatively not violent, will not come up. However, the force used should be as 'surgical' as possible – realizing, at the same time, that such precision is generally impossible – so that only the absolute minimum amount of force is used, and that which is used is proportional to the situation which is being remedied. Also, the forces should only stay as long as it takes to stop the mass violence and loss of life. Sometimes, this might mean deposing a ruling despot and perhaps putting a country under UN trusteeship for a time.

5) *Respect for Self-Determination.* The intervening entity must respect the values and institutions of the people. It cannot attempt to impose its own political or other system on the people. It must 'enter into the purposes of the people' and not try to frustrate them.

6) *Outcome Better than Previous Situation.* Related to respect for self-determination, the government which comes into power must have the support of the people – be democratic, however one defines that, or include some notion of popular sovereignty – and the situation in general must be 'better'.

7) *Exhaustion of Other Remedies.* The intervening entity must try all other avenues of peaceful conflict resolution before resorting to force. These would include UN resolutions and diplomatic missions, as well as economic sanctions.[105] Yet, there might also be instances where, because the threat is so massive and the situation is evolving so

rapidly, that there might not be time to implement a wide array of other measures before resorting to more forceful action.

ACCESS, INTERVENTION AND THE NEW SOVEREIGNTY

The above discussion has demonstrated three things. First, individuals have a right to receive humanitarian assistance. Second, international organizations have a right, in certain instances, to gain access to provide such assistance without regard for the wishes of the government as well as to engage in more far-reaching intervention in certain types of instances. Third, the international community may have not only a right but an obligation to provide assistance and to intervene in cases of widespread gross violations of human rights.

These conclusions have far-reaching implications for the theory and practice of sovereignty. Former UN Secretary-General Boutros-Ghali recently framed the issue this way:

> The international law of human rights was conceived of initially as a body of rights and obligations applying essentially to the relationship between a State and its citizens and other persons within its jurisdiction under the tutelage of the international community. Recognition of a right of humanitarian access as a human right would require introducing new elements into this relationship between the individual and the State, either by recognizing the individual as having rights which can be asserted against entities beyond the State, or recognizing obligations of the State which go beyond its duties to persons within its territory.[106]

This combines the questions of the rights of individuals and obligations towards those individuals. Individuals are conceived of as having a different relationship with the wider community beyond the state. In addition, states have obligations toward individuals within the wider community beyond their supposed sovereign realm. That is, the state is no longer the absolute mediating focus between the individual and the international community. Rather, the welfare of individuals is the direct concern of the international community, and states, as members of the international community, have obligations towards those individuals when the international community determines they are in need.

These rights and obligations come into play when a state, or at least certain actions of a state, has been found to be illegitimate within the framework of the New Sovereignty. That is, when a state violates human rights or cannot meet its obligations *vis a vis* its citizens, those citizens have a right to ask for and receive assistance and the international community has a right and obligation to respond in a manner most befitting the particular situation, which may involve ignoring the sovereignty of the state in favour of the sovereignty of individuals and groups. This is the most direct and damaging challenge to the sovereignty discourse with its traditional notions of state sovereignty, and represents a significant paradigm shift in the way the relationship between the individual and the international community is conceived, as well as the way the legitimate loci of power and authority are constructed.

In practice, this challenge has been taken up by the international community in ambiguous and sometimes contradictory ways. In the cases of Bangladesh and Uganda, India and Tanzania engaged in what some see as illustrative cases of humanitarian intervention, although neither country used this argument. In the case of the Kurds, the international community responded, somewhat reluctantly, with a clear violation of Iraqi sovereignty. In Somalia, to the extent that one could talk about Somali sovereignty, the international community, again, took action on humanitarian grounds which undermined the norm of non-intervention. In both of these cases, findings of threats to international peace and security (based, especially, on refugee flows) rather than specific humanitarian criteria were used to justify the interventions. In other instances, there have been cases where UNHCR and many NGOs have either pushed the limits of state sovereignty or ignored it altogether when attempting to gain humanitarian access to affected populations. Sometimes this is recognized by humanitarian practitioners as violating sovereignty, but other times a more benign gloss is put on these activities so as not to raise the ire of governments. In still other situations, the international community has done little to deal with widespread violations of human rights, even when there seems to be consensus that it can and should act.

Humanitarian intervention in the post-Cold War era has been extremely selective, and will probably continue to be so. Some would argue that this fact, itself, is enough to call into question the legitimacy of such actions. However, this is too simplistic a reaction. It is likely that the world will continue to see more Rwandas and Bosnias and Somalias. The international community is not going to intervene in certain powerful states, nor is it going to respond in the same fashion to all humanitarian emergencies. Forsaking action in all situations because the powerful states may only choose to act in a few is an abdication of the responsibility which I have tried to lay out in this book. Coherent and consistent responses to all situations would enhance the legitimacy of humanitarian interventions and allay the fears of some regarding inconsistency. However, we are not living in particularly coherent times, and this situation is likely to continue for some time as the emerging global order begins to take shape.

It may be that even as a normative revolution is taking place with regard to the rights and responsibilities inherent in claims to sovereignty, the will of the global community to adjust to this reorientation has not kept up. Or, as one UN official has put it, human rights has won the struggle with sovereignty but does not know what to do with the victory.[107]

5 The Institutional Foundations of the New Sovereignty

In the previous chapters I have made two related arguments about the evolving balance between human rights and state sovereignty. From a normative perspective I have argued that sovereignty includes an obligation to uphold basic human rights, popular sovereignty and self-determination. In practice, the international community has taken a wide variety of actions, however ambiguous, which indicate a shift in the balance between sovereignty and human rights. Yet, there is still a great disjunction between humanitarian needs worldwide and the international institutional capacity and the will to deal with these needs.

Many of the issues and proposed changes are interrelated. However, to maintain a certain conceptual clarity and consistency with the rest of the book, I will discuss possible changes related to the issues discussed in Chapters 2–4 in turn, as well as their implications for sovereignty.

SELF-DETERMINATION

Communal assertions for self-determination are widespread and persistent. The existing institutional arrangements and agreement among different communities on the modes of conflict resolution, as well as the exclusivity of the identities in question, will determine whether or not a communal conflict can be resolved in a non-violent manner and, more importantly, whether the framework can respond to future changes in the inter-communal context. That is, if there is general agreement that the electoral arrangements within a country can accommodate various types of communal claims, then the need for further international intrusion is minimal. On the other hand, if this agreement is not present, if the identities involved are perceived as being mutually exclusive, or if there is communal discrimination, then the international community will need to be more creative, as well as more forceful, in its approach to dealing with such conflicts.

This will require two things. First, the international community must more forthrightly accept a revision of the concept of sovereignty which recognizes that self-determination is not a one time event and is not restricted to decolonization, that there are many forms of self-determination beyond independent statehood, and that in some cases independent statehood may be an option. This recognition requires a much more nuanced conceptualization of the 'internal' aspects of sovereignty, where the loci of power and authority do not reside solely at the level of the state, but may also move 'downward' toward sub-state groupings. Further, as in Breton's 'logical state', it also requires a recognition that identities cross borders and that such identities, while challenging state authority, must be guaranteed their full expression.

Second, in cases where competing communal claims appear intractable, more impartial institutional capacities must be created or strengthened to mediate such claims. Erskine Childers has suggested three types of steps which may help resolve such conflicts – strengthening the knowledge and capabilities of the UN Secretariat, expanding NGO competency, and creating machinery 'to provide a climate of confidence that states wishing to resolve such frontier issues will have *impartial and disinterested assistance through the UN and/or special regional bodies; and that seeking such assistance is not in any way derogatory but indeed a laudatory initiative by governments'.*[1] Regionally, while there has been an ambiguous record thus far, there have been some innovative proposals, including one for a Conference on Security, Stability, Development and Cooperation in Africa, which stated that: 'An African Peace Council should be formed and charged with the task of ensuring that peace and harmony reign in the continent, and a state of intra-African and inter-African tranquillity is created and maintained.' It would be 'empowered (and) given discretion to effect a measure of intervention in national security problems of member states' and would determine whether mediation and/or African peacekeeping operations might be appropriate.[2] Talk of even a 'measure of intervention' within Africa is certainly a step beyond insistence on maintaining the absolute sovereignty of post-colonial states.

A similar position, the High Commissioner on National Minorities (HCNM), was created within the Conference on Security and Cooperation in Europe at the 1992 Helsinki summit. According to the mandate, the High Commissioner is to investigate issues relating to national minorities and possible communal conflict before they reach a crisis point. He or she can talk to individuals and representatives of groups (except for those who condone 'terrorism'), attempt to mediate among the parties, and, if necessary, put a problem on the agenda of the Committee of Senior Officials for further action. While some see restrictions put on the High Commissioner's abilities to act as a possible problem, it is nonetheless significant that an international organization like the CSCE (now OSCE) has created a position to investigate matters which previously have been viewed as within the sovereign prerogative of states.[3] In fact, as Max van der Stoel, the current High Commissioner, who has investigated or attempted to de-escalate a number of different conflicts in Eastern Europe and the former Soviet Union, has written: 'the domestic domain of the individual state is an integral part of the public CSCE domain'.[4]

In 1994 the CSCE decided to send a 3,000 troop peacekeeping force to Nagorno-Karabakh to ensure that communal fighting between Armenians and Azerbaijanis did not erupt again. Although the force was never deployed, this decision represented an expansion of its activities and focus, and entailed a further recognition that 'internal' communal conflicts are a continuing threat to international peace and security and thus require international solutions.[5]

Beyond regional arrangements, however, a UN body may also be needed. Rather than turning to the Security Council for this function, a different and more impartial UN body not involved with enforcement should be created. One possibility might be turning the UN Trusteeship Council, which has essentially outlived its usefulness,[6] into a body called the Council on Self-Determination which would 'be mandated to study, with creativity and sensitivity, *all* problems of political identity of distinct communities, so that it does not have the image of either a court or even a resort only for specific disputes'.[7] This depoliticized, nonjuridical image would be particularly important since such issues are very threatening to states, and states might be more inclined to either bring issues of self-determination to such a body, or agree to participate in such a discussion if another party to a dispute brought up the issue. A state may not be willing to initiate such a discussion, but once a discussion is under way, it may feel compelled to participate. Even if the state in question did not participate, the Council could still investigate, prepare a report, and forward its findings and recommendations to other appropriate UN bodies, including the Security Council.

A UN body with such a mandate would signal a definite shift in the thinking about sovereignty, minority rights and the inviolability of borders. It would be an institutionalized recognition that issues involving communal rights are not 'essentially domestic'. Further, the Council would have within its purview the authority to suggest instances where not only autonomy but also secession might be an appropriate response to a particular situation. Certainly a recognition of this possibility by the international community would mean that a critical component of sovereignty – the inviolability of borders – was not as set as had been thought.

The new Council on Self-Determination might also have one duty
left over from its previous incarnation as the Trusteeship Council. There
may be instances where either because a country has completely fallen
apart or because a particular territory is so contested that it is the focus
of continued violence, the international community may have to step
in, at least temporarily, and run the country or territory as an international trust. The former case would involve an instance like Somalia,
where the entire fabric of civil society seemed to have fallen apart and
violence was rampant. In a case such as this, the focus would be on administration rather than imposing a police force on a particular territory.
Yet, in order for peaceful administration to occur, a police force may be
needed, albeit one with a more up-front mandate than was the case in
Somalia. However, any kind of trusteeship or protectorate needs the
acceptance of the people. Without it, one could run into problems such
as in Somalia where at least certain segments of the population were very
anti-UN.

One recent instance where the UN acted as an administrator while
trying to help the country restore order and legitimate government is in
Cambodia.[8] The United Nations Transitional Authority in Cambodia
(UNTAC) had widespread authority to return refugees, demobilize the
various factions, oversee the administration of the country, engage in
human rights monitoring, and conduct elections. From a legal standpoint,
the UN did not give itself all of this authority. Rather, it was given to it by
the Supreme National Council, which was comprised of the Vietnamese-
imposed government and the three Cambodian resistance groups. Since
the Security Council was not willing to take action under Chapter VII
without agreement of the parties involved, and since Article 78 of the UN
Charter prevents UN trusteeship of a member state, the UN had to be
invited into Cambodia. However, this required a recognized legitimate
government, and this was not forthcoming since the *de facto* government
which controlled most of the territory was not recognized by the UN (and,
in fact, the resistance was seated at the UN). Thus, the Supreme National
Council was created by the factions, in consultation with the UN and relevant states, to 'delegate to UNTAC the authority needed to implement
the settlement'.[9] The international community thus created a fiction to
enable the UN to do something which according to its charter and traditional notions of state sovereignty it cannot do. This is surely an unprecedented and extraordinary undertaking, and it indicates that while the
international community continues to insist on at least a veneer of sovereignty in all instances, it will work around the question of sovereignty
when necessary.

Instances where a territory or city is subject to such virulent competing claims that no peaceful resolution seems possible may also necessitate international trusteeship. Perhaps Jerusalem, for example, on which Jews, Muslims and Christians make claims, should be put under international control. This would allow all groups to have access to the city while taking it out of the realm of violent contention for exclusive control. In fact, the 1947 Palestine partition plan did provide for a separate status for Jerusalem, but that aspect was never implemented.[10]

Other conflict situations might require at least temporary international control of a city or other territory. Towards the end of the civil war in Ethiopia, there were proposals to 'internationalize' the port of Massawa in the province of Eritrea. It was the main port for delivery of relief supplies to the northern part of Ethiopia, and was the focus of many battles between rebel and government forces, which prevented the delivery of needed assistance. However, the proposals, supported by the US and Soviet Union, which would have entailed a UN presence to ensure that famine relief could move through the port, were never implemented, because of intransigence by the warring groups.[11] In cases such as Massawa or, indeed, the 'safe areas' in Bosnia-Herzegovina, the focus for authority over these territories would not be with the Council on Self-Determination but with the peacekeeping forces on the ground.

Taking a slightly different tact, Helman and Ratner point to three types of possible UN guardianship. These are governance assistance, delegation of governmental authority, and direct UN trusteeship. In the first instance, the UN would provide personnel to help states which, while having a certain degree of internal control, also are experiencing economic breakdown and political unrest. They would provide technical training, help to foster democratic processes, and assist in economic change. Delegation of governmental authority would include a situation like Cambodia, which was truly a 'failed state', incapable of governance and maintaining order. In these instances, local elites would retain some authority while significant administrative authority would be given to the UN. Finally, there may be instances where full-scale trusteeship may be in order, to be administered either directly by the UN, or by a regional organization, like the European Union, with a grant of authority from the UN. While the Trusteeship Council (or a variation) might be able to carry out the required functions, it requires a change in the Charter. Thus, they argue that the Security Council is the only UN organ available to do the job, along with a new UN management facility. All of these different options would be oriented toward the goal of the state involved reacquiring the ability to govern itself and manage conflict without resorting to violence, human rights abuses, and the other civil ills which afflict numerous states.[12]

Such trusteeship arrangements would open up a new way of thinking about authority over a particular territory. Rather than having authority reside with a particular state, the international community as a whole would administer the territory to ensure that the rights of different groups were upheld, leading to a diminution of communal conflict and, ultimately, the withdrawal of international trusteeship.

Jarat Chopra uses a slightly different framework to conceptualize what he calls 'peace-maintenance'. Peace-maintenance operations respond to the need for 'a transnational capability to exercise political authority as a means of internal conflict resolution, establishing order and fostering justice',[13] and come in four different types: assistance, partnership, control and governorship. An assistance operation 'provides international standards for the development of national institutions' for a local administration which is in partial disarray. Partnership operations are 'first among equals' in situations where there is a powerful local authority, and have 'the final say in selective direction' as a colonial power withdraws or an authoritarian regime reforms itself. In the third type of operation, control is exercised over particular bureaucratic structures, such as the police, military and judiciary, and can 'take corrective action' when the process is violated. Finally, governorship refers to a situation where 'the peace-maintenance authority assumes full responsibilities for conducting the affairs of government'.[14] Rather than serving as a form of neo-colonialism, peace-maintenance operations as Chopra envisions them would act as 'an international guarantor of a kind of internal self-determination'.[15] Implementation of such peace-maintenance operations would be a recognition that the concept of sovereignty is changing to such as an extent that 'the scope of "international" is widening to the point that UN political authority becomes a necessity rather than an infringement'.[16]

Finally, mention must be made of one of the developments occurring in the European Union. As discussed in Chapter 2, the EU has specific bodies which channel resources to sub-state regions within Europe, bypassing states and allowing such regions to develop more autonomously from the states of which they are a part, thus aiding the continual process of self-determination and undermining somewhat state control over their development. While the EU may have sufficient resources to do that in Europe, other regions may not and so a UN body set up specifically to aid this aspect of the process of self-determination might be useful. This will be a particularly contested idea, especially insofar as states see it as a threat to their sovereign control. However, states may also see it as a way of providing resources to groups where the basis for communal claims has been lack of access to resources.

DISPLACEMENT

The movement of people, and especially forced displacement, has resulted in institutional innovations which are, in turn, leading to a reconceptualization of sovereignty. International organizations have adapted in such a way that sovereign borders have become less important. Most striking is the instance of the cross-border Preventive Zones between Somalia, Kenya and Ethiopia. These zones, which were set up by UNHCR to engage in preventive aid activities which would create the conditions to stop the flows of refugees coming from Somalia, demonstrate a way in which borders are seen as increasingly irrelevant in dealing with refugee situations. In this way, UNHCR was able to prevent internally displaced persons from becoming refugees.

UNHCR has also been engaged in other preventive activities, such as in Tajikistan, which, like other former Soviet republics, have experienced communal conflict and civil war, creating large numbers of refugees and IDPs. In Tajikistan in 1992, 500,000 people became internally displaced, including 60,000 who eventually became refugees in Afghanistan. The prospect of displacement was particularly worrying because the diverse ethnic makeup of all of the states in the region threatened to further inflame the ongoing communal conflict with more influxes of refugees. UNHCR, in conjunction with other UN agencies, worked to create the conditions to allow the return of refugees to Tajikistan as well as IDPs to their homes, while also engaging in activities to prevent the conditions which would push more people from their homes and create more refugees.[17] Similar preventive activities have occurred in the borders regions of Afghanistan/Pakistan and Armenia/Azerbaijan.[18] In the Former Yugoslav Republic of Macedonia, human rights monitors and UN peacekeepers have helped to maintain a relatively calm atmosphere, preventing an overflow of hostilities from other parts of the former Yugoslavia and thus preventing what might otherwise be widespread displacement.[19]

In Sri Lanka, UNHCR set up Open Relief Centres (ORCs), with the informal acceptance of the parties to the armed conflict, in a couple of key locations in north-east Sri Lanka in 1990 to aid returnees from India and the internally displaced, both of whom had been rendered vulnerable by the continuing civil war. One of their functions was also to provide alternatives to flight to India. It is unclear how successful this goal might have been since soon after the ORCs were established, India set up a naval blockade, preventing potential refugees from entering India. Overall, though, the ORCs have been successful in providing aid to vulnerable populations in the middle of an armed conflict.[20]

On the other hand, there are countervailing trends, as well as areas where institutional innovation has been inadequate. States are attempting to gain greater control over their borders and have become more exclusionary. As a result, the institution of asylum is being undermined. One way to renew the institution of asylum and ensure that all of those in need are ensured of asylum protection is to create a system whereby determination of asylum claims are taken out of the hands of states and where the burden of dealing with refugees falls more on those who have the resources. In one proposed international system, states would have an obligation to provide first asylum to all internationally recognized refugees who seek it. That is, when a refugee who has been recognized as such by competent international authorities seeks asylum, a state is required to admit that individual. In this way, the principle of *non-refoulement,* which is currently violated with impunity, would be upheld.[21]

After the granting of first asylum, however, dealing with refugee populations would become more of an international problem, addressed in a more globally equitable manner than is currently the case. States would have to 'accept their fair share of those refugees who cannot readily be received in the country of first asylum'.[22] Most developing countries, which frequently are countries of first asylum, would not have many obligations beyond that first stage, whereas more developed countries would be obligated to accept more refugees, at least on a medium-term basis. This time frame is crucial because a renewed system of asylum can provide an interim measure of protection until refugees can be repatriated. In this way, states would have an initial and medium-term humanitarian obligation to provide protection for refugees, and that obligation would be overseen by an international body with authoritative decision-making powers with respect to refugee status and movement. A variation on this proposal envisions a system whereby states (mostly in the North) might be able to fulfill their responsibilities by providing aid to refugee receiving countries (mostly in the South). This raises many issues, not the least of which is whether Northern states would just be buying off their international responsibilities. However, it would, at the same time, ensure that countries of asylum could expect to receive assistance to deal with mass refugee flows, which they cannot count on under the present system.[23]

In addition to asylum, a second major humanitarian issue with regard to the movement of people is that of the internally displaced. No international institution has a mandate to deal with them. As a result, their needs are met on an ad hoc basis by whatever agency happens to be in the area dealing with other humanitarian issues, particularly refugees. In most cases, the agency has been UNHCR, which has been provided with an ad hoc mandate from either the Secretary-General or the General Assembly.

UNHCR has developed specific criteria to guide its decisions on becoming involved with the internally displaced. These are:

- A specific request from the Secretary-General or the General Assembly, or the activities must flow from the needs of other operations.
- UNHCR must have the relevant expertise.
- All of the parties involved – both state and non-state actors – must consent.
- The resources are limited to those appropriated for the activities.

In addition, UNHCR should only take the lead when there is a link between the situation and the organization's mandate, such as in cases where:

- IDPs are mixed with returnee populations.
- The situation has caused both refugees and IDP flows, or where internal displacement may lead to a refugee situation (part of UNHCR's prevention activities).

Finally, the following principles underlie UNHCR's decisions to become involved in situations of internal displacement:

- The option to seek asylum should still be present.
- UNHCR has full access to affected populations, along with adequate security.
- UNHCR must be able to intercede directly with governments.[24]

The fact that these criteria have been developed, and followed, indicates a continuing and expanding involvement with some of the most inaccessible populations in need of humanitarian assistance, as well as an increasing willingness on the part of the international community to support involvement in situations which might have been considered 'domestic' and not within the purview of the UN. UNHCR has, in fact, recognized its deepening involvement with IDPs and other war victims who are not refugees in the strict sense by using the terms 'persons of concern' or 'populations' to refer to all of the people it assists.[25]

Within UNHCR, there has been little support for providing UNHCR a general mandate to deal with IDPs. UNHCR is already stretched to the limit and permanently broadening its mandate would weaken a focus which has been successful in the past. Further, since IDPs stay within countries of origin, any agency dealing with them confronts sovereignty issues in a more direct way than may be the case with refugees, thus complicating the quest for access to affected populations. At one point, the mandate to deal with the internally displaced was given to the UN Development Program (UNDP). However, it became apparent that UNDP does not have the operational capabilities to adequately respond to the needs of IDPs.[26]

UNHCR has favoured continuing ad hoc practices in dealing with the internally displaced (although it and others within the UN have recently proposed a more formal recognition of UNHCR's position as the *de facto* lead humanitarian agency in most humanitarian crises by moving more functions to UNHCR[27]). Yet, there are displaced populations – both refugees and IDPs – that UNHCR does not have access to. Regarding IDPs, this may be at least partially because these populations are not connected to refugee populations and thus it is harder to make a case for them falling under UNHCR's competence. Further, IDPs do raise significant questions with regard to sovereignty and access, and while UNHCR has been able to engage in some innovative activities to finesse the issue at times, sovereignty still remains a difficult issue to deal with. For this reason, the internally displaced perhaps should come under the aegis of a humanitarian agency with a more direct mandate to deal with issues of access across borders.

The lack of a focal point for IDPs in the UN system was partially rectified with the appointment of Francis Deng as the Representative of the Secretary-General on Internally Displaced Persons. This position, mandated by Resolution 1992/73 of the Commission on Human Rights and subsequently approved by the Economic and Social Council in July 1992, was a recognition that the internally displaced are, indeed, a matter of international concern and that they 'are in need of relief assistance and protection'.[28] The Representative's role is 'to undertake fact-finding missions, intercede directly with governments, publish reports about the situation and treatment of internally displaced people, and bring violations to the attention of human rights bodies and the Security Council'.[29] However, it is unclear the extent to which the Representative has or could actually address some of the operational and other issues related to aiding the internally displaced, which brings me to the next set of institutional concerns.

ACCESS AND INTERVENTION

Two sets of interrelated concerns must be addressed regarding humanitarian access and intervention. These are the purely operational aspects of
gaining access to affected populations, and questions of how to deal with
situations where just providing humanitarian assistance is not enough.
Broader issues of protection and root causes are raised. The connection
between access and intervention comes when force may be needed just to
provide humanitarian assistance rather than protection.

There is a right to receive humanitarian assistance as well as a concomitant right to provide such assistance. The ICRC and other humanitarian organizations have engaged in innovative activities to put this right into
practice. The use of humanitarian corridors or corridors of tranquillity
have been useful in getting aid to affected populations. However, there
have still been many instances where such access has either not been forthcoming or has taken a long time to negotiate and may be implemented only
haltingly.[30]

There are two main approaches to dealing with the access issue. The
first involves focusing on the UN to provide coordination and an umbrella
for a wide range of organizations to work under. Frederick Cuny has suggested that the position of High Commissioner for War Victims be created. In addition to those displaced by conflict, this new office would also
be responsible for those who remain in conflict situations. This would relieve UNHCR of some of its burden with respect to IDPs and allow it to
focus on aiding those within its original mandate. While in many cases the
needs of refugees and IDPs may not be much different, the fact that IDPs
do stay within their country of origin means that the approaches to gaining
access must be different. An agency with a specific mandate to address
questions of sovereignty more directly would allow the international community to gain access to affected populations more quickly and would
help prevent refugee flows.[31] As Cuny argues: 'The artificial and restrictive definitions of refugees now can be replaced by a more protective and
expansive approach, without frontiers.'[32]

Such an approach would go hand in hand with a proliferation of NGOs
and an expansion in their roles, especially National Red Cross and Red
Crescent Societies. Humanitarian organizations have tended to 'bear the
brunt of operations', without, in many cases, adequate security. This is
likely to continue, although perhaps with greater security provided by humanitarian peacekeeping operations.[33] The UN would provide the focal
point for humanitarian operations in conflict situations. The High Commissioner for War Victims would negotiate access to affected populations,

enabling UN and NGO humanitarian activities in areas of conflict. If the UN does not create a specific organization to deal with IDPs, Cuny believes that the International Organization for Migration, which is an intergovernmental organization that facilitates the movement of people, including refugees, may expand its role. He notes that it has already been working on the issue of the internally displaced in many African countries and 'can focus on a wide range of issues dealing with migration and spans the gap between refugees and internally displaced persons'.[34] This vision of humanitarian activities would, in the best case, focus on a new UN actor which would provide an umbrella under which a wide variety of actors could work. Even if a High Commissioner for War Victims or similar agency were not established, the UN and other intergovernmental organizations will continue to play a lead role in humanitarian relief.

Yet, many see significant shortcomings in UN leadership regarding humanitarian activities. Some of the criticism focuses on the Inter-Agency Standing Committee (IASC) created by Resolution 46-182, which is supposed to coordinate responses to humanitarian crises. This committee, with the Department of Humanitarian Affairs (DHA) coordinating, includes a number of different UN agencies dealing with humanitarian issues, as well as relevant NGOs. In this way, the IASC transcends the UN system. However, Cuny believes that the DHA has just resulted in more bureaucracy.[35] James Ingram agrees with this criticism, and sees even more fundamental problems with the UN humanitarian framework. He argues that the coordination necessary to respond requires not a committee but a 'military-type response' where a single individual can direct the operation.[36] The UN is not suited to engage in this type of humanitarian operation, at least partly because the structure of the UN is such that all of the different agencies are semi-autonomous, are beholden to their governing boards made up of governmental representatives, and may have conflicting goals and mandates. In addition, donor governments require detailed accounting which may come into conflict with speedy action.[37] He comes to the conclusion that '[t]here is no reason why a coordinated international humanitarian response should be built around the United Nations'.[38]

Others have come to a similar conclusion. One individual intimately tied to coordinating humanitarian operations believes that the UN may not be able play a sole or even dominant role in humanitarian relief. The UN does not have the will, capacity, respect or resources to be a major player in humanitarian action, and perhaps should focus on negotiation and other political activities.[39] Certainly, the UN is constrained by fiscal requirements and has also demonstrated an uneven will to deal with humanitarian crises. In addition, as a political body, it is perceived as less than neutral.

This is not always the case. For example, in Cambodia UNHCR was able to do a great deal precisely because it was perceived as neutral.[40] However, in many cases it may be difficult for a UN agency to convince either a government or rebel organization of its neutrality. It may still be perceived as a coercive body with an agenda beyond saving lives, and in many cases this perception would be right because, as an organization of states, it is also concerned with security issues, and these may conflict with the interests of the parties involved.[41]

Because of these problems, Ingram argues that NGOs should take the lead in negotiating access (in fact, as I noted in previous chapters, NGOs have done exactly this and are frequently on the ground in humanitarian crises before the UN). Specifically, he advocates the ICRC becoming such a focus. In order to do this, it would have to become more internationalized, moving away from its status as a solely Swiss organization. This would enable it to 'enjoy more confidence with developing countries and therefore be more effective in negotiating access to all victims of internal conflict . . .'.[42] Once the ICRC was able to gain access, the UN and NGOs would work under the ICRC umbrella in providing protection and relief. The UN could focus on resolving conflicts and its political nature would not get in the way of humanitarian action. In instances where the ICRC could not negotiate the needed access, the UN, through the Security Council, could initiate more forceful action. Ingram recognizes that the ICRC might be unwilling to initiate such a restructuring and that a change in its mandate might imperil its role in maintaining international humanitarian law. Thus, he suggests that some other organization like the ICRC might be set up for this purpose.[43]

Both Cuny and Ingram propose strengthened humanitarian systems which are a mixture of the UN and NGOs. The difference comes with emphasis on actors. A hybrid of both proposals, taking some of the more innovative features of each, would probably prove the best starting point for humanitarian action. There is a definite need for a UN agency with competence to deal with IDPs and other victims of war, especially internal war. The current framework of the Special Representative of the Secretary-General on Internally Displaced Persons could fulfill at least part of this role. The Special Representative could play a coordinating role among UN agencies and NGOs, but could also intercede directly with governments. As the direct representative of the Secretary-General, perhaps he or she could more easily and directly express the fact that the plight of the internally displaced has become the legitimate interest of the international community. Yet, this office does not have any operational capability to actually aid IDPs, such as UNHCR has.

A recent proposal by Kofi Anan, the current UN Secretary-General, purports to address some of these issues, at least indirectly. He has proposed disbanding (actually just renaming) DHA and transferring its few operational responsibilities to other parts of the UN, while its coordination role would be taken over by a United Nations Humanitarian Assistance Coordinator (UNHAC), responsible to the Secretary-General.[44] UNHAC would be responsible for policy development and coordination of all humanitarian issues, including those outside of the mandate of any UN agency, such as IDPs. In carrying out its activities, it would have to maintain liaison with, among others, the UN Department of Peacekeeping Operations (DPKO), demonstrating the continuing connection between humanitarian activities and peacekeeping.[45] It is unclear exactly how this proposal will be implemented, what responsibilities will ultimately end up where, and whether they actually represent much of an improvement or change over current arrangements. If the broad outlines of this proposal are implemented, however, it appears that humanitarian operations will continue to operate in essentially the same manner as in the past, with the UNHAC designating a lead agency to deal with specific humanitarian crises. In many cases this will be UNHCR, and UNHCR will continue to aid mixed populations of refugees, IDPs, and other populations in need. While the UNHAC will have responsibility for IDPs, it is not clear that the position will have a greater mandate to confront the sovereignty issues related to IDPs.

However, there may be instances where UN leadership may not be welcome or may be an impediment to humanitarian action. In these cases, an NGO which is perceived as more neutral might have better luck gaining access. If necessary, UN action could still be resorted to, including forceful military action. However, before that is considered, I will discuss briefly what might be seen as an intermediary step between complete and free access and a resort to military action. This is the developing area of humanitarian peacekeeping.

Traditional UN peacekeeping has, to a large extent, been concerned with observing cease-fires and providing a peaceful atmosphere for negotiations. Most of the hostile parties have been states. Some situations, however, have involved internal conflict. Currently, most conflicts, whether or not they are wholly so, have a significant internal dimension, providing significant challenges to peacekeeping. In addition to keeping apart belligerents, peacekeeping might be used for more direct humanitarian purposes, such as providing relief to civilians in adverse situations, including a combat environment.

Gordenker and Weiss identify two ways in which peacekeeping can contribute to humanitarian relief – 'normal' security-related operations and non-traditional technical services. Security-related operations would 'maintain safe conditions for threatened persons or groups'. This would include regular police functions, as well as addressing the conditions which caused the emergency in the first place, such as guarding areas where negotiations were going on or where government or rebel activities might otherwise have an adverse affect on the population, and basically gathering intelligence relevant to humanitarian assistance programs. The security function might also include providing for the physical security of humanitarian workers. A basic premise of peacekeeping has been that the forces be neutral, soldiers without enemies and sometimes without guns, maintaining a purely defensive posture. However, 'the performance of security functions in connection with a humanitarian emergency could make the UN's blue berets or other outside military unit everyone's enemy'.[46] Certainly this was the concern of those involved in Bosnia-Herzegovina. UN peacekeepers had a hard enough time gaining access to affected populations and guarding convoys, and increased aggressiveness in the military aspects of its humanitarian operations would have made them even greater targets.

Provision of technical services involves directly engaging in activities such as transport, communications and medical services. All military forces engage in these activities, and some countries, notably Sweden, Switzerland and France have units specifically organized for humanitarian assistance. They can respond very quickly to provide communications, logistics and medical care. This category could include transporting food to remote locations. Administrative functions could also be carried out for a short period of time. Local and national governments may be resistant to such activities and see them as an encroachment on their authority. However, such activities have been carried out in the past by peacekeeping forces or their civilian components, notably in the Congo and Cyprus.[47] The UN Force In Cyprus (UNFICYP) was the first UN force where the military carried out 'such a comprehensive military economic assistance operation that one party in a dispute was physically enabled to pursue its livelihood and maintain an adequate standard of living'.[48] Cambodia is another place where the UN has sent in peacekeeping forces to carry out these activities.

The UN has also had more recent experience with humanitarian peacekeeping. The Somalian experience must be considered a success insofar as the massive starvation throughout the country ended as a result of the protection of aid convoys by US troops. Problems came as a result of wider enforcement action, which was not planned for in a coherent way. In Bosnia-Herzegovina, several thousand peacekeepers protected aid convoys with, one could argue, very limited success. Aid convoys were prevented from gaining access to affected populations by one or another of the combatants. It was impossible to separate a resolution of the humanitarian crisis from an end to the war. This created tension between support for wider military action to end the fighting and protect Muslim populations, and concern for the peacekeepers on the ground who would become even greater targets if the UN took more forceful action.[49]

In such a situation where questions of neutrality are no longer relevant, more forceful humanitarian intervention, as opposed to peacekeeping, must be considered. Two considerations must be taken into account when examining the institutional foundations for military intervention – the perception of legitimacy and the actual ability to carry out a full-scale humanitarian intervention. Such activities are most likely to come from the UN, so that will be my focus.

Regarding legitimacy, relying solely on the Security Council for the basis for action will do little to calm fears in the developing world that the action is nothing more than neo-colonialism under a multilateral guise. This is partly a function of both the current make-up of the Security Council, with its Western domination, and the way it has very selectively chosen to act. In addition, the Council has lost credibility because of its inability to respond adequately or quickly in many situations. One way to address these legitimate concerns is to involve the General Assembly more in the process. All law and policy dealing with human rights and humanitarian issues comes from the General Assembly. Because of this, perhaps the General Assembly should retain this legislative role by determining if an intervention is needed and then giving that recommendation to the Security Council, which would then consider how to carry out the operation.[50] This would help to allay fears that decisions would be made without significant Third World input. However, it might also drag out the process even more, for certainly a body of 15 will come to decisions quicker than a body of 185 (unless action was precluded because of a veto in the Security Council). One way to deal with this problem as well as the concerns regarding legitimacy would be to enlarge the Security Council and add one or more permanent members from the Third World. This step might enhance the legitimacy of Security Council decisions in the eyes of Third World states.[51]

Ensuring that the UN has the actual capabilities to carry out such actions may necessitate several changes. Article 47 of the UN Charter provides for a Military Staff Committee (MSC) to coordinate military planning. The MSC has not been utilized; yet, in order for coherent planning to take place, perhaps it should be more permanently constituted. Further, the original Charter provisions say that it should be comprised of the permanent members of the Security Council plus whatever other members might be required. There should be an effort to ensure that non-permanent members are always represented so that a more balanced view is represented.[52] Reviving the MSC is highly controversial because the role of the permanent members and others who contribute troops to an operation has not been established. In addition, there is much dissatisfaction with the UN's operational ability in terms of enforcement activities, and actual enforcement activities under MSC command may be unlikely, 'but the body could serve as a useful, informal source of military expertise for the secretary-general and his staff'.[53] Yet, there is a need for more centralized, coherent planning for enforcement actions, and the MSC provides a Charter-based way to ensure that this begins to occur.

A major stumbling block in any kind of peacekeeping or enforcement action is obtaining the necessary troops. This can either stop an operation before it gets started or significantly slow down its implementation. The Charter has a provision whereby member states designate certain forces ahead of time to be used for enforcement activities. Recently, a number of states have made such arrangements, although the forces are restricted to peacekeeping functions, and states still have discretion regarding to which operations to contribute. This is due, at least partly, to reluctance on the part of states to put troops in situations where casualties would be a virtual certainty. One way of addressing this would be to have an individually recruited standing UN force, which would could be deployed at short notice. This would substantially increase the UN's operational capabilities and allow it to intervene earlier in a much more forceful manner.[54]

Implementing humanitarian access and intervention may be thought of as moving along a continuum which measures not only the amount of force necessary but also the extent to which sovereignty is affected in both its internal and external aspects. Negotiating access, whether on the part of the UN or an NGO, can be a delicate exercise which may require forthright discussions of sovereignty with the relevant parties. At the same time, however, the issues may be framed in terms of responsibilities, and insofar as governments and others see the necessity of maintaining the perception that they are upholding their humanitarian responsibilities, one can discern a shift in general global acceptance of the evolving nature of sovereignty. Further, if a new focal point within the UN is created to deal with IDPs and other victims of conflict, it will signal even greater international interest in once internal humanitarian matters. Humanitarian peacekeeping may be seen as a bridge between access and intervention. It may require a certain level of acceptance by all of the parties involved. Yet, it

involves the intrusion of police or military forces into the affairs of a supposedly sovereign country. Full-scale humanitarian intervention involves
the greatest amount of force. It also involves the global community making a statement to the effect that mass starvation or genocide do not fall
within the realm of legitimate state activity and that the global community
is empowered and even compelled, to take action which falls far outside
the sovereignty discourse in order to address the situation.

There are several types of situations, then, which will require differing
amounts of force and entail differing challenges to the sovereignty discourse by the international community. The following is a partial list:

1) Consent of the parties involved.

2) Reluctant consent of the various parties. This might include situations
   such as Somalia or Liberia. However, in those situations resistance
   has ensued, and the intervening parties were drawn into the conflict
   and fighting.

3) No consent, no resistance. This includes situations such where the
   government (or other parties) does not consent to humanitarian action, but also does not offer resistance to the action.

4) No consent, active resistance. In the case of Ethiopia, it was the government which offered resistance. In Bosnia, on the other hand, the internationally recognized *de jure* if not *de facto* government assented
   to UN humanitarian action and it was opposition forces that resisted
   these measures.

5) Full-scale intervention in the face of active opposition.

Humanitarian peacekeeping falls into the low and middle range of activities. Traditional peacekeeping has required consent from the various
parties involved. The experiences in Bosnia demonstrate what can happen
when that consent is not forthcoming. There are at least three types of situation where peacekeeping with a humanitarian component may be implemented in the future. The first is where peacekeeping and humanitarian
activities are significant components of an overall political framework,
such as UNTAC in Cambodia. Second is the introduction of a peacekeeping force to prevent further conflict, such as in Tajikistan where
peacekeeping was combined with humanitarian activities to calm the situation, address the refugee crisis and prevent the spread of the conflict to

neighbouring states.[55] Finally, such humanitarian peacekeeping activities will occur in places like Bosnia or Somalia, where ongoing conflict or anarchy makes it difficult to negotiate humanitarian access and deal with all of the competing interests.

It is this last type of situation which demonstrates forcefully that even with dramatic changes in the global political landscape and partial re-orientations of state and international policy toward humanitarian issues, political and humanitarian interests frequently do not coincide. While the peacekeeping troops in Bosnia did provide significant humanitarian services, the fact that their mandate and capabilities were severely circumscribed demonstrates a lack of will to stop genocide, as does the lack of response in Rwanda. Thus, even when a humanitarian crisis is perceived as falling outside the sovereignty discourse, this provides no guarantee that the appropriate steps will be taken to address the situation.

INSTITUTIONAL INNOVATION AND SOVEREIGNTY

The institutional changes discussed above, both proposed and actual, have had and will continue to have, an impact on the theory and practice of sovereignty. With respect to self-determination, in Chapter 2 I pointed to three policy changes or institutional innovations which have opened up the discussion of what self-determination entails, providing a space to examine the relationship between self-determination, human rights and sovereignty. The first change, the CSCE declaration on the former Yugoslavia, partially eroded the right of a state to combat self-determination claims and keep itself together. Second, the General Assembly has provided for the right of minorities to engage in contacts across state frontiers, a right which, depending upon how it is implemented, could have consequences for the ability of states to control borders. Third, the developing trend, especially within the European Union, toward the support of sub-state regions by intergovernmental organizations also supports the relocation of power and authority away from the state toward other types of communities.

Yet, these developments do not address many of the conflicts and concerns with respect to communal assertions. Providing a focal point within the UN, such as a Council on Self-Determination, would allow such questions to be addressed in a more coherent way. It would also entail a further recognition that self-determination is not a one time thing and could mean different things at different times in different situations, thus moving away from the state-centric focus which has dominated discussion of self-determination. This, in turn, would require a recognition of the rights of many different types of communities with respect to the state and perhaps moving certain aspects of power and authority away from the state. In addition, in certain types of situations where communal claims are perceived as completely mutually exclusive, a form of international trusteeship might be necessary to ensure that no one group is able to gain control over a particular territory and domination over the others who have similar claims. This would entail recognition of a type of global sovereignty, where the global community as a whole exercises power and authority over a particular area, as it does today, to a certain extent, over the seas or Antarctica.

The trends with regard to refugees and other aspects of human migration have been mixed. States have been increasingly aggressive in preventing migrants of all types from crossing their borders, although this is becoming a losing battle, as the numbers of the displaced increase and people are able to evade even expanded border patrols. Yet, the international community has broadened mandates and come to see borders as somewhat less important in dealing with refugees and the internally displaced. Preventive zones have ignored borders as refugees, IDPs and other war victims are seen as part of a whole, rather than as separate problems defined by sovereign borders. However, two problems remain. The first is related to the trend of closing borders. The Haitian example is only the most vivid demonstration that governments are not living up to their asylum obligations. Creating an international authority with the competence to decide asylum claims would ensure that states complied with their obligations. It would also have the effect of taking a basic component of the sovereignty discourse – complete control over borders – at least partially out of the hands of states. This control might be further eroded as states are obliged to provide refuge to those who cannot be accommodated by countries of first asylum. Even if the focus were on ultimate repatriation, some portion of the refugee population would permanently 'disappear' into countries of refuge, thus subverting the ability of states to decide who become at least *de facto* members of their community.

The second problem is related to the larger problem of gaining access to those in need under conditions of conflict. In effect, I have outlined a multi-level and multi-focal strategy for gaining such access. It relies, as now, on a mixture of UN and NGO action, although with a somewhat new institutional array. Providing humanitarian aid has meant combining confidential and public negotiation, overt and covert activities, forcible and nonforcible action, and finessing or ignoring the issues of sovereignty and borders. Under international law there is a right to receive and provide humanitarian assistance. This, in and of itself, represents a theoretical restriction on state sovereignty. However, concrete action has, at times, provided a more direct challenge to sovereignty. Even when the issue of sovereignty does not come up overtly, there is still a recognition that humanitarian actions are subverting states' sovereign claims.

Yet, the failures in gaining access in situations such as Bosnia, stopping genocidal massacres and the inadequacies of the current system mean that if the global community is serious about ameliorating some of the worst humanitarian disasters, other changes will have to be made. Such changes, which focus on upgrading the ability of the United Nations to respond quickly and forcefully to a wide range of humanitarian crises and human rights abuses will mean that the global community will have taken one more step toward recognizing a new conception of sovereignty. Rather than claiming 'domestic jurisdiction', governments would be held accountable for their actions. This is happening haltingly now. The rights and needs of individuals are increasingly becoming legitimate topics for global discussion and action; yet, the concrete international responses have been ambiguous, contradictory and all too often too late. Implementing some of the changes outlined above would provide a clearer course for humanitarian action. At the same time, it would also provide a clearer indication that the New Sovereignty – with its renewed focus on human rights and its multiple loci of power and authority – is being recognized.

The theory and practice of sovereignty will continue to be ambiguous and contradictory. Even with the movement towards a recognition of human rights and humanitarian principles as constitutive of legitimate claims to authority, such recognition will still not occur in every instance and even when it does and even if some of the institutional innovations described above are implemented, the responses by the global community to humanitarian crises will not be uniform. Many of the changes discussed above will not occur soon, if at all. States continue to want to hold onto their sovereign privilege to control borders and to prevent intervention of any type and the extent to which most states have an interest in providing troops to dangerous intervention activities is not clear. However, recent developments in international law and institutions, and the actions taken in a wide variety of situations, lead to the conclusion that the sovereignty discourse is becoming and will continue to become less relevant to those caught in communal conflict, refugee situations, and other humanitarian crises.

6 Concluding Observations on the New Sovereignty

The international scene has experienced vast and unprecedented change in recent decades. The declining salience of state power, the proliferation of NGOs, global telecommunications, widespread communal conflict, and large-scale environmental and humanitarian disasters have all contributed to a sense that some of the questions regarding the very basis of the international community which many had thought were settled, especially with respect to the loci of power and authority, are now much more up for grabs. The most fundamental of these questions has to do with the concept of state sovereignty which has been held to be the basic constitutive element of the international system. As I have demonstrated in this book, however, this concept is under significant challenge on a wide variety of fronts related to human rights and other humanitarian concerns.

I have made three different types of arguments regarding the connection between human rights and sovereignty. First are those having to do with normative concerns. I have argued that by recognizing the state as a socially constructed entity and looking at the resulting social purpose of the state, we can derive three constitutive elements for claims to sovereignty – upholding human rights, popular sovereignty and self-determination. It is only when these three elements are present that an entity can legitimately claim a certain kind of power and authority.

The second type of argument has to do with more empirical concerns – the development of international law, state practice and other incursions which force discussion outside the sovereignty discourse. International law has recast the relationship between the individual and the state, as well as between the individual and the broader international community. State practice and actions taken by the United Nations have, however ambiguously, pointed to a redefinition of what a claim to sovereignty means. Refugee flows and other human migration have demonstrated that borders are becoming increasingly irrelevant for large portions of humanity. Widespread communal conflict offers clear indication that the current construction of communities and the power and authority which supposedly are inherent within these communities do not correspond to the way in which many individuals and groups experience the world, or at least strive to experience the world.

Third, I have touched on a few ways in which international institutional innovation has contributed to a reconsideration of the parameters of

187

sovereignty. Further, I have briefly examined a few ways in which international institutions either may need to be changed or new ones created to deal with humanitarian issues and how these changes might impact on the theory and practice of sovereignty.

These arguments have been spread across several different issue areas which may overlap at times, but may also seem unrelated. Perhaps, then, it is appropriate to bring these different threads together. My focus is on how normative and empirical perspectives on issues related to human rights, self-determination, human migration and international action to respond to humanitarian crises are forcing a recasting of the concept of sovereignty.

A general focus on human rights leads in several different directions. First, within the sovereignty discourse, the state is the focal point of power and authority. It is the ultimate arbiter of its own actions within its territory, not subject to outside intervention. A concern with human rights, however, results in a much different construction of the loci of legitimate power and authority. This concern has come from a couple of different perspectives which have reinforced each other. States, like other types of communities, rather than being natural entities as some would maintain, are social constructions. Because of this, they must have some purpose which derives from their construction. That is, communities of all types are created to respond to various needs and pressures. In the case of the state, the social purpose is to provide for the well-being of its inhabitants. From this purpose comes the principle that the state's claim to legitimacy rests upon its will and ability to carry out this purpose. That is, if a state violates this purpose by transgressing human rights it can no longer claim legitimacy or a right to non-intervention. Further, this social purpose can be tied to the various types of international organizations the states have created and because of this, these organizations have an obligation to ensure that the social purpose of the states which comprise them is upheld.

A redefinition of the relationship between individuals, states and the international community is also occurring more empirically. The Universal Declaration of Human Rights, the international human rights covenants, numerous other human rights declarations, as well as the body of international humanitarian law, represent a codification of an evolving balance between individuals and states, and actions on behalf of human rights contribute to a reification of this codification. Human rights are generally seen as restrictions on state power. That is, there are certain things which states are not permitted to do to their inhabitants. From one perspective, this is a restriction on state sovereignty. From another, it is a recognition that legitimate claims to sovereignty entail maintaining certain types of conduct and this means that sovereignty is something different than what it has been in the past. What this something different is is still not entirely clear, nor are the implications for how the international community will deal with violations of this new conception of sovereignty which it is currently engaged in creating.

A second trajectory which a concern for human rights leads us to has to do with self-determination. Having the ability to decide how one is going to live communally is an important right in and of itself, as well as necessary in upholding other types of rights. The salience of this issue is demonstrated by widespread communal conflict. The need to uphold group rights is a restriction on the state, which traditionally has been the subject of self-determination. Further, however, various groups are making different types of communal claims and struggling for different kinds of outcomes. In fact, self-determination does not mean the same thing all of the time. Rather, it is, first, an ongoing process which must be reassessed and renewed from time to time. Second, the possible arrangements arising out of a claim to self-determination are varied, some leading to statehood and some to various forms of sub-state autonomy or, in a few instances, international trusteeship. Further, these seemingly disintegrative trajectories, while at one level in conflict with integrative, globalizing trajectories, are also supported by the latter, as when, for example, the European Union transfers resources to sub-state autonomous regions within its member countries, thus enabling certain types of communities to further pursue different communal trajectories. All of this means that in the quest for community, power and authority is being transferred away from the state. This is being done directly as sub-state communities gain autonomy directly from the state, and indirectly as suprastate entities enhance this autonomy with resources from these same states or restrict the ability of states to exercise authority over certain communities.

Further, the relevance of borders for many types of communities is increasingly in doubt. The colonial era left a legacy of divided communities. When colonies became independent – especially in Africa – the resulting states were geographically situated such that many communities straddled borders. This has meant that in the quest for community, borders have become an impediment rather than an enabling factor. Such split communities, as well as many instances where groups have been thrown together in majority-minority relationships, have resulted in what has appeared to be chronic communal conflict. Thus, artificial borders, reified by the concept of sovereignty, have created situations where borders are actually dysfunctional for the attainment and maintenance of certain types of communities, as well as upholding human rights. However, even as some states are attempting to isolate communities, adjustments are being made to enable transnational communities to maintain contact and identity.

Yet, communal conflict is still on the rise and has contributed to yet another trajectory of humanitarian concern – the movement of people. This has essentially two components which put it within a human rights and humanitarian framework. The first, and most visible, has to do with refugees and others fleeing oppression and armed conflict. The second involves the extent to which a general right to cross borders is a human rights issue and enhances other human rights. Regarding the first, communal conflict, human rights abuses and other humanitarian disasters, as well as severe economic dislocation, impel people to move across borders. The massive increase in the number of the displaced in recent years has, on the one hand, illuminated these problems. On the other, it has also demonstrated that states have what seems to be a decreasing ability to control their borders. In response, states have attempted to close their borders, or at least severely restrict who can gain access. In some instances, they have attempted to 'push out' their borders in response to a perceived tidal wave of refugees and other migrants. Yet, it is a losing battle. States have only been partially successful in preventing undesirables from crossing their borders. And once the displaced cross a border – whether legally or illegally – they frequently lose themselves inside the country, severely restricting the ability of states to decide who become at least *de facto* members of their community.

These attempts have come at the expense of certain humanitarian obligations of states – to such an extent, in fact, that there is now a widely perceived crisis of asylum. That is states, either because of xenophobia, lack of ideological imperatives, or a basic inability to deal with massive influxes of people – or a mix of the three – have backed away from obligations to review asylum claims and, instead, have undermined the principle of *non-refoulement.*

The increasing numbers of the displaced, while leading states to close borders, have also resulted in action on the part of international agencies which recognizes that borders are increasingly irrelevant in addressing these issues. Cross-border operations have resulted in incursions of sovereignty in order to deal with the internally displaced. In addition, such operations have also at times recognized a contiguous geographical area encompassing parts of two or more countries as forming the most rational sphere for humanitarian action. Thus, UNHCR and other agencies move between Kenya and

Somalia, tending to the needs of all within the region, including refugees, IDPs and others, in order to pursue an overall strategy of assistance, protection and prevention, with little regard for state borders.

Beyond this, however, some have called for a more coherent and even response to refugees and asylum seekers which, while recognizing the limitations of certain states to respond in the medium- and long-term to refugees, would also take away at least part of the ability of states to control who crosses their borders. Further, such a system would, in the process, institutionalize an expanded array of international distributional obligations on the part of states.

Even though the increasing practice of states to close their borders has introduced a significant element of ambiguity into the process, the actual movement of refugees across borders, and the actions taken on the part of the international community to respond to the humanitarian crisis of the displaced, indicate a realization that the dimensions of the problem of the displaced require a framework which goes beyond a strict adherence to sovereign borders. Further, there are other considerations related to human rights and the distribution of resources which lead to the conclusion that borders should be much more open than they currently are. That is, the recognized right to leave one's country is meaningless without a concomitant right of entry to other countries. In addition, those in need outside of the borders of particular states may be able to make claims to gain access to those countries.

The question of open borders also raises questions with regard to the rights of communities. After all, sovereign borders, theoretically at least, make the development and maintenance of community possible. The argument made by many is that allowing more 'outsiders' into a country disrupts this process. What is relevant here is the recognition that community development – that is, self-determination – is a *process*, rather than a fixed end-point. Communities do change, and often change as a result of immigration; in fact, these changes frequently occur along borders. Further, while different types of communities do have rights, these rights are not absolute and do not mean that they can be protected against all changes. Other questions of human rights, humanitarian issues and distributive justice impinge upon communal rights. Thus, what may be more important is the possibility of community versus a situation where that possibility were precluded. Opening borders wider further undermines the concept of state sovereignty by calling into question a basic principle of that concept, namely the ability of states to control access to membership in the state. It also makes possible the expression of trans-border communal identity.

The issue of crossing borders takes on a much different dimension when discussing what other options the international community may have to deal with various humanitarian crises. This also represents yet another way in which human rights and humanitarian concerns require a rethinking of sovereignty. In fact, questions of humanitarian access and intervention pose both indirect and direct challenges to the sovereignty discourse, especially insofar as the norm of non-intervention is perceived as increasingly anachronistic in a wide variety of situations.

This view has arisen from two different sources. The first has to do with normative concerns. That is, divorced from other contexts, there is an increasing feeling that as human rights become more entrenched, these rights are meaningless without a concomitant commitment on the part of some entity to ensure that they are upheld. The international community is the proper place to turn for this commitment. The balance between human rights and state sovereignty has changed such that it is now easier to talk about intervening and violating previously inviolable borders for humanitarian purposes. Further, international governmental organizations, by virtue of their status as creations of states – and therefore their connection to the social purpose of the entities which created them – and particularly the UN, have not only a right but an obligation to intervene on behalf of human rights, thus giving meaning to the rights which are, more or less, universally recognized.

The second source for the view that non-intervention is less salient than it used to be comes from the growing realization that humanitarian crises are intimately related to security issues. Questions regarding self-determination can lead to violent communal conflict, which can spill over borders, both in the form of more widespread fighting, as well as massive flows of refugees. Refugees, while disrupting communal life can also lead to greater conflict within the country of refuge. Human rights abuses can lead to either communal conflict with its attendant ills, or directly to refugee situations.

The responses to humanitarian crises have been varied, incomplete and contradictory. In attempting to gain access to affected populations humanitarian organizations, in general, do not directly raise the issue of sovereignty and do not characterize what they are doing as impinging upon sovereignty, although certainly some governments see it this way. Yet, some of those involved do acknowledge that their activities do violate the sovereignty of the state in which they are operating. Or, and perhaps even more relevant for the core theoretical concerns of this book, they argue that their activities fit within the framework of sovereignty because valid claims to sovereignty involve responsibilities toward members of the community as well as rights. These responsibilities are partially represented within international humanitarian law, which recognizes a right to receive humanitarian aid on the part of affected individuals, and a right of humanitarian organizations to offer such assistance, which governments must accept.

Yet, gaining access to populations and providing humanitarian assistance may only help to prolong a conflict and not address root causes of the problem. In addition, there are many instances where it is not possible to gain access and provide adequate security for humanitarian workers. Regarding the latter, various approaches have been used. In Somalia, before the infusion of US troops, many agencies such as the ICRC had to resort to hiring the very groups which created an insecure environment in the first place to protect their convoys, raising certain ethical questions as well as practical considerations. Although it appeared to go awry later on, the initial intervention by US troops under the auspices of the UN was very successful in ensuring that humanitarian aid was delivered to where it was needed. As a result, the most pressing humanitarian problem – widespread starvation – ceased to be an issue, although of course many other problems still affect the country. This can be contrasted with the relative inaction and restraint on the mandate of humanitarian peacekeeping forces in Bosnia-Herzegovina, or the resounding silence by the United Nations in response to the Rwanda genocide. In cases such as Bosnia-Herzegovina and Rwanda, full-scale humanitarian intervention may be required. The United Nations has thus far been unwilling to commit the necessary resources and frame issues in such a way as to recognize a coherent and consistent right and responsibility of humanitarian intervention. Yet, the right exists and if one is to take seriously the protection of human rights, the responsibility exists also.

This has obvious implications for the theory and practice of sovereignty. The norm of non-intervention, which has been a cornerstone of the sovereignty discourse, is undermined. Further, it infuses the evolving concept of sovereignty with elements of human rights and humanitarian responsibilities. It also redefines the relationship between the international community and the individuals by bypassing, to a certain extent, the mediating authority of the state.

The core issue is where rights and responsibilities as well as power and authority will and should reside in the future. While the 'should' usually is far ahead of the 'will', there appears to be a certain convergence between the two. The normative aspect of the equation includes a redefinition of the relationship between individuals, groups, communities, states and the overall global community. The sovereignty discourse has assigned a preeminent position to the state. That is, it has been identified as the ultimate arbiter of the exercise of power and authority. Yet, claims to sovereignty – which cannot be absolute in any case – must involve three principles – human rights, popular sovereignty and self-determination. Any entity which does not carry out its responsibilities according to these principles cannot make a legitimate claim to authority. This is a significant departure from the sovereignty discourse in and of itself. Further, even when it can make such a claim, its claims to sovereignty are tempered by other claims to sovereignty which may overlap. In fact, the very act of recognizing the principle of self-determination for a wide range of communities necessarily means recognizing numerous loci of semi-sovereign power and authority. In addition, this does not mean only sub-state entities. Rather, trans-state communities also have a right to communal expression and contact, and the global community as a whole also forms one of many centres of power and authority.

Regarding the empirical aspects of the normative/empirical convergence, the sovereignty discourse has been undermined and will continue to be undermined, in numerous ways. State power, in general, has lost much salience, as communications, economic, environmental and other concerns intrude. Globalizing and localizing tendencies are relocating power and authority. Nowhere is this more evident, yet ambiguous, than in the areas of human rights and humanitarian issues. International law recognizes rights of people and communities which transcend state authority and traditional conceptions of sovereignty. And, the international community as a whole has transgressed sovereign borders in the name of human rights, or at least with a recognition that human rights issues do not fall within 'domestic jurisdiction'. Yet, it seems that while human rights has won the battle with sovereignty, it does not know what to do with the victory. That is, while human rights and humanitarian principles are increasingly recognized, and statehood is increasingly imbued with responsibility as well as rights, for many around the world the victory appears hollow indeed. For every instance where humanitarian principles have been implemented in practice, one can name many more where the international community has shown little will to act and atrocities have continued unabated.

Yet, the back of sovereignty has been broken. Its days as an absolute ordering principle are over. The concept of sovereignty has been evolving and will continue to evolve. The New Sovereignty increasingly includes greater respect for human rights and humanitarian principles. In addition, the sovereignty of the future will recognize a much wider array of loci of power and authority, such that rather than being able to point to a single sovereign centre, a much more ambiguous situation will emerge where states, sub-state and trans-state communities, NGOs, international organizations and other actors will all hold a piece of a continually changing global puzzle.

Notes

NOTE TO INTRODUCTION

1. F.H. Hinsley defines sovereignty as 'final and absolute authority in the po-
    litical comunity'. F.H. Hinsley, *Sovereignty*, (New York: Cambridge Uni-
    versity Press, 1986) p. 125.

NOTES TO CHAPTER 1

1. F.H. Hinsley, *Sovereignty,* (New York: Cambridge University Press,
    1986): p. 125.
2. Joseph A. Camilleri, 'Rethinking Sovereignty in a Shrinking, Fragmented
    World', in R.B.J. Walker and Saul Mendlovitz, eds, *Contending Sovereign-
    ties: Redefining Political Community*, (Boulder, CO: L. Rienner Publishers,
    1990): p. 39.
3. Hinsley, p. 1.
4. Ibid., p. 2.
5. Ibid., pp. 215, 219.
6. Harold J. Laski, *A Grammar of Politics*, (London: George Allen & Unwin,
    1941): p. 41.
7. Which, curiously enough, Hinsley also recognized. Hinsley notes that 'sov-
    ereignty is not a fact' (1), and that 'Sovereignty at its first inception has still
    been only a new solution of an existing problem.' (25).
8. Mary Catherine Bateson, 'Beyond Sovereignty: An Emerging Global Civil-
    ization', in Walker and Mendlovitz, eds, p. 150.
9. Walter B. Wriston, 'Technology and Sovereignty', *Foreign Affairs,* 67
    (Winter 1988–9): p. 63.
10. Joseph A. Camilleri and Jim Falk, *The End of Sovereignty?: The Politics of
    a Shrinking and Fragmenting World*, (Brookfield, VT: Ashgate Publishing
    Company, 1992): p. 11.
11. The following is a very brief overview of the development of the concept of
    sovereignty. For more in-depth analyses see Hinsley, *Sovereignty*; Nicho-
    las Greenwood Onuf, 'Sovereignty: Outline of a Conceptual History', *Al-
    ternatives*, 16 (4 1991): pp. 425–46; Jens Bartelson, *A Genealogy of
    Sovereignty*, (Cambridge: Cambridge University Press, 1995); Hendrik
    Spruyt, *The Sovereign State and Its Competitors: An Analysis of Systems
    Change*, (Princeton: Princeton University Press, 1994).
12. Camilleri and Falk, p. 13.
13. Ibid., p. 12.
14. Ibid., pp. 12–14; Hinsley, 100, 130.
15. Camilleri and Falk, pp. 14–15; Hinsley, 8–22. Both Grotius and Vattel,
    two of the first theorists to put forward comprehensive statements of
    international law also saw the state as a natural entity. See Peter F. Butler,
    'The Individual and International Relations', in James Mayall, ed., *The*

Community of States: A Study in International Political Theory, (London: George Allen and Unwin, 1982): p. 117.

16. See, for example, Camilleri and Falk, pp. 19–20.
17. Thomas Hobbes, *Leviathan*, Richard Tuck, ed., (Cambridge: Cambridge University Press, 1991): p. 93.
18. See Jean Bodin, *On Sovereignty: Four Chapters from the Six Books of the Commonwealth*, Julian H. Franklin, trans., (Cambridge: Cambridge University Press, 1992).
19. Hinsley, pp. 112–13, 121–5, 141–57, 181; Camilleri, pp. 15–18; Camilleri and Falk, pp. 16–21; Onuf, 437–8.
20. However, some political philosophers wrote about the importance of non-intervention in the 19th century. See, for example, John Stuart Mill, 'A Few Words on Non-Intervention', in John Stuart Mill, *Essays on Equality, Law, and Education*, John M. Robson, ed., (Toronto: University of Toronto Press, 1984): pp. 111–24.
21. See Alan James, *Sovereign Statehood: The Basis of International Society*, (London: Allen & Unwin, 1986): Chapter 2.
22. Robert Keohane, *Sovereignty, Interdependence and International Institutions*, Working Paper no. 1 (Center for International Affairs, Harvard University, Spring 1991): pp. 1–4.
23. Ruth Lapidoth, 'Sovereignty in Transition', *Journal of International Affairs*, 45 (Winter 1992): p. 325.
24. Ibid., p. 329.
25. The United Nations General Assembly described this principle in the 'Declaration on Principles of International Law Concerning Friendly Relations and Co-operation among States in Accordance with the Charter of the United Nations' (Resolution 2625 (XXV) 24 October 1970): 'All States enjoy sovereign equality. They have equal rights and duties and are equal members of the international community, notwithstanding differences of an economic, social, political or other nature.'
26. Again, the 'Declaration on Principles of International Law' states: 'No state or group of states has the right to intervene, directly or indirectly, for any reason whatever in the internal or external affairs of any other states.'
27. Lapidoth, pp. 329–31.
28. Quoted in Onuf, p. 425.
29. Camilleri and Falk, p. 44.
30. Quoted in Camilleri and Falk, p. 47.
31. Onuf, p. 426.
32. Camilleri, p. 26.
33. Ibid., pp. 26–7.
34. Camilleri and Falk, p. 48.
35. Richard Falk, *Explorations at the Edge of Time*, (Philadelphia: Temple University Press, 1992): p. 30 (italics in original).
36. Ibid., p. 5.
37. Philip Allott, *Eunomia: New Order for a New World*, (New York: Oxford University Press, 1990): pp. 4–13.
38. Anthony Giddens, *The Consequences of Modernity*, (Stanford: Stanford University Press, 1990): p. 2.

39. This is not to say that metanarratives cannot be challenged, or that they cannot be overcome. Certainly environmentalism is a significant force today. However, it is still difficult in many instances for environmental concerns to make inroads against the development/growth paradigm which still predominates, even as the concept of sustainable development gains adherents.
40. Quentin Skinner, quoted in Onuf, p. 428.
41. Camilleri and Falk, pp. 48–53, 62–3.
42. Thomas J. Biersteker and Cynthia Weber, eds, *State Sovereignty as Social Construct*, (Cambridge: Cambridge University Press, 1996).
43. Ibid., p. 2.
44. Ibid., p. 11.
45. Ibid., p. 53.
46. Alexander Wendt, 'Anarchy Is What States Make of It: The Social Construction of Power Politics', *International Organization,* 46 (Spring 1992): p. 413.
47. Walter Truett Anderson, *Reality Isn't What It Used To Be: Theatrical Politics, Ready-to-Wear Religion, Global Myths, Primitive Chic, and Other Wonders of the Postmodern World,* (San Francisco: HarperSanFrancisco, 1990): p. 39.
48. Ibid.
49. James Der Derian, 'The Boundaries of Knowledge and Power in International Relations', in James Der Derian and Michael J. Shapiro, eds, *International/Intertextual Relations: Postmodern Readings of World Politics,* (Lexington, MA: Lexington Books, 1989): p. 4.
50. Allott, p. 302.
51. Camilleri and Falk, p. 11.
52. Anderson, p. 25.
53. Richard K. Ashley, 'Untying the Sovereign State: A Double Reading of the Anarchy Problematique', *Millennium: Journal of International Studies,* 17 (Summer 1988): p. 230.
54. Camilleri and Falk, p. 39.
55. For further discussions and critiques of postmodernism and international relations see: Ashley; Camilleri and Falk, Chapter 3; Der Derian and Shapiro; Falk, *Explorations at the Edge of Time*; Pauline Rosenau, 'Once Again Into the Fray: International Relations Confronts the Humanities', *Millennium,* 19 (1 1990): pp. 83–110; Pauline Rosenau, *Postmodernism and the Social Sciences: Insights, Inroads, and Intrusions,* (Princeton: Princeton University Press, 1992); Roger D. Spegele, 'Richard Ashley's Discourse for International Relations', *Millennium,* 21 (2 1992): pp. 147–82. For an overview of how the postmodern condition is evident in numerous aspects of contemporary life see Truett, *Reality Isn't What It Used To Be.* Anthony Giddens, in *The Consequences of Modernity,* argues that rather than experiencing postmodernity we are, instead, in a period of 'high modernity' in which modern thought is going through a phase of 'self-clarification' and 'radicalisation'. He also places the globalizing tendencies which the world experiences within a modern framework. Yet, this focus on globalization ignores the concomitant localizing or fragmenting processes which have also taken hold. See Giddens, especially pp. 45–52, 177.

Finally, my discussion will not be in a 'traditional' postmodern mode, for to do so would be to engage in, as Pauline Rosenau puts it, the 'intentional stylistic ambiguity (some would say obscurantism) that characterizes post-structural, post-modernist writing' (p. 84).

56. Camilleri and Falk, p. 53.
57. Wendt, p. 425.
58. Camilleri and Falk, p. 3, 31.
59. James N. Rosenau, 'Sovereignty in a Turbulent World', presented at the Conference on National Sovereignty and Collective Intervention, (Dartmouth College, 18–20 May 1992): p. 3.
60. Falk, *Explorations at the Edge of Time*, pp. 12–14.
61. R.B.J. Walker and Saul H. Mendlovitz, 'Interrogating State Sovereignty', in Walker and Mendlovitz, eds, p. 3.
62. Ibid., pp. 3–4.
63. Keohane, *Sovereignty, Interdependence and International Institutions*, pp. 1–9.
64. Mark W. Zacher, 'The Decaying Pillars of the Westphalian Temple: Implications for International Order and Governance', in James N. Rosenau and Ernest-Otto Czempiel, eds, *Governance without Government*, (New York: Cambridge University Press, 1992): p. 60 (italics in original). L. Ali Khan makes a distinction between institutional and normative enmeshment. Institutional enmeshment involves the type of activity Zacher cites, whereby 'nation-states and state coalitions relinquish their wilful independence in exchange for the benefits of cooperative enmeshment at the regional and global levels'. Normative enmeshment involves 'networks of common values at both regional and global levels', and encompasses not only human rights norms, but also many other interests, particularly in the economic realm. L. Ali Khan, *The Extinction of Nation-States: A World without Borders*, (The Hague: Kluwer Law International, 1996): p. 134. More generally, see pp. 133–62.
65. Ibid., pp. 65–6, 99. Of course, the number of states entering into those bilateral treaties tripled between 1946 and 1975.
66. James N. Rosenau, 'Subtle Sources of Global Interdependence: Changing Criteria of Evidence, Legitimacy, and Patriotism', in James N. Rosenau and Hylke Tromp, eds, *Interdependence and Conflict in World Politics*, (Brookfield, VT: Glower Publishing Company, 1989): p. 32.
67. Vojin Dimitrijevic, 'Human Rights, Interdependence and International Norm-Setting', in Rosenau and Tromp, eds, p. 121.
68. Jessica Tuchman Mathews, 'Redefining Security', *Foreign Affairs*, 68 (Spring 1989): p. 168.
69. Ibid., pp. 168–70; Gareth Porter and Janet Welsh Brown, *Global Environmental Politics*, (Boulder, CO: Westview Press, 1991): pp. 92–7.
70. Mathews, 'Redefining Security', pp. 168–9; Porter and Brown, pp. 74–8.
71. Marlise Simons, 'Winds Toss Africa's Soil, Feeding Lands Far Away', *The New York Times*, (29 October 1992): p. 1, 6.
72. Marlise Simons, 'Massive Ozone and Smog Defile South Atlantic Sky', *The New York Times*, (12 October 1992): p. 1, 6.
73. Mathews, 'Redefining Security', p. 162.
74. Wriston, 'Technology and Sovereignty,' p. 75.

75. Ibid., p. 67.
76. Gamani Corea, 'Global Stakes Require a New Consensus', *ifda Dossier*, 78 (July/September 1990): p. 77.
77. On the role the Internet is playing in the human rights movement, see Jamie F. Metzl, 'Information Technology and Human Rights', *Human Rights Quarterly*, 18 (November 1996): pp. 705–46.
78. Walter B. Wriston, *The Twilight of Sovereignty: How the Information Revolution Is Transforming Our World*, (New York: Charles Scribner's Sons, 1992): p. xii.
79. Some states and municipalities are attempting to regulate the Internet, preventing their citizens from gaining access to 'corrupting' influences, such as China's attempt to create a 'Virtual Wall of China'. That is, a territorial entity is trying to regulate something which is inherently nonterritorial, and thus this enterprise is probably doomed. Joshua Gordon, 'East Asian Censors Want to Net the Internet', *The Christian Science Monitor,* [Online], (12 November 1996), Available: http://www.csmonitor.com; Sheila Tefft, 'China Attempts to Have Its Net and Censor It Too', *The Christian Science Monitor*, [Online], (5 August 1996), Available: http://www.csmonitor. com.
80. As Jessica T. Mathews points out: 'By drastically reducing the importance of proximity, the new technologies change people's perceptions of community. Fax machines, satellite hookups, and the Internet connect people across borders with exceptionally growing ease while separating them from natural and historical associations within nations.' Jessica T. Mathews, 'Power Shift', *Foreign Affairs,* 76 (January/February 1997): pp. 51–2.
81. Thierry Breton, *The Pentecost Project,* Mark Howson, trans., (New York: Henry Holt and Company, 1987): p. 58.
82. Ibid., p. 60.
83. Consider, though, the Vatican Web site (http://www.vatican.va), an instance of a transnational community (logical state) using new communications capabilities to strengthen, through more direct communication, an already existing global identity with both territorial and nonterritorial elements. Or, take Partenia (http://www.partenia.fr/indexU.html), a 'Virtual Diocese', which represents an act of resistance on the part of the former bishop of Evreux in France, who ran afoul of the Vatican authorities and was symbolically banished by the Vatican to Partenia, a theoretical diocese in the middle of the Saudi Arabian desert where, for centuries, dissident clergy within the Catholic Church have been banished.

    Many self-determination movements have also established a presence on the Internet. See the Fourth World Documentation Project (http://www. halcyon.com/FWDP/fwdp.html) for a comprehensive list of self-determination movements with a presence on the Internet. See also Crawford and Kekula Crawford, 'Self-Determination in the Information Age' [Online], (3 May 1995), Available: http://www.cernet.edu.cn/HMP/PAPER/230/html/paper. html.
84. Wriston, *The Twilight of Sovereignty,* p. 7.
85. Wriston, 'Technology and Sovereignty', p. 71. See also Wriston, *The Twilight of Sovereignty,* pp. 8–9.
86. Wriston, 'Technology and Sovereignty', p. 71.
87. Wriston, *The Twilight of Sovereignty,* p. 9.

88. Ibid., p. xii.
89. James N. Rosenau, 'Individual Aspirations and Collective Outcomes: Notes for a Micro-Macro Theory of World Politics', presented at the 1992 Annual Meeting of the American Political Science Association, (Chicago, 3–6 September 1992): p. 18.
90. Robert Reich talks in terms of 'global webs' of production where 'products are international composites' and points to 'the coming irrelevance of corporate nationality'. Robert B. Reich, *The Work of Nations: Preparing Ourselves for 21st-Century Capitalism,* (New York: Vintage Books, 1992): pp. 110–53.
91. Camilleri and Falk, p. 77.
92. Robert Jackson, *Quasi-States: Sovereignty, International Relations, and the Third World,* (New York: Cambridge University Press, 1990): p. 178.
93. Camilleri and Falk, p. 98.
94. Ibid., p. 99.
95. Of course the very term terrorist is applied in a politically-laden way. Ronald Reagan's portrayal of the Nicaraguan *contras* as 'freedom fighters' has further underlined the adage: 'One person's "terrorist" is another person's "freedom fighter".' The current usage of the term also precludes recognizing that most activity that might be labeled as 'terrorist' is actually undertaken by governments against their own – or other states' – people. Thus, once again one can see the sovereignty discourse at work as it covers up and marginalizes 'non-terrorist' terror-inducing actions on the part of states.
96. Camilleri and Falk, p. 142.
97. See Keohane, p. 11; Alexander Motyl, 'The Modernity of Nationalism: Nations, States and Nation-States in the Contemporary World', *Journal of International Affairs,* 45 (Winter 1992): pp. 318–9.
98. For an overview of natural law and its relationship to international relations, see Joseph Boyle, 'Natural Law and International Ethics', in Terry Nardin and David R. Mapel, eds, *Traditions of International Ethics,* (Cambridge: Cambridge University Press, 1992): pp. 112–35.
99. However, Eric Heinze notes that human rights law can, at a certain point, go beyond state's wishes: 'Unlike most other traditional branches of law, international human rights law is not intended merely to recapitulate the wishes and practices of States. It arises from the positive consent of nations; yet, once born, it is not necessarily constrained by those nations' individual objectives. It does, so to speak, take on a life of its own.' Eric Heinze, 'Beyond Parapraxes: Right and Wrong Approaches to the Universality of Human Rights Law', *Netherlands Quarterly of Human Rights,* 12 (4 1994): p. 381. Even though I argue that positive international law cannot provide an overall basis for grounding human rights restrictions on state behaviour, this does not mean that human rights law is not crucial in delineating current practice, future aspirations and bases for action on human rights grounds. The role of human rights law and the extent to which it may have 'taken on a life of its own' will be discussed below.
100. Allott, p. 256.
101. Ingrid Delupis, *International Law and the Independent State,* (New York: Crane, Russak, 1974): p. 5.

102. Thomas G. Weiss and Jarat Chopra, 'Sovereignty Is No Longer Sacrosanct: Codifying Humanitarian Intervention', *Ethics & International Affairs*, 6 (1992): p. 106.
103. Ibid.
104. Stanley Hoffman, 'A New World and its Troubles', *Foreign Affairs*, 69 (Fall 1990): pp. 120–1.
105. See Gerhard von Glahn, *Law Among Nations: An Introduction to Public International Law*, 5th edn, (New York: Macmillan Publishing Company, 1986): pp. 356–9, 384–408.
106. Jeffrey D. Myhre, *The Antarctic Treaty System: Politics, Law, and Diplomacy*, (Boulder, CO: Westview Press, 1986): pp. 14, 15; Malcom W. Browne, 'France and Australia Kill Pact on Limited Antarctic Mining and Oil Drilling', *The New York Times*, (25 September 1989): p. 10; Sudhir K. Chopra, 'Antarctica as a Commons Regime: A Conceptual Framework for Cooperation and Coexistence,' in Christopher C. Joyner and Sudhir K. Chopra, eds, *The Antarctic Legal Regime*, (Dordrecht, The Netherlands: Martinus Nijhoff Publishers, 1988): p. 172.
107. United Nations, *The United Nations Treaties on Outer Space*, (New York: United Nations, 1984).
108. Khan, p. 163.
109. Ibid.
110. Ibid., pp. 163–89.
111. Of course, in some of these places there are no people. A population is one of the main components of statehood, and therefore of a claim to sovereignty traditionally conceived. However, the fact that there may sometime be people there, or that there may be strategic or other reasons to gain sovereign control over these places, means that these multiple jurisdictional arrangements may still hold significance for the wider theory and practice of sovereignty.
112. Jackson, p. 29.
113. Ibid., p. 21.
114. Ibid., p. 22–3.
115. Ibid., p. 104.
116. Ibid., p. 183.
117. Ibid., p. 150.
118. Almost all US states have trade offices in other countries, whereas only four had them in 1970. Mathews, 'Power Shift', p. 61. See also James O. Goldsborough, 'California's Foreign Policy', *Foreign Affairs*, 72 (Spring 1993): pp. 88–96.
119. Ivo D. Duchacek, 'Perforated Sovereignties: Towards a Typology of New Actors in International Relations', in Hans J. Michelmann and Panayotis Soldatos, eds, *Federalism and International Relations: The Role of Subnational Units*, (Oxford: Clarendon Press, 1990): pp. 1–33.
120. Panayotis Soldatos, 'An Explanatory Framework for the Study of Federated States as Foreign-policy Actors', in Michelmann and Soldatos, eds, p. 40.
121. Duchacek, p. 14.
122. Herbert Kitschelt, 'New Social Movements in West Germany and the United States', *Political Power and Social Theory*, 5 (1985): pp. 273–324.

123. Camilleri, p. 35.
124. Ibid., pp. 35–6. See also Alberto Melucci, 'The New Social Movements: A Theoretical Approach', *Social Science Information,* 19 (2 1980): pp. 199–226; Hanspeter Kriesi, 'The Interdependence of Structure and Action: Some Reflections on the State of the Art', *International Social Movement Research,* 1 (1988): pp. 349–368; Claus Offe, 'New Social Movements: Challenging the Boundaries of Institutional Politics', *Social Research,* 52 (Winter 1985): pp. 817–868. On *transnational* social movements see Jackie Smith, Charles Chatfield, and Ron Pagnucco, eds, *Transnational Social Movements and World Politics: Solidarity Beyond the State,* (Syracuse: Syracuse University Press, 1997).
125. James N. Rosenau, 'The Relocation of Authority in a Shrinking World', *Comparative Politics,* 24 (April 1992): p. 262
126. James N. Rosenau, 'Citizenship in a Changing Global Order', in Rosenau and Czempiel, eds, p. 286.
127. Richard Falk, 'Evasions of Sovereignty', in Walker and Mendlovitz, eds, p. 69.
128. Thom Kuehls, *Beyond Sovereign Territory: The Space of Ecopolitics,* (Minneapolis: University of Minnesota Press, 1996): p. 54. On Greenpeace more generally, see pp. 49–55.
129. Falk, *Explorations at the Edge of Time,* p. 97.
130. Camilleri and Falk, p. 232.
131. Falk, 'Evasions of Sovereignty', pp. 70–5.
132. Robin Wright, 'The Outer Limits?' *The Los Angeles Times,* (25 August 1992): p. 1.
133. Ernest Gellner, *Nations and Nationalism,* (Ithaca, NY: Cornell University Press, 1983): pp. 44–5.
134. George Demko, quoted in Wright, p. 4.
135. Lawrence T. Farley, *Plebiscites and Sovereignty: The Crisis of Political Illegitimacy,* (Boulder, CO: Westview Press, 1986): p. 7.
136. David B. Knight, quoted in Wright, p. 4.
137. Julian Minghi, quoted in Wright, p. 4.
138. Ibid.
139. Farley, p. xii.
140. Camilleri and Falk, pp. 24–8.
141. On the changing importance of territory for national security see Timothy Luke, 'The Discipline of Security Studies and the Codes of Containment: Learning From Kuwait', *Alternatives,* 16 (Summer 1991): pp. 315–44.
142. James N. Rosenau, 'The State in an Era of Cascading Politics: Wavering Concept, Widening Competence, Withering Colossus, or Weathering Change?' *Comparative Political Studies,* 21 (April 1988): p. 13.
143. Ibid., pp. 28–33. Rosenau also identifies four different strategies that states use in adapting to various internal and external challenges: acquiescent, intransigent, preservative and promotive (pp. 34–40).
144. Camilleri, p. 33.
145. Falk, *Explorations at the End of Time,* pp. 58–62.
146. Ibid., p. 57.
147. Ibid.
148. Ibid., pp. 93–5.

149. Rosenau, 'Citizenship in a Changing Global Order', in Rosenau and Czempiel, eds, p. 282.
150. James N. Rosenau, 'Normative Challenges in a Turbulent World', *Ethics & International Affairs,* 6 (1992): p. 9.
151. Rosenau, 'The Relocation of Authority in a Shrinking World', p. 256.
152. Rosenau, 'Citizenship in a Changing Global Order', in Rosenau and Czempiel, eds, p. 282.
153. This is similar to various social contract theories. However, whereas Locke used natural law to provide a base for the intrinsic rights of people over state-centric positive law, I want to suggest that these rights can be derived from the social purpose of the state itself rather than a nebulous and unidentifiable natural order of things.
154. Michael Walzer, *Just and Unjust Wars,* New York: Basic Books, 1977, pp. 53–8.
155. Allott, p. 313.
156. Claude Lefort, *The Political Forms of Modern Society: Bureaucracy, Democracy, Totalitarianism,* John B. Thompson, ed., (Cambridge, MA: The MIT Press, 1986): p. 243.
157. Ibid., p. 242.
158. Ibid., p. 255
159. Ibid., p. 256.
160. W. Michael Reisman, 'Sovereignty and Human Rights in Contemporary International Law', *American Journal of International Law,* 84 (October 1990): 867.
161. Delupis, p. 132.
162. Ibid., p. 133.
163. World Conference on Human Rights, *The Vienna Declaration and Programme of Action,* (United Nations Department of Public Information, June, 1993): 30.
164. Delupis, p. 133.
165. Jackson, p. 143.
166. Reisman, p. 868.
167. Ibid., p. 869.
168. Thomas Pickering, quoted in Ibid., p. 874.
169. Jarat Chopra, 'The New Subjects of International Law', *Brown Foreign Affairs Journal,* (Spring 1991): p. 30. Chopra also points out that national liberation movements also have a degree of legal personality (29).
170. Camilleri, p. 22.
171. Quoted in United Nations, 'The Limits of Sovereignty', (United Nations Department of Public Information, February 1992): p. 1.
172. Michael Walzer, 'The Moral Standing of States: A Response to Four Critics', *Philosophy & Public Affairs,* 9 (Spring 1980): p. 223.
173. Weiss and Chopra, 'Sovereignty Is No Longer Sacrosanct', p. 107.
174. Ibid.
175. Farley, p. 145.
176. This does not, however, necessarily mean Western-style democracy. For example, one could argue that various 'traditional' societies, such as in Africa, are 'democratic' even though they do not take the forms associated with democracy in the West, such as elected parliaments and presidents.

See, for example, George B.N. Ayittey, *Africa Betrayed*, (New York: St. Martin's Press, 1992).
177. Ibid., p. 17.
178. Jackson, p. 153.
179. Ibid., p. 156. See also pp. 154–9.
180. Ibid., pp. 150–1.
181. Farley, pp. 10.
182. Allott, p. 292 (italics in original).
183. Lapidoth, p. 336.
184. For example, the 1970 Declaration on Principles of International Law provides for 'the principle of equal rights and self-determination of peoples'. Article 1 of the International Covenants on Economic, Social and Cultural Rights, and on Civil and Political Rights, state: 'All peoples have the right to self-determination.' See Lapidoth, pp. 337–8.
185. For example, the UN prevented the secession of Katanga from the Congo while, at the same time, supporting Congo's liberation from Belgium. See Allen Buchanan, 'Self-Determination and the Right to Secede', *Journal of International Affairs*, 45 (Winter 1992): p. 349.
186. Hurst Hannum, *Autonomy, Sovereignty, and Self-Determination: The Accommodation of Conflicting Rights*, (Philadelphia: University of Pennsylvania Press, 1990): p. 47.
187. Rosenau, 'Normative Challenges in a Turbulent World', p. 3.
188. Yet, Jackson believes that such arrangements may have been useful in the post-colonial era in dealing with the problems in a number of former colonies. Jackson, p. 202.
189. The situation in Haiti after the 1991 elections indicates that, perhaps, the UN should have played a role beyond supervision for a while after the elections.
190. Benedict Anderson, *Imagined Communities: Reflections on the Origins and Spread of Nationalism*, (New York: Verso, 1991): p. 6.
191. Viewing the earth as a political unit is historically contingent, and, to a large extent, the ability to act on such an understanding may not have been possible until the middle part of this century with the advent of space flight. Surely indicative is the reaction of the first Apollo astronauts who remarked that they could not discern state boundaries from outer space.
192. Richard Falk, *Revitalizing International Law*, (Ames, Iowa: Iowa State University Press, 1989): p. 10.
193. Quoted in United Nations, 'The Limits of Sovereignty', p. 3.
194. Quoted in Ibid. (italics added).
195. United Nations, 'The Limits of Sovereignty', pp. 3–4.
196. Quoted in Ibid., p. 2.
197. Quoted in Thomas G. Weiss and Jarat Chopra, 'Sovereignty Under Seige: from Intervention to Humanitarian Space', presented at the Conference on National Sovereignty and Collective Intervention, (Dartmouth College, 18–20 May 1992): p. 2 (italics added).
198. Weiss and Chopra, 'Sovereignty Under Seige', p. 3.
199. Weiss and Chopra, 'Sovereignty Is No Longer Sacrosanct', p. 101.
200. Weiss and Chopra, 'Sovereignty Under Seige', pp. 36–7. This argument will be made in more detail in Chapter 4.

201. Allott, p. xvii.
202. Part of the debate with regard to universality and cultural contexts of human rights has revolved around the idea that human rights are somehow 'Western' ideas being hegemonically pushed on the rest of the world. That is, the Enlightenment basis for human rights is not applicable to other cultures which have different historical and cultural traditions. One particular argument can be made within the context of this book to address this. The ideas developed in the Enlightenment onwards with respect to human rights, freedom, and so on have been integrally entwined with the development of the modern state form and sovereignty. Thus, those who would use the state form and claim to act on the basis of sovereignty must also take into account the traditions which go with it. That is, if one accepts the state form and wants to play the sovereignty game, one must also accept the limits which go along with participation.

A second argument is to simply repeat the truism that all major religions, cultures and ethical systems have some notion of the sanctity and rights of the person. Most of these systems have evolved outside of the rather recent era of Western hegemony, and thus could not be considered to have been the result of North-South power relations which the leaders of many human rights abusing states claim they are a victim of today. That is, the idea of human rights exists beyond particular cultural contexts, and what is occurring today is the attempt to reconcile various ideas into a globally relevant one as cultures become more globally entwined.

On the universality of human rights see also: Heinze, 'Beyond Parapraxes: Right and Wrong Approaches to the University of Human Rights Law', and Pieter van Dijk, 'A Common Standard of Achievement: About Universal Validity and Uniform Interpretation of International Human Rights Norms', *Netherlands Quarterly of Human Rights*, 13 (2 1995): pp. 105–21.
203. Falk, *Explorations at the Edge of Time*, p. 6.
204. Ibid.
205. James N. Rosenau, 'Global Changes and Theoretical Challenges: Toward a Postinternational Politics for the 1990s', in Ernst-Otto Czempiel and James N. Rosenau, eds, *Global Changes and Theoretical Challenges: Approaches to World Politics for the 1990s*, (Lexington, MA: Lexington Books, 1989): pp. 2–3.
206. Francis Fukuyama, 'The End of History?' *The National Interest*, 16 (Summer 1989): pp. 3–18.

NOTES TO CHAPTER 2

1. 'Why do the nations imagine vain and foolish things?' Camille Saint-Saëns, *Christmas Oratorio, Op. 12*.
2. Quoted in Lee C. Buchheit, *Secession: The Legitimacy of Self-Determination*, (New Haven: Yale University Press, 1978): p. 9.
3. Michael Walzer, 'The New Tribalism: Notes on a Difficult Problem', *Dissent* 39 (Spring 1992): p. 164.

4. Kumar Rupesinghe, 'The Disappearing Boundaries Between Internal and External Conflicts', in Kumar Rupesinghe, ed., *Internal Conflict and Governance*, (New York: St. Martin's Press, 1992): p. 13.
5. Donald L. Horowitz, *Ethnic Groups in Conflict*, (Los Angeles: University of California Press, 1985): p. 13.
6. Hurst Hannum, *Autonomy, Sovereignty, and Self-Determination: The Accommodation of Conflicting Rights*, (Philadelphia: University of Pennsylvania Press, 1990): p. 4.
7. Eric J. Hobsbawm, *Nations and Nationalism Since 1780: Programme, Myth, Reality*, (New York: Cambridge University Press, 1990): p. 160.
8. James G. Kellas, *The Politics of Nationalism and Ethnicity*, (New York: St. Martin's Press, 1991): p. 4.
9. Horowitz, p. 41. More generally see pp. 41–54.
10. Ibid., pp. 41–2.
11. Ibid., p. 52.
12. Enid Schildkrout quoted in Ibid., p. 53.
13. Horowitz, p. 53.
14. Rupesinghe in Rupesinghe, ed., p. 19.
15. Horowitz, p. 56.
16. Elise Boulding, 'Introduction', in Rupesinghe, ed., p. xv.
17. Ibid., p. xx, footnote 1. She also mentions the '10,000 societies' sometimes talked about by anthropologists.
18. Daniel Patrick Moynihan, *Pandaemonium*, (New York: Oxford University Press, 1993): p. 4.
19. Ibid., pp. 4–5.
20. Hobsbawm, *Nations and Nationalism since 1780*, p. 6.
21. Ernest Gellner, *Nations and Nationalism*, (Ithaca: Cornell University Press, 1983): p. 7.
22. Neil MacCormick, 'Is Nationalism Philosophically Credible?' in William Twining, ed., *Issues of Self-Determination*, (Aberdeen: Aberdeen University Press, 1991): p. 16.
23. Gellner, p. 6.
24. Ibid., pp. 48–9.
25. James Mayall and Mark Simpson, 'Ethnicity is not Enough: Reflections on Protracted Secessionism in the Third World', *International Journal of Comparative Sociology*, XXXIII (January–April 1992): p. 10.
26. Kellas, pp. 27–8.
27. Eric Hobsbawm, 'Whose Fault-Line Is It Anyway?' *New Statesman and Society*, 5 (24 April 1992): p. 23 (italics in original).
28. Gellner, pp. 48–9 (italics in original).
29. Quoted in Hobsbawm, 'Whose Fault-Line Is It Anyway?' p. 23.
30. Quoted in Alexander J. Motyl, 'The Modernity of Nationalism: Nations, States and Nation-States in the Contemporary World,' *Journal of International Affairs*, 45 (Winter 1992): p. 310, footnote 10.
31. Hedva Ben-Israel, 'Nationalism in Historic Perspective', *Journal of International Affairs*, 45 (Winter 1992): p. 374.
32. Hobsbawm, *Nations and Nationalism since 1780*, p. 9.
33. Ben-Israel, p. 380.
34. Gellner, pp. 34, 39. More generally see pp. 19–52.

35. Hobsbawm, *Nations and Nationalism since 1780*, pp. 110–11.
36. Ibid., p. 111.
37. Ibid., pp. 9–10.
38. Gellner, p. 6.
39. Hannum, p. 35.
40. Robin Wright, 'The New Tribalism All Over the World', *Sacramento Bee* [Online], Forum, (13 June 1993): F1, Available: Nexis.
41. At least one of these groups – Muslims – had not self-identified themselves as such before the war. In fact, many of the 'Muslims' were such in name only, having become much more secular. Rather, it was in the process of the Serbian and Croatian nationalist myth-making projects that they had their ethnicity thrust upon them. In addition, 'Bosnians' also included Catholics (Croats) and Orthodox (Serbs), thus making the Bosnian identity even more complex.
42. See Teresa Rakowska-Harmstone, 'Chickens Coming Home To Roost: A Perspective on Soviet Ethnic Relations', *Journal of International Affairs*, 45 (Winter 1992): pp. 529–33.
43. Hobsbawm, *Nations and Nationalism since 1780*, p. 153.
44. Rupesinghe in Rupesinghe, ed., pp. 14–20.
45. See Ibid., pp. 13–14; Ted R. Gurr, 'The Internationalization of Protracted Communal Conflicts Since 1945: Which Groups, Where, and How', in Manus I. Midlarsky, ed., *The Internationalization of Communal Strife*, (New York: Routledge, 1992): pp. 8–14; Myron Weiner, 'Peoples and States in a New Ethnic Order?' *Third World Quarterly*, 13 (2 1992): pp. 318–20; and Morton H. Halperin and David J. Scheffer with Patricia L. Small, *Self-Determination in the New World Order*, (Washington, DC: Carnegie Endowment for International Peace, 1992): pp. 49–52, 123–60.
46. Lapidoth, pp. 332–3.
47. The most recent referendum on Quebec sovereignty, in October 1995, was somewhat ambiguous in its goal, but was rejected by a very small margin of the population in the province. It is unclear whether and when there will be another referendum and what the outcome would be.
48. See Maurice Pinard, 'The Dramatic Reemergence of the Quebec Independence Movement', *Journal of International Affairs*, 45 (Winter 1992): pp. 471–97; Robert Siegel, 'Quebec Residents Do Battle Over Language' [Radio Transcript], *NPR: All Things Considered* [Online], (3 June 1993), Available: Nexis; Jennifer Ludden, 'Quebec May Loosen Tough Laws Restricting English Use' [Radio Transcript], *NPR: Morning Edition* [Online], (24 May 1993), Available: Nexis.
49. See Halperin et al., pp. 143–4; Alexander MacLeod, 'A Dis-United Kingdom?' *The Christian Science Monitor* [Online], (September 1997), Available: http://www.csmonitor.com; 'The News in Brief', *The Christian Science Monitor* [Online], (22 September 1997), Available: http://www.csmonitor.com.
50. See Buchheit, pp. 198–214.
51. In the early 1960s, the basis for the secessionist movement had been religious – the Muslims resisted becoming part of Ethiopia. However, as Addis Ababa attempted to impose Amharic on the Tigrinya speaking population

of Eritrea and engaged in other repressive actions, the Christian portion of the Eritrean population joined with the Muslims, and a nationalist movement, based partly on a shared history as an Italian colony and partly on shared repression from the centre, emerged. See John Markakis, 'Nationalities and the State in Ethiopia', *Third World Quarterly*, 11 (October 1989): pp. 119–30; Paul B. Henz, 'Eritrea: The Endless War', *The Washington Quarterly*, 9 (Spring 1986): pp. 23–36.

52. Naomi Chazan, 'Introduction', in Naomi Chazan, ed., *Irredentism and International Politics*, (Boulder: Lynne Rienner Publishers, 1991): p. 1.

53. Ibid., p. 2.

54. Hedva Ben-Israel, 'Irredentism: Nationalism Reexamined', in Chazan, ed., p. 24.

55. Donald L. Horowitz, 'Irredentas and Secessions: Adjacent Phenomena, Neglected Connections', in Chazan, ed., pp. 9–22.

56. Chazan in Chazan, ed., p. 2.

57. Horowitz in Chazan, ed., pp. 16–17.

58. Halperin et al, p. 52.

59. Horowitz, p. xi.

60. Rupesinghe, p. 10. And this figure pales in comparison to the up to one million people killed in Rwanda within just a few weeks during the civil war in 1994, or the many tens of thousands killed in the former Yugoslavia.

61. Which is frequently just a euphemism for genocide.

62. Andrew Bell-Fialkoff, 'A Brief History of Ethnic Cleansing', *Foreign Affairs*, 72 (Summer 1993): p. 110.

63. Quoted in Moynihan, p. 16.

64. Ibid. For example, Bell-Fialkoff notes that the first instance of ethnic cleansing as state policy occurred in the 7th century BC in Assyria and has continued ever since all over the world. Frequently, such as during the Middle Ages, it has been based on religion, although at other times it has been related more to general territorial expansion, including 'the slow dispersal and annihilation of North America's indigenous population' (p. 110).

65. Bell-Fialkoff, pp. 110–15.

66. 'Bosnia War Displaces Millions', *The Associated Press* [Online], (13 March 1994), Available USENET: clari.news.gov.international.

67. Gurr in Midlarsky, ed., p. 18.

68. Howard Adelman, 'Ethnicity and Refugees', in U.S. Committee for Refugees, *World Refugee Survey – 1992*, (New York: US Committee for Refugees, 1992): p. 6.

69. For an expanded discussion of the origins and development of Article 21 see Allan Rosas, 'Article 21', in Asborne Eide et al., eds, *The Universal Declaration of Human Rights: A Commentary*, (Oxford: Scandinavia University Press, 1992): pp. 299–317.

70. Aureliu Cristescu, *The Right to Self-Determination: Historical and Current Development on the Basis of United Nations Instruments*, Study prepared by Aureliu Cristescu, Special Rapporteur of the Sub-Commission on Prevention of Discrimination and protection of Minorities, (New York: United Nations, 1981): pp. 8–9, 119.

71. James Crawford, quoted in Halperin et al., p. 25.

72. Hannum, p. 40; Cristescu, pp. 46–7; Halperin. p. 22.
73. It referred to 'race, creed, or colour'.
74. Halperin et al, pp. 23–4.
75. See Issa G. Shivji, 'The Right of Peoples to Self-determination: An African Perspective', in Twining, ed., pp. 40–2. See also Robert Jackson, *Quasi-States: Sovereignty, International Relations, and the Third World*, (New York: Cambridge University Press, 1990).
76. For example, as noted earlier in this chapter, the UN Human Rights Commission ruled that English speakers in Quebec had their rights violated by certain language laws propagated by the provincial government and that they can resume using English on various kinds of signs in public. Thus, the *Quebecois* have rights with regard to the majority English speakers within federal Canada, and English speakers have rights with regard to French speakers in Quebec.
77. CSCE, Fifth Meeting of the Committee of Senior Officials, Journal No. 1, Annex 2, Prague, 1992.
78. Shivji in Twining, ed., p. 33.
79. Cristescu, p. 22.
80. Ibid.
81. Ruth Lapidoth, 'Sovereignty in Transition', *Journal of International Affairs*, 45 (Winter 1992): p. 343.
82. Héctor Gros Espiell, *The Right to Self-Determination: Implementation of United Nations Resolution,* study prepared by Héctor Gros Espiell, Special Rapporteur of the Sub-Commission on Prevention of Discrimination and protection of Minorities, (New York: United Nations, 1980): p. 3, 11.
83. Ibid., p. 13.
84. Ibid., p. 14.
85. Cristescu, p. 26.
86. Ibid.
87. Buchheit, pp. 97–127; Lapidoth, p. 340; Halperin et al, pp. 13–15.
88. However, the United States, in interceding in the late stages of the fall of the Mengistu regime, hoped to prevent such an outcome which might set a precedent for other secessionist movements, favouring autonomy for Eritrea instead.
89. Buccheit, p. 41.
90. See, for example: Buchheit; Buchanan; Chazan; Etzioni; Heraclides; Lapidoth; Mayall and Simpson, pp. 5–25; and Ralph R. Premdas, S.W.R. de A. Samarasinghe, and Alan B. Anderson, eds, *Secessionist Movements in Comparative Perspective*, (New York: St. Martin's Press, 1990).
91. Quoted in Lawrence T. Farley, *Plebiscites and Sovereignty: The Crisis of Political Illegitimacy,* (Boulder: Westview Press, 1986): p. 5.
92. See Farley, pp. 4–6; Buchheit, pp. 62–73, esp. note 57, p. 63; Hannum, pp. 28–32.
93. Quoted in Moynihan, p. 83.
94. Buchheit, p. 64.
95. Hobsbawm, *Nations and Nationalism since 1780*, pp. 132–3.
96. M.B. Ramose, 'Self-determination in Decolonisation', in Twining, ed., p. 28.

97. Walzer, 'The New Tribalism', p. 165 (italics in original).
98. Ibid. It is interesting to note, however, that Walzer applies his theory of self-determination to all groups except the Palestinians, thus demonstrating the ideological – and contradictory – basis for much discussion of self-determination. Edward Said, 'Michael Walzer's *Exodus and Revolution: The Cannanite Option*', in Edward W. Said and Christopher Hitchens, eds, *Blaming the Victims: Spurious Scholarship and the Palestinian Question,* (New York: Verso, 1988): pp. 161–78.
99. MacCormick in Twining, ed., p. 17.
100. Horowitz, p. xiii.
101. Walzer, 'The New Tribalism', p. 171 (italics added).
102. See Bell-Fialkoff, especially pp. 120–1. He notes how differences and similarities can be changed and exploited depending on the context:

> The hollowness and exaggeration of these [historical] claims are revealed as each side will alternately emphasize their common roots when it indeed suits its purposes. Before the war, for example, when the Serbs still hoped to keep Bosnia in Yugoslavia, the media frequently highlighted similarities with the Muslims, while Croats often stressed that Bosnia had been part of historical Croatia and that most Bosnian Muslims were originally of Croatian descent (p. 121).

> These supposed common roots do not seem to count for much right now, as differences are resurrected, constructed, or manipulated.

103. Buchheit, p. 17.
104. For a discussion of this concept see: Michael Hechter, *Internal Colonialism: The Celtic Fringe in British National Development, 1536–1966,* (Berkley: University of California Press, 1977).
105. Farley, p. 19.
106. Espiell, p. 9.
107. Hannum, pp. 71–2. See pages 50–73 for an in-depth discussion of minority rights.
108. Ibid., p. 50.
109. Moynihan, p. 21.
110. Halperin et al, p. 47.
111. Hannum, pp. 80–81, 89.
112. R.S. Bhalla, 'The Right to Self-determination in International Law', in Twining, ed., p. 100.
113. Hannum, p. 31.
114. Moynihan, p. 147.
115. Joxerramon Bengoetxea, 'Nationalism and Self-Determination: The Basque Case', in Twining, ed., p. 138.
116. Cristescu, p. 4.
117. Michael Walzer, 'The Moral Standing of States', *Philosophy & Public Affairs*, 9 (Spring 1980): pp. 226.
118. Ben-Israel, p. 374, 389.
119. Buchanan, p. 353.
120. Ibid.
121. Ibid., pp. 354–56.

122.   Ibid., p. 357. In addition, Buchanan points out that Québécois claims for secession would also come into conflict with other self-determination claims made by the indigenous peoples:

Any attempt by the Québécois to argue for secession on grounds of rectificatory justice would be quite shaky, since the French took the territory by conquest from the native inhabitants just as the English took it from them. . . . [and] it may turn out that even if the Québécois have a right to secede, they are only entitled to part of the territory now within the boundaries of Quebec. (p. 357)

Indeed, most indigenous groups within Quebec want to stay part of Canada should Quebec ever secede.

123.   Ibid., pp. 557–8.
124.   Walzer, 'The New Tribalism', p. 168.
125.   Quoted in Jeff Greenwald, 'The Unrepresented Nations and Peoples Organization: Diplomacy's Cutting Edge', *Whole Earth Review,* 77 (Winter 1992): p. 35.
126.   See for example: Michael Chisolm and David Smith, eds, *Shared Space, Divided Space: Essays on Conflict and Territorial Organization,* (London: Unwin Hyman, 1990); Hannum; Horowitz; Arend Lijphart, *Democracy in Plural Societies,* (New Haven, CT: Yale University Press, 1977); Joseph V. Montville, ed., *Conflict and Peacemaking in International Societies*, (Lexington, MA: Lexington Books, 1990); Rupesinghe, ed.; Sammy Smooha and Theodore Hanf, 'The Diverse Modes of Conflict-regulation in Deeply Divided Societies', *International Journal of Comparative Sociology,* XXXIII (January–April 1992): pp. 26–47.
127.   See Lijphart.
128.   Ben-Israel, p. 388.
129.   James Crawford, *The Creation of States in International Law*, (New York: Oxford University Press, 1979): p. 85.
130.   Farley, p. 9.
131.   Lapidoth, p. 325.
132.   Huw Thomas, 'Perestroika in the Western Wing – Nationalism and National Rights within the European Community', in Twining, ed., p. 155.
133.   Jeanie J. Bukowski, 'A Community of the Regions? European Integration Reexamined: The Case of Spain', presented at the 1993 Annual Meeting of the Midwest Political Science Association, (Chicago, April 15, 1993). See also Barry Jones and Michael Keating, eds, *The European Union and the Regions,* (Oxford: Clarendon Press, 1995).
134.   Thomas in Twining, ed., p. 157.
135.   Weiner, p. 332
136.   Thomas in Twining, ed., p. 159.
137.   Weiner, p. 332.
138.   See, for example: Richard A. Falk, *A Study of Future Worlds,* (New York: The Free Press, 1975); Richard A. Falk, 'Toward a New World Order: Modest Methods and Drastic Visions', in Saul H. Mendlovitz, ed., *On the Creation of a Just World Order: Preferred World for the 1990's,* (New York: The Free Press, 1975); Johan Galtung, *The True World: A*

Transnational Perspective, (New York: The Free Press, 1980); Ali A. Mazrui, *A World Federation of Cultures: An African Perspective,* (New York: The Free Press, 1976); Gustavo Lagos and Horacio H. Godoy, *Revolution of Being: A Latin American View of the Future,* (New York: The Free Press, 1977). All of these texts are part of the World Order Models Project (WOMP). The goal of WOMP is to provide glimpses of preferred futures or 'relevant utopias' with an eye toward attaining certain values: minimization of violence, maximization of economic welfare, and maximization of social justice.

139.   Hobsbawm, *Nations and Nationalism since 1780*, p. 163.
140.   Ibid., p. 182.
141.   See, for example, Samuel P. Huntington, 'The Clash of Civilizations?' *Foreign Affairs*, 72 (Summer 1993): pp. 22–49.
142.   Quoted in Moynihan, p. 111.
143.   Motyl, p. 316
144.   Hobsbawm, *Nations and Nationalism since 1780*, p. 157.
145.   Walzer, 'The New Tribalism', p. 168, 171.

NOTES TO CHAPTER 3

1.   Daniel Warner, *An Ethic of Responsibility in International Relations*, (Boulder, CO: Lynne Rienner, 1991): p. 128.

2.   Joseph H. Carens, 'Aliens and Citizens: The Case for Open Borders', *The Review of Politics*, 49 (Spring 1987): p. 251.

3.   Many times borders are, indeed, constructed physically, as well as metaphorically and metaphysically. The Berlin Wall was a concrete manifestation of the Iron Curtain, and the fences between the United States and Mexico are concrete representations of the 'Tortilla Curtain'.

4.   Brian Barry 'A Reader's Guide', in Brian Barry and Robert E. Goodin, eds, *Free Movement: Ethical Issues in the Transnational Migration of People and Money*, (University Park, PA: Pennsylvania State University Press, 1992): p. 3.

5.   In fact, some of these measures can have the opposite effect, such as the US Immigration Reform and Control Act (IRCA) of 1986 which was supposed to reduce illegal immigration by putting sanctions on employers who hired undocumented workers, and which legalized previously illegal undocumented workers. As the government recognized the reality and the necessity (in terms of the need for inexpensive labour) of the movement of undocumented people across its borders, it actually created the conditions for even greater movement. See Jeffrey S. Passel, Frank D. Bean, and Barry Edmonston, 'Undocumented Migration Since IRCA: A Overall Assessment', in Jeffrey S. Passel, Frank D. Bean, and Barry Edmonston, eds, *Undocumented Migration to the United States: IRCA and the Experience of the 1980s,* (Lanham, MD: University Press of America, 1990): p. 263. More recently, the US Attorney General, Janet Reno, seemed to recognize the government's inability to effectively control illegal immigration:

'The bottom line is: we will not reduce the flow of illegal immigrants until these immigrants find better jobs in Mexico.' 'Reno Says No Reduction of Illegal Immigrants', *Reuters* [Online], (7 October 1993), Available: Nexis.

6. Robert E. Goodin, 'If People Were Money...' in Barry and Goodin, p. 7.

7. Gil Loescher, *Refugee Movements and International Security*, (London: Brassey's for the International Institute for Strategic Studies, 1992): p. 9; United Nations High Commissioner for Refugees, *The State of the World's Refugees: The Challenge of Protection* (hereafter referred to as UNHCR), (New York: Penguin Books, 1993): pp. 1–2; United Nations High Commissioner for Refugees, *The State of the World's Refugees: In Search of Solutions,* (New York: Oxford University Press, 1995): pp. 40, 248; UNHCR, *REFWORLD* [Online], Available: http://www.unhcr.ch/refworld/refbib/refstat/1996/table01.htm. Figures are for 1 January of the stated year.

8. UNHCR, p. 24.

9. However, as figures from the US Committee for Refugees show, there is actually a higher percentage of those in a refugee-like situation in Jordan, where one out of three in the country are Palestinians, who do not fall under the mandate of UNHCR but rather under the UN Relief and Works Agency for Palestine Refugees in the Near East. Loescher, p. 72; UNHCR, REFWORLD; US Committee for Refugees, *World Refugee Survey – 1996*, (Washington, DC: US Committee for Refugees, 1996): p. 7.

10. 'Movements of People in the 1990s: Challenges for Policy Makers', Final Report of the *North-South Roundtable on Movements of People in the 1990s: Challenges for Policy Makers*, 1991, pp. 11–72; UNHCR, pp. 83, 123, 149–54; 'Great Exoduses Since WWII', *The Associated Press* [Online], (16 July 1994), Available USENET: clari.news.immigration; United States, Agency for International Development, Bureau for Humanitarian Response, Office of U.S. Foreign Disaster Assistance, 'Rwanda – Civil Strife/Displaced Persons', Situation Report No. 3, Fiscal Year 1995, 30 January 1995, Available: http://www.intac.com/PubService/rwanda/OFDA/OFDA-8.html.

11. 'Analytic Report of the Secretary-General on Internally Displaced Persons', Commission on Human Rights, Economic and Social Committee of the United Nations, E/CN.4/1992/23, (14 February 1992): p. 10.

12. Loescher, p. 31.

13. Ibid., pp. 10–16.

14. UNHCR, pp. 162–7.

15. Ibid., p. 68.

16. Ibid.

17. Marjolein Brink, Mutiara Pasariboe, Philip Muus, and Lieke Verstrate, 'Reception Policies for Persons in Need of International Protection in Western European States', Research Project Commissioned by the United Nations High Commissioner for Refugees (UNHCR), Centre for Migration Research, Department of Human Geography, University of Amsterdam, (October 1993): p. 33; Doris Meissner, 'Managing Migrations', *Foreign Policy*, 86 (Spring 1992): pp. 69–70.

18. 'Poll Find Anti-Immigrant Bias', *The Associated Press* [Online], (23 May 1994), Available USENET: clari.news.immigration.

19. Loescher, p. 50.

20. US Committee for Refugees, *World Refugee Survey – 1993*, (Washington, DC: US Committee for Refugees, 1993): pp. 63–4. In fact, in January 1994, Kenyan President Daniel Arap Moi declared that refugees had 'engaged in acts of lawlessness' and were a threat to the country's security, and he called for some of them to be moved to other countries. 'Moi Tells UN to Move Refugees in Kenya to Other Countries', *Agence France Presse* [Online], (19 January 1994), Available: Nexis.

21. Loescher, p. 41.

22. David A. Martin, 'Effects of International Law on Migration Policy and Practice: The Uses of Hypocrisy', *International Migration Review,* 23 (Fall 1989): pp. 548–9.

23. Howard Adelman, 'Refuge or Asylum: A Philosophical Perspective', *Journal of Refugee Studies*, 1 (1 1988): p. 10.

24. The morality or immorality of this, which many consider to be pure exploitation, does not detract from the fact of this aspect of the interdependence along the border.

25. Tim Golden, 'U.S. Blockade of Workers Enrages Mexican Town', *The New York Times* [Online], (1 October 1993): 3, Available: Nexis.

26. Oscar J. Mart´nez, *Troublesome Border*, (Tuscon: University of Arizona Press, 1988): p. 134.

27. Ibid., p. 136.

28. Ibid., p. 2.

29. Sebastian Rotella, 'Texas Border Crackdown Stems Tide, Raises Tensions', *Los Angeles Times*, [Online], (2 October 1993): p. 1, Available: Nexis.

30. Golden, p. 3; Rotella, p. 1.

31. 'Operation Gatekeeper' Starts', *The Associated Press* [Online], (1 October 1994), Available USENET: clari.news.immigration; B. Drummond Ayres, Jr., 'Flow of Illegal Aliens Rises as the Peso Falls', *The New York Times*, (4 February 1995): p. 6; Golden; Glenn F. Bunting, 'Plan for National Guard At Border Gains Support', *Los Angeles Times* [Online], (19 October 1993): p. 3, Available: Nexis; Howard LaFranchi, 'America Puts Up Chain-Links Along a Once-Friendly Border', *The Christian Science Monitor* [Online], (13 February 1996), Available: http://www.csmonitor.com; Sam Walker, 'Beefier Border Patrol Hasn't Weakened Allure of a US Job', *The Christian Science Monitor* [Online], (12 December 1996), Available: http://www.csmonitor.com.

32. UNHCR, pp. 152, 159. The ten countries are: Austria, Belgium, Denmark, France, Germany, Netherlands, Norway, Sweden, Switzerland and United Kingdom. About half of the asylum seekers came from three former Eastern bloc countries – the former Yugoslavia, Romania, and Poland – and Turkey.

33. Sadako Ogata, 'Emergencies, Displacement and Solutions', Presented at the North South Roundtable on Movements of People in the 1990s: Challenges for Policy Makers, (December 1991): p. 3.

34. UNHCR official, October 1993.

35. Martin, p. 576.

36. M.T. Mapuranga, 'Mass Movements of People in the Nineties: Problems, Prospects and New Challenges – A View from Africa', Presented at the North South Roundtable on Movements of People in the 1990s: Challenges for Policy Makers, (December 1991): p. 9.

37. Marc Sandalow, 'INS Chief Says Illegals' Goal Isn't Welfare', *The San Francisco Chronicle* [Online], (30 October 1993): p. 1, Available: Nexis.

38. Meissner, p. 68.

39. UNHCR official, October 1993.

40. The draft Convention on the Crossing of External Frontiers has yet to be signed by all the member states, although it may be superceded by other EU-wide provisions. Demetrios G. Papademetriou, *Coming Together or Pulling Apart: The European Union's Struggle with Immigration and Asylum,* (Washington, DC: Carnegie Endowment for International Peace, 1996): pp. 24–7, 39–47, 95–7. See also Elspeth Guild, *The Developing Immigration and Asylum Policies of the European Union: Adopted Conventions, Resolutions, Recommendations, Decisions and Conclusions,* (The Hague: Kluwer Law International, 1996). The US and Canada have also concluded a draft agreement regarding asylum claims. Under this agreement, any asylum seeker who makes a claim in one country after entering the other must be returned to the first country where the asylum claim will be heard. When it was first negotiated it was not signed as a result of pressure from NGOs in both countries, and it is not clear exactly when it will go into effect.

41. UNHCR, pp. 84–5; 'Turkish Kurds Seek Refuge in North Iraq', *Reuters* [Online], (22 May 1994), Available USENET: clari.news. immigration.

42. UNHCR, p. 99.

43. See Alan Dowty, *Closed Borders: The Contemporary Assault on Freedom of Movement,* (New Haven: Yale University Press, 1987): 213–14.

44. 'German Gov. And Church At War', *The Associated Press* [Online], (14 May 1994), Available USENET: clari.news.conflict. For a comprehensive look at US policy for the four decades after World War II see Gil Loescher and John A. Scanlan, *Calculated Kindness: Refugees and America's Half-Open Door, 1945 to the Present,* (New York: The Free Press, 1986).

45. James C. Hathaway, 'The Emerging Politics of Non-Entrée', *Refugees,* (December 1992): p. 41.

46. Juan P. Osuna and Christine M. Hanson, 'US Refugee Policy: Where We've Been, Where We're Going', in *World Refugee Survey – 1993,* pp. 42–5.

47. UNHCR, p. 32.

48. Ogata, 'Emergencies, Displacement and Solutions', p. 2. In fact, if I had to identify one theme which was common to all my interviews with UNHCR officials and those at other humanitarian organizations in Geneva it would be, as one interviewee put it, the 'crisis of asylum'.

49. Interviews with UNHCR officials, October and November 1993.

50. Ibid., p. 4.

51. Martin, p. 559.

52. Mapuranga, p. 3.

53. Ogata, 'Emergencies, Displacement and Solutions', p. 2.
54. For an overview of refugees' rights and state compliance with those rights, see James C. Hathaway and John A. Dent, *Refugee Rights: Report on a Comparative Survey,* (Tornoto: York Lanes Press, 1995).
55. For example, Article 14 (1) of the UDHR states: 'Everyone has the right to seek and enjoy in other countries asylum from persecution'.
56. United States official, November 1993. Rather, its purpose was to deal with the European refugees left over from World War II.
57. For a discussion of temporary protection, see 'The Temporary Protection of Refugees: A Solution-Oriented and Rights Regarding Approach', Refugee Law Research Unit, Centre for Refugee Studies, York University, July 1996.
58. The Immigration Act of 1990 specifically created a 'temporary protected status' for those who fled their countries because the situation in the country was too dangerous, including armed conflict and environmental disaster. Osuna and Hanson in *World Refugee Survey – 1993*, p. 42. See also Bill Frelick and Barbara Kohnen, 'Filling the Gap: Temporary Protected Status', (Washington, DC: U.S. Committee for Refugees, 1994).
59. United States official, November 1993.
60. In fact, the INS does not monitor whether or not those granted temporary protected status return home after their grant is up. Frelick and Kohnen, p. 15.
61. UNHCR, p. 122.
62. Ibid.
63. UNHCR official, November 1993.
64. UNHCR official, October 1993.
65. UNHCR official, October 1993.
66. James C. Hathaway, 'Reconceiving Refugee Law as Human Rights Protection', *Journal of Refugee Studies* 4 (2 1991): p. 115.
67. UNHCR official, October 1993.
68. Hathaway, 'Reconceiving Refugee Law as Human Rights Protection', p. 114.
69. UNHCR official, November 1993.
70. Bill Frelick, 'Preventing Refugee Flows: Protection or Peril', in *World Refugee Survey – 1993*, p. 8.
71. It is Southern states which experience such humanitarian incursions while Northern states are the ones generally aided by UNHCR to keep out refugees.
72. UNHCR, p. 133.
73. Ibid.
74. UNHCR, p. 79.
75. UNHCR, p. 149.
76. 'Notes on the Preventive Zone Concept', UNHCR Memorandum, (1 October 1992): pp. 1–2.
77. United Nations High Commissioner for Refugees, A *New Approach in the Horn of Africa: The Preventive Zone Concept*, (July 1992).
78. Ibid.
79. 'Notes on the Preventive Zone Concept', p. 5.
80. UNHCR officials, October and November 1993.

81. Charles Beitz, 'Bounded Morality', *International Organization*, 33 (Summer 1979): p. 420.
82. Ann Dummett, 'The Transnational Migration of People Seen from within a Natural Law Tradition', in Barry and Goodin, p. 171.
83. Carens, 'Aliens and Citizens', p. 252. In *Closed Borders,* Alan Dowty discusses this concept of serfdom – what he calls the 'new serfdom' – in a slightly different light. He argues that there are a number of states which restrict the right to leave or expel people based upon state goals such as nation-building and cultural homogeneity: 'What the new serfdom does serve is the pursuit of total control and perfect homogeneity' (p. 226). In this way, people are treated like serfs, with little say in their destiny: 'The tragic irony was that most who moved did not want to, and most who wanted to move could not. It was, indeed, a new serfdom (p. 56).'
84. Beitz, 'Bounded Morality', p. 417.
85. Michael Walzer, 'The Distribution of Membership', in Peter Brown and Henry Shue, eds, *Boundaries: National Autonomy and its Limits*, (Totawa, NJ: Rowan and Littlefield, 1981): p. 32.
86. Quoted in Dummett, p. 175.
87. Recently, California tried to cut welfare benefits for those coming from other states. This policy was overturned by a federal court, as was a similar Minnesota law, because, as one judge said, it 'places a penalty on migration'. 'California Welfare Cuts Banned', *The Associated Press* [Online], (4 May 1994), Available USENET: clari.news. immigration.
88. Carens, 'Aliens and Citizens', pp. 266–7.
89. Karl Schoenberger, 'Cascadia' Borders on the Future', *Los Angeles Times* [Online], (1 November 1993): p. 1, Available: Nexis.
90. Ernest Callenbach was one of the first to conceive of the Pacific Northwest as an environmental utopia in his 1975 novel *Ecotopia.*
91. Joseph H. Carens, 'Migration and Morality: A Liberal Egalitarian Perspective', in Barry and Goodin, eds, p. 28.
92. These refugees have also been the victim of the blurring of the line between asylum seekers and economic migrants. Similar movements have arisen in other countries, such as Germany and Sweden, in reaction to the tightening of asylum policies. See 'German Gov. And Church At War'; 'Germans Break Laws To Give Aid', *The Associated Press* [Online], (10 May 1994), Available USENET: clari.news.immigration; 'Swedes Hide Bosnian Refugees', *The Associated Press* [Online], (23 March 1995), Available USENET: clari.news.immigration.
93. Mark Gibney, *Strangers or Friends: Principles for a New Alien Admission Policy,* (Westport, CT: Greenwood Press, Inc., 1986): p. 9.
94. 'Governors Seek Aid for Aliens', *The Associated Press* [Online], (22 June 1994), Available USENET: clari.news.immigration.
95. Gibney, pp. 6–9.
96. Ibid., p. 15.
97. Ibid.
98. Ibid., pp. 9–10.
99. Quoted in Goodin, p. 13.
100. Ibid.

101. Dummett, p. 173.
102. Even though many states cannot control their borders to the degree they would wish, thereby allowing many people in against the wishes of the state, this would not fulfill the conditions necessary to ensure the right to leave because those in the second country are there illegally and thus have no right to stay if the authorities caught up with them.
103. Aristide R. Zolberg, 'The Next Waves: Migration Theory for a Changing World', *International Migration Review*, 23 (Fall 1989): p. 425.
104. Daniel Warner, in Daniel Warner and James Hathaway, 'Refugee Law and Human Rights: Warner and Hathaway in Debate', *Journal of Refugee Studies*, 5 (2 1992): p. 164.
105. Adelman, 'Refuge or Asylum', p. 16 (italics in original).
106. Gibney, p. 79.
107. Ibid., p. 85.
108. Ibid., p. 87.
109. The US did admit many Nicaraguans, but on ideological grounds rather than any sense of obligation to those its had harmed.
110. Gibney, p. 89.
111. Ibid., pp. 92–98.
112. Ibid., p. 103.
113. Henry Shue quoted in Ibid.
114. This is similar to the principle of international distributive justice. See Beitz, 'Bounded Morality', pp. 416–22; Charles R. Beitz, 'International Distributive Justice', in Steven Luper-Foy, ed., *Problems of International Justice*, (Boulder: Westview Press, 1988): pp. 27–54.
115. Gibney, pp. 5, 36, 103–7.
116. Warner in Warner and Hathaway, p. 166.
117. For an in-depth study of how one particular community – the city of Miami – changed as a result of immigration see Guillermo J. Grenier and Alex Stepick III, *Miami Now! Immigration, Ethnicity, and Social Change*, (Gainseville, FL: University of Florida Press, 1992). As the editors point out in the introduction: 'The history of Miami since the early 1960s has been affected thoroughly by one particular phenomenon – immigration. In fact, the latter half of the twentieth century can be divided into two basic parts: before the immigrants and after the immigrants (p. 3).'
118. Carens, 'Aliens and Citizens', p. 268.
119. James Hathaway in Warner and Hathaway, p. 170.
120. 'German Gov. And Church At War'. During 1993 about 40,000 people were deported, compared 12,000 in the previous year. See also Stefan Telöken, 'The Domino Effect', *Refugees*, (December 1993): pp. 38–40; 'Germany Tightens Laws on Asylum', *Facts on File World News Digest* [Online], (3 June 1993), Available: Nexis.
121. 'New Law Gives German Border Force More Power', *The Reuter European Community Report* [Online], (24 June 1994), Available: Nexis.
122. Adelman, p. 14.
123. US Committee for Refugees, *World Refugee Survey – 1994*, (Washington, DC: US Committee for Refugees, 1994): pp. 134–7. In fact, USCR concludes that: 'Practical difficulties in administration and contrary court

decisions suggested that Germany would continue to host a sizeable number of refugees for the foreseeable future (136).'

124. Of course, they usually become members of the underclass.

125. For a discussion of what Rainer Bauböck calls 'transnational citizenship', see Rainer Bauböck, *Transnational Citizenship: Membership and Rights in International Migration*, (Brookfield, VT: Edward Elgar Publishing Company, 1994). On the evolving notion of European citizenship, see Yasemin Soysal, *Limits of Citizenship: Migrants and Postnational Membership in Europe*, (Chicago: University of Chicago Press, 1994); Antje Wiener, *Building Institutions: The Developing Practice of European Citizenship*, Dissertation, Department of Political Science, Carleton University, 1995.

NOTES TO CHAPTER 4

1. Sadako Ogata, United Nations High Commissioner for Refugees, 'Address to the Conference on Humanitarian Intervention, Sovereignty and the Future of International Society', Dartmouth College, 18 May 1992, p. 5.

2. Director of US Office of Foreign Disaster Assistance, quoted in *Internally Displaced in Africa*, (Washington, DC: Refugee Policy Group): p. 37.

3. Following is a *partial* review of the recent literature: Howard Adelman, 'Humanitarian Intervention: The Case of the Kurds', *International Journal of Refugee Law* 4 (1 1992): pp. 4–38; Payam Akhavan, 'Lessons from Iraqi Kurdistan: Self-Determination and Humanitarian Intervention Against Genocide', *Netherlands Quarterly of Human Rights* 11 (1 1993): pp. 4–62; Charles A. Allen, 'Civilian Starvation and Relief During Armed Conflict: The Modern Humanitarian Law', *Georgia Journal of International and Comparative Law* 19 (Spring 1989): pp. 1–85; Michael J. Bazyler, 'Reexamining the Doctrine of Humanitarian Intervention in Light of the Atrocities in Kampuchea and Ethiopia', *Stanford Journal of International Law* 23 (Summer 1987): pp. 547–619; Mario Bettati, 'The Right of Humanitarian Intervention or the Right of Free Access to Victims?' *The Review* 49 (1992): pp. 1–11; Antonio Donini, 'Beyond Neutrality: On the Compatability of Military Intervention and Humanitarian Assistance', *The Fletcher Forum* (Summer/Fall 1995): pp. 31–45; Jack Donnelly, 'Human Rights Humanitarian Intervention and American Foreign Policy', *Journal of International Affairs* 37 (Winter 1984): pp. 311–28; H. Scott Fairley, 'State Actors, Humanitarian Intervention and International Law', *Georgia Journal of International and Comparative Law* 10 (Winter 1980): pp. 29–63; Elizabeth G. Ferris, ed., *The Challenge to Intervene: A New Role for the United Nations*? (Uppsala: Life & Peace Institute, 1992); Ian Forbes and Mark Hoffman, eds, *Political Theory, International Relations, and the Ethics of Intervention*, (New York: St. Martin's Press, 1993); Thomas R. Gillespie, 'Unwanted Responsibility: Humanitarian Intervention to Advance Human Rights', *Peace & Change* 18 (July 1993): pp. 219–46; Sohail H. Hashmi, 'Is There an Islamic Ethic

of Humanitarian Intervention?' *Ethics & International Affairs,* 7 (1993): pp. 55–73; J. Bryan Hehir, 'Intervention: From Theories to Cases', *Ethics & International Affairs* 9 (1995): pp. 1–13; Luis Kutner, 'World Habeas Corpus and Humanitarian Intervention', *Valparaiso University Law Review* 19 (Spring 1985): pp. 593–631; Pierre Laberge, 'Humanitarian Intervention: Three Ethical Positions', *Ethics & International Affairs* 9 (1995): pp. 15–35; Guenter Lewy, 'The Case for Humanitarian Intervention', *Orbis* 37 (Fall 1993): pp. 621–32; Richard B. Lillich, ed., *Humanitarian Intervention and the United Nations,* (Charlottesville: University of Virginia Press, 1973); Gene M. Lyons and Michael Mastanduno, eds, *Beyond Westphalia? State Sovereignty and International Intervention,* (Baltimore: The Johns Hopkins University Press, 1995); Samuel M. Makinda, *Seeking Peace from Chaos: Humanitarian Intervention in Somalia,* International Peace Academy, Occasional Paper Series, (Boulder, CO: Lynne Rienner Publishers, 1993); Michael Mandelbaum 'The Reluctance to Intervene', *Foreign Policy* 95 (Summer 1994): pp. 3–18; Andrew S. Natsios, 'Food Through Force: Humanitarian Intervention and U.S. Policy', *The Washington Quarterly* 17 (Winter 1994): pp. 129–44; Kelly-Kate Pease and David P. Forsythe, 'Humanitarian Intervention and International Law', *Austrian Journal of Public and International Law* 45 (1993): pp. 1–20; Thomas W. Pogge, 'An Institutional Approach to Humanitarian Intervention', *Public Affairs Quarterly* 6 (January 1992): pp. 89–103; Oliver Ramsbotham and Tom Woodhouse, *Humanitarian Intervention in Contemporary Conflict: A Reconceptualization,* (Cambridge: Polity Press, 1996); Laura W. Reed and Carl Kaysen, eds, *Emerging Norms of Justified Intervention: A Collection of Essays from a Project of the American Academy of Arts and Sciences,* (Cambridge, MA: Committee on International Security Studies, 1993); Adam Roberts, 'Humanitarian War: Military Intervention and Human Rights', *International Affairs* 69 (July 1993): pp. 429–49; Nigel Rodley, ed., *To Loose the Bands of Wickedness: International Intervention in Defense of Human Rights,* (London: Brassey's Defense Publishers, 1992); David. J. Scheffer, 'Toward a Modern Doctrine of Humanitarian Intervention', *University of Toledo Law Review* 23 (2 1992): pp. 253–92; M. Sornarajah, 'Internal Colonialism and Humanitarian Intervention', *Georgia Journal of International and Comparative Law* 11 (Winter 1981): pp. 45–77; Fernando R. Teson, *Humanitarian Intervention: An Inquiry into Law and Morality,* (Dobbs Ferry, NY: Transnational Publishers, Inc., 1988); Michael Walzer, *Just and Unjust Wars,* (New York: Basic Books, 1977); Thomas G. Weiss and Jarat Chopra, 'Sovereignty Is No Longer Sacrosanct: Codifying Humanitarian Intervention', *Ethics & International Affairs* 6 (1992): pp. 95–117; Nicholas J. Wheeler, 'Pluralist or Solidarist Conceptions on International Society: Bull and Vincent on Humanitarian Intervention', *Millennium: Journal of International Studies* 21 (3 1992): pp. 463–87.

4. Anne-Marie Slaughter Burley, 'Commentary on "Changing Conceptions of Intervention in International Law"', in Reed and Kaysen, eds, p. 111.

5. Richard Falk, 'The Legitimacy of Legislative Intervention by the United Nations', in Roland J. Stanger, ed., *Essays on Intervention* (Ohio State University Press, 1964): p. 36.

6.   Frank Newman in Lillich, ed., p. 111.
7.   Kutner, p. 611.
8.   Quoted in Pease and Forsythe, p. 3.
9.   Pease and Forsythe, p. 3.
10. Robert A. Pastor, 'Forward to the Beginning: Widening the Scope for Glo-
     bal Collective Action', in Reed and Kaysen, eds, p. 138.
11. One case, in particular, is put forward as a positive example of this excep-
     tion. This is the case of the Congo in 1964. In this case, there was a civil war
     going on in the Congo and the rebels took 2,000 noncombatant resident
     aliens hostage to get concessions from the government. After the rebels
     threatened to kill the hostages, Belgian paratroopers, using US planes and
     British facilities went into the rebel area – at the invitation of the central
     Congo government – to rescue the hostages, which occurred within four days.
     The foreign troops were promptly removed. Although African members of
     the UN condemned this action, it is generally viewed as being lawful. See
     Bazyler, pp. 587–88; Lillich, ed., p. 57. Other examples of this kind of inter-
     vention labelled, at least partly, as humanitarian intervention, are the inva-
     sions by the US of the Dominican Republic in 1965, Grenada in 1983 and
     Panama in 1989. In reality, the humanitarian label was nothing more than a
     fig leaf for other motives. As Fairley observes about the Dominican case:

     this precedent appears less credible than the Congo example for a number
     of reasons: many more people perished after, rather than before, the Amer-
     ican intervention [as was the case with the invasion of Panama]; the duration
     of the intervention by American troops was prolonged far beyond the time
     required to ensure the safety of the lives and property of American and oth-
     ers [as was also the case in Grenada, where, in addition to 'rescuing' the
     medical students which the US claimed were in danger, the US troops also
     overthrew the government which it did not like]. . . .

     Fairley, p. 50. See also Bazyler, p. 586; Lillich, ed. p. 56.
        Yet, another observer perceives a boost for the doctrine of humanitarian
     intervention in the Dominican case: 'The value of the Dominican Crisis to the
     doctrine of humanitarian intervention lies not only in providing an illustra-
     tion of an abuse of the doctrine but also in the fact that a Great Power
     considered the doctrine sufficiently viable to excuse its intervention.'
     Sornarajah, p. 67.
12. Take, for example, the Corfu Channel Case of 1949, where Albania, in
     1946, had laid mines which sank two British destroyers. In the judgement,
     the International Court of Justice, while finding for Britain, dismissed
     Britain's claim of an

     alleged right of intervention as the manifestation of a policy by force, such
     as has, in the past, given rise to most serious abuses and as such cannot,
     whatever be the present defects in international organization, find a place in
     international law. Intervention is perhaps still less admissible in the par-
     ticular form it would take here; for, from the nature of things, it would be
     reserved for the most powerful States, and might easily lead to perverting
     the administration of international justice itself.

     See Bazyler, p. 575

13. The term unilateral intervention includes bloc intervention. The motivations and interests of one state will probably be the same for a group of like-minded states.

14. Stanley Hoffman, 'The Problem of Intervention', in Hedley Bull, ed., *Intervention in World Politics*, (New York: Oxford University Press, 1984): p. 24.

15. Quoted in Bazyler, p. 577.

16. Teson, p. 5 (italics in original).

17. Bazyler, pp. 578–81.

18. Discussion of self-interest in this manner is meant to reflect the current reality that, in general, states do not include the protection of human rights as a major factor in calculating national interest. This may be changing somewhat, as states have to deal with the fallout of human rights abuses, especially refugees crossing their borders, or as others see the upholding of humans rights as conducive to long-term international stability and democratic processes of decision-making. A new view of self-interest may emerge in the future; however, since self-interest does not, in general include human rights, the ensuing discussion will be premised on this reality.

19. Aristide Zolberg, Astri Suhrke and Sergio Aguayo, *Escape From Violence*, (New York: Oxford University Press, 1989): p. 144.

20. Quoted in Fairley, p. 52.

21. Bazyler, p. 589.

22. Fairley, p. 52.

23. Bazyler, pp. 589–90.

24. See Bazyler, pp. 590–2; Donnelly, pp. 316–17.

25. Martha Finnemore, 'Constructing Norms of Humanitarian Intervention', prepared for delivery at the 1994 Annual Meeting of the International Studies Association, Washington, DC, 29 March–1 April 1994, p. 33.

26. In Lillich, ed., p. 33.

27. Ibid., p. 73.

28. Ibid., pp. 71–2.

29. Akhavan, p. 49.

30. In Lillich, ed., p. 85.

31. Ibid., pp. 49–50.

32. Ibid., p. 107.

33. Ibid., p. 108.

34. R.J. Vincent, *Nonintervention and International Order*, (Princeton: Princeton University Press, 1974): p. 345.

35. However, one could argue that the way the United States acted with respect to the UN in obtaining its blessing in prosecuting the Gulf War was an abuse of the system.

36. Pastor, p. 134. (italics in original)

37. French representative to the UN Security Council, quoted in Akhavan, p. 44.

38. Akhavan, p. 44. The preamble to Resolution 688 made reference to 'the repression of the Iraqi civilian population in many parts of Iraq, including most recently in Kurdish populated areas, which led to a massive flow of refugees towards and across international frontiers and to cross-border incursions, which threaten international peace and security in the region....'

39. Adelman, p. 19; Akhavan, p. 45.
40. Adelman, pp. 19–21; Akhavan, pp. 44–5.
41. Adelman, p. 4.
42. Of course, given the rhetorical (and, one could argue, military) excesses which the United States, especially, directed at the Iraqi regime, and given the initial reluctance to be involved in the humanitarian mission, one could also argue that this was just a situation where the US was just taking advantage of an opportunity to undermine its sworn enemy.
43. However, some have argued that domestic political factors within the United States played a significant role in the timing, as well as the actual fact, of the intervention. Certainly, there was a long period of time before the intervention during which the US could have acted and did not. One might also point to the 'CNN Effect'. That is, to many it appears that the United States and the rest of the world may only respond to humanitarian emergencies when the world media focus on a particular situation, showing graphic pictures on the evening news, thus leading to domestic pressure to 'do something'. If this is so, then humanitarian responses will continue to be highly selective. However, it may also point to a situation where domestic pressure is felt on the international scene. Further, it may also force a partial reconceptualization of the way 'state' action actually occurs. That is, rather than just focusing analysis on how the apex of power in a particular country – presidents, prime ministers, etc. – reacts to a given humanitarian disaster, it may also be important to include the role of the media and publics as crucial determinants of foreign policy. To the extent that President Bush felt pressure to intervene in a situation where there were no 'vital strategic interests', this should be seen at least partly as an exercise in popular sovereignty, and the subsequent action as an expression of the will of the country as a whole. On the role of the media in humanitarian crises see Robert I. Rotberg and Thomas G. Weiss, eds, *From Massacres to Genocide: The Media, Public Policy, and Humanitarian Crises*, (Washington, DC: The Brookings Institution, 1996).
44. For an in-depth discussion of the situation in the former Yugoslavia see James B. Steinberg, 'Yugoslavia', in Lori Fisler Damrosch, ed., *Enforcing Restraint: Collective Intervention in Internal Conflicts*, (New York: Council on Foreign Relations, 1993): pp. 27–76.
45. 'U.S. Bombs Bosnian Serbs', *The Associated Press* [Online], (10 April 1994), Available USENET: clari.news.fighting.
46. 'NATO Strikes At Serb Base', *The Associated Press* [Online], (26 May 1995), Available USENET: clari.world.organizations; 'Chronology of Conflict in Former Yugoslavia', *Reuters* [Online], (5 October 1995), Available: USENET Newsgroup: clari.world.organizations.
47. See Steinberg, in Damrosch, ed., pp. 52–5.
48. Three months before the genocide began, the commander of the UN Mission for Rwanda (UNAMIR), Gen. Romeo Dallaire, sent a cable to UN headquarters in New York warning that a genocide was being planned. In fact, Dallaire's informant, a 'very very important' government official, claimed that his forces could kill up to 1,000 people in 20 minutes. Cable from General Romeo Dallaire, UNAMIR\Kigali to Baril\DPKO\UNations, New York, regarding 'Request for Protection for Informant', 11 January 1994.

49. In fact, senior officials questioned the credibility of the informant. Howard Adelman and Astri Suhrke, 'Early Warning and Conflict Management: Genocide in Rwanda', Study 2 of the Joint Evaluation of Emergency Assistance to Rwanda, *International Response to Conflict and Genocide: Lessons from the Rwanda Experience,* in the *Journal of Humanitarian Assistance* [Online], (March 1996): footnote 64, Available: http://131.111.106.147/policy/pb021.htm.

50. For an overview of the Rwanda crisis and UNAMIR, see 'United Nations Assistance Mission in Rwanda', Program on Peacekeeping Policy, George Mason University [Online], Available: http://ralph.gmu.edu/cfpa/peace/unamir.html; Joint Evaluation of Emergency Assistance to Rwanda, *International Response to Conflict and Genocide: Lessons from the Rwanda Experience,* in the *Journal of Humanitarian Assistance* [Online], (March 1996), Available: http://131.111.106.147/jpb.htm.

51. Bruce D. Jones, '"Intervention without Borders": Humanitarian Intervention in Rwanda, 1990–94', *Millennium: Journal of International Studies,* 24 (2 1995): pp. 226–33.

52. Ibid., pp. 231–2; Gérard Prunier, '"Opération Turquoise": A Humanitarian Escape from a Political Dead End', workshop on *Genocide in Rwanda: International Responsibilities and Responses,* Washington, DC, 8–9 December 1995.

53. Lori Fisler Damrosch, 'Epilogue', in Damrosch, ed., pp. 375.

54. Ibid.

55. Ibid.

56. 'Towards a Rapid Reaction Capability for the United Nations', Government of Canada, Department of Foreign Affairs and International Trade [Online], (September 1995), Available: http://www.dfait-maeci.gc.ca/english/news/newsletr/un/rap1.htm.

57. For example, there was much debate during the Somalian operation about the nature of Somalian society, especially with respect to whether its social structures can or cannot be fit within traditional Western conceptions of social and political organization, which might have consequences for how negotiations and other activities should be undertaken. The OAU might be more sensitive to these issues.

58. Lillich, p. 100.

59. Quoted in Bazyler, p. 614, note 320.

60. Thomas G. Weiss, David P. Forsythe and Roger A. Coate, *The United Nations and Changing World Politics,* (Boulder, CO: Westview Press, 1994): pp. 33–9.

61. 'Caribbean: Caricom Countries Pledge Support for Invasion of Haiti', *Inter Press Service,* [Online], (30 August, 1994), Available: Nexis; 'Rio Group: Presidents Call for Haitian Regime to Step Down', *Inter Press Service* [Online], (10 September 1994), Available: Nexis; 'Haiti Accord Greeted with Relief in Latin America', *Reuters North America Wire Service* [Online], (19 September 1994), Available: Nexis; 'Haiti: Latin America Leaders Breathe Sigh of Relief', *Inter Press Service* [Online], (19 September 1994), Available: Nexis. For an in-depth discussion of the role of the OAS during the first two years after Aristide was removed from power see Domingo E. Acevedo, 'Haiti', in Damrosch, ed., pp. 119–56.

62. Gwynne Dyer, 'Beyond Haiti; Armies in the Western Hemisphere Take Note: Coups Will Not Be Tolerated', *The Gazette (Montreal)* [Online], (20 September 1994): B3, Available: Nexis.

63. 'OAU Questions Exclusively African Force for Rwanda', *Reuters* [Online], (5 May 1994), Available USENET: clari.world.africa.

64. David Wippman, 'Enforcing the Peace: ECOWAS and the Liberian Civil War', in Damrosch, ed., pp. 164–75.

65. Ibid., pp. 175–81.

66. Quoted in Ibid., p. 181.

67. Arthur C. Helton, 'The Legality of Providing Humanitarian Assistance Without the Consent of the Sovereign', *International Journal of Refugee Law*, 4 (3 1992): p. 375.

68. Denise Plattner, 'Assistance to the Civilian Population: The Development and Present State of International Humanitarian Law', *International Review of the Red Cross*, (May–June 1992): p. 251; Maurice Torrelli, 'From Humanitarian Assistance to "*Intervention on Humanitarian Grounds*"?' *International Review of the Red Cross*, (May–June 1992): p. 231.

69. Plattner, p. 261.

70. Torrelli, p. 232.

71. Plattner, p. 260. (italics added)

72. Ibid., p. 258.

73. Ibid., p. 257.

74. Michael Bothe, 'Relief Actions: The Position of the Recipient State', in Fritz Kalshoven, ed., *Assisting the Victims of Armed Conflicts and Other Disasters*, (Dordrecht: Martinus Nijhoff Publishers, 1989): p. 96.

75. Torrelli, p. 233.

76. Quoted in Ibid., p. 234.

77. Ibid.

78. ICRC official, November 1993.

79. UNHCR officials, November 1993.

80. UNHCR official, November 1993.

81. Adelman, p. 19.

82. UNHCR official, November 1993.

83. See Kurt Mills, 'Humanitarian Intervention: Responding to the Situation in Ethiopia', Occasional Paper 3:OP:3, Joan B. Kroc Institute for International Peace Studies, University of Notre Dame, Fall 1992, especially pp. 29–43. For an in-depth look at the role of humanitarian organizations in Ethiopia, see William DeMars, *Helping People in a People's War: Humanitarian Organizations and the Ethiopian Conflict, 1980–1988*, Dissertation, Department of Government and International Studies, University of Notre Dame, 1993.

84. *Internally Displaced in Africa*, p. 42.

85. Bernard Kouchner, 'Morals of Urgent Need', in Kalshoven, ed., pp. 56–7.

86. See Ibid. See also Bernard Kouchner and Mario Bettati, *Le Devoir d'ingérence: peut-on les laisser mourir?* (Paris: Denoël, 1987).

87. Quoted in Torrelli, p. 229.

88. Torrelli, p. 245.

89. Quoted in Larry Minear, *Humanitarianism Under Siege: A Critical Review of Operation Lifeline Sudan,* (Trenton, NJ: Red Sea Press, 1991): p. 99.

90. Several interviews, October and November 1993.
91. ICRC official, November 1993.
92. Walzer, *Just and Unjust Wars*, p. 88.
93. Michael Walzer, 'The Moral Standing of States: A Response to Four Critics', *Philosophy & Public Affairs*, 9 (Spring 1980): p. 220.
94. Juha Räikkä, 'On National Self-Determination: Some Problems of Walzer's Definition of Nation', in William Twining, ed., *Issues of Self-Determination*, (Aberdeen: Aberdeen University Press, 1991): p. 22.
95. Ibid.
96. Akhavan, p. 46.
97. This latter option, of course, would have significant consequences for the surrounding states which have significant Kurdish populations.
98. Of course, this ignores the question of 'better' according to whom. Presumably, it would be better according to the people who were engaging in the struggle for self-determination and not according to those who were intervening on their behalf. The intervening entity must 'support the development of political forms perceived as just by . . . [the] indigenous populations'. Alan H. Goldman, 'Foreign Intervention', in Steven Luper-Foy, ed., *Problems of International Justice*, (Boulder, CO: Westview Press, 1988): p. 202.
99. Walzer, *Just and Unjust Wars*, p. 104.
100. Ibid., pp. 101, 106.
101. Ibid., p. 106.
102. These criteria are similar, but not identical, to criteria put forward by a number of other observers. See, for example, Bazyler, pp. 598–607; Barabara Harff, *Genocide and Human Rights: International Legal and Political Issues*, Vol. 20, No. 3, Monograph Series in World Affairs, (Denver: University of Denver, 1984): pp. 24–5; Sornarajah, especially pp. 73–7 (focuses on instances of self-determination and secession); Ramsbotham and Woodhouse, pp. 225–31; David J. Scheffer, 'Challenges Confronting Collective Security: Humanitarian Intervention', in *Post-Gulf War Challenges to the UN Collective Security System: Three Views on the Issue of Humanitarian Intervention*, (Washington, DC: United States Institute of Peace, 1992): pp. 1–14.
103. As Harff (p. 12) points out: 'It is difficult enough to identify the elements of genocide – a diverse set of deadly strategies on which states embark to eliminate certain unwanted people – without requiring an answer to the question, "how many?" A criterion which requires "counting the dead" implies that genocide [or other widespread gross violations of human rights] cannot be diagnosed until after the fact, and thus defeats the purpose of recognizing and, more ambitiously, stopping genocidal practices.'
104. I have not addressed the question of monitoring or deciding when genocide or other gross violations of human rights are occurring. Recognizing, publicizing, and getting relevant decision-makers to recognize and act upon such abuses can be a complicated and sometimes politically-laden process. On defining and recognizing genocide see Helen Fein, ed., *Genocide Watch*, (New Haven: Yale University Press, 1992). See also Harff, pp. 14–17 for some of the shortcomings of the definition of genocide in the Genocide Convention.
105. See Harff, pp. 79–80 for a clear delineation of what these actions should be in the case of potential or actual genocide.

106. *Analytic Report of the Secretary-General on Internally Displaced Persons,* Commission on Human Rights, Economic and Social Committee of the United Nations, E/CN.4/1992/23, 1992, p. 25.
107. UN official, November 1993.

NOTES TO CHAPTER 5

1. Erskine Childers, 'UN Mechanisms and Capacities for Intervention', in Elizabeth G. Ferris, ed., *The Challenge to Intervene: A New Role for the United Nations?* (Uppsala: Life and Peace Institute, 1992): p. 51 (italics in original).
2. Ibid., pp. 51–2, footnote 18.
3. See Erika Schlager, 'Conflict Resolution in the CSCE', Occasional Paper 5:OP:4, Joan B. Kroc Institute for International Peace Studies, University of Notre Dame, (March 1993): pp. 14–5; Conference on Security and Cooperation in Europe, 'The Challenges of Change – Helsinki Summit Declaration', [Online], (July 1992), Available: gopher://gopher.nato.int/ Other International Organizations/CSCE/Backgrounds/Follow-up & Summit Documents/1992 Helsinki – The Challenges of Changes. On the role of the HCNM, see also: Rachel Brett, 'Human Rights and the OSCE', *Human Rights Quarterly*, 18 (3 1996): pp. 668–93; Jane Wright, 'The OSCE and the Protection of Minority Rights', *Human Rights Quarterly*, 18 (1 1996): pp. 190–205.
4. Max van der Stoel, 'Preventing Conflict and Building Peace: A Challenge for the CSCE', *NATO Review*, 42 (August 1994): pp. 10–11.
5. Jane Perlez, 'No Unity on Balkans at Europe Summit', *New York Times*, (7 December 1994): p. 8; S. Neil MacFarlane and Larry Minear, *Humanitarian Action and Politics: The Case of Nagorno-Karabakh*, Occasional Paper No. 25, Thomas J. Watson Institute for International Studies, Brown University, 1997.
6. It suspended its operations after the last trust territory, Palau, became self-governing in October 1994. The UN Secretary-General proposes that the Trusteeship Council 'be reconstituted as the forum through which Member states exercise their collective trusteeship for the integrity of the global environment and common areas such as the oceans, atmosphere, and outer space', thus recognizing global sovereignty over the common heritage of mankind. 'Renewing the United Nations: A Programme for Reform', Report of the United Nations Secretary-General [Online], (A/51/950), 16 July 1997, Available: http:// www.un.org/reform.
7. Childers in Ferris, ed., p. 53 (italics in original).
8. For an in-depth discussion of the Cambodian peace accords and subsequent developments see: Steven B. Ratner, 'Cambodia', in Lori Fisler Damrosch, ed., *Enforcing Restraint: Collective Intervention in Internal Conflicts,* (New York: Council on Foreign Relations Press, 1993): pp. 241–73 and Steven R. Ratner, 'The Cambodia Settlement Agreements', *The American Journal of International Law*, 87 (January 1993): pp. 1–41.

9. Ibid.
10. Gerald B. Helman and Steven R. Ratner, 'Saving Failed States', *Foreign Policy*, 89 (Winter 1992–93): p. 6.
11. See Kurt Mills, 'Humanitarian Intervention: Responding to the Situation in Ethiopia', Occasional Paper 3:OP:3, Joan B. Kroc Institute for International Peace Studies, University of Notre Dame, (Fall 1992): p. 40.
12. Helman and Ratner, pp. 12–20.
13. Jarat Chopra, 'Peace-Maintenance: The Last Stage of Development', *Global Society*, 11 (2 1997): p. 185.
14. Ibid., pp. 200–1.
15. Jarat Chopra, 'The space of peace-maintenance', *Political Geography*, 15 (3/4 1996): p. 339.
16. Ibid., p. 355.
17. United Nation High Commissioner for Refugees, *The State of the World's Refugees: The Challenge of Protection*, (New York: Penguin Books, 1993): pp. 134–5 (hereafter referred to as UNHCR).
18. United Nations High Commissioner for Refugees, *UNHCR's Operational Experience with Internally Displaced Persons*, (1994): pp. 21–4.
19. UNHCR, pp. 128–9.
20. UNHCR,*UNHCR's Operational Experience with Internally Displaced Persons*, pp. 47–9.
21. James C. Hathaway, 'Reconceiving Refugee Law as Human Rights Protection', *Journal of Refugee Studies*, 4 (2 1991): pp. 113–31.
22. Ibid., p. 127.
23. For an in-depth discussion of the issues involved in international fiscal burden sharing and responsibility sharing for refugee protection, see 'Common But Differentiated Responsibility: A Model for Enhanced International Refugee Protection Within Interest Convergence Groups', Refugee Law Research Unit, Centre for Refugee Studies, York University, March 1996.
24. UNHCR, *UNHCR's Operational Experience with Internally Displaced Persons*, Annex 1, pp. 3–4.
25. Only half of UNHCR's 'persons of concern' are refugees. Thomas G. Weiss and Amir Pasic, 'Reinventing UNHCR: Enterprising Humanitarians in the Former Yugoslavia, 1991–1995', *Global Governance*, 3 (January–April 1997): pp. 43, 50. As the authors note, 'The casualties of Yugoslavia's wars received benefits because of their needs and not because of their legal classification' (p. 51). In fact, most of the people UNHCR assisted in the former Yugoslavia were not refugees.
26. UNHCR officials, October and November 1993.
27. UNHCR, 'Message from the High Commissioner to all staff on UN Reform', 14 July 1997. Recent proposals in this area will be discussed below.
28. Francis M. Deng, 'Protecting the Internally Displaced: A Challenge for the United Nations', a Study by the Representative of the Secretary-General on Internally Displaced Persons, United Nations, 1993, p. 3. See also Francis M. Deng, *Protecting the Dispossessed: A Challenge for the International Community*, (Washington, DC: The Brookings Institution, 1993).
29. United Nations High Commissioner for Refugees, 'UNHCR's Role in Protecting and Assisting Internally Displaced People', Central Evaluation Section Discussion Paper, EVAL/IDP/13, November 1993, p. 24.

30. James O. C. Jonah, 'Humanitarian Intervention', in Thomas G. Weiss and Larry Minear, eds, *Humanitarianism Across Borders: Sustaining Civilians in Times of War*, (Boulder, CO: Lynne Rienner Publishers, Inc., 1993): p. 70.
31. Frederick C. Cuny, 'Humanitarian Assistance in the Post-Cold War Era', in Weiss and Minear, eds, pp. 166–7.
32. Ibid., p. 167.
33. Ibid., p. 162. Thomas Weiss proposes a different structure. While fighting was going on, UN humanitarian agencies such as UNHCR and UNICEF would not be present. Rather, a new entity, whose members have specific training and expertise, would be created to operate in conflict situations to deliver humanitarian aid. This Humanitarian Protection Force 'would comprise a core of soldiers and civilians in possession of expertise and body army'. It would report to the Security Council, rather than the Secretary-General, thus partially insulating the Secretary-General from some of the polical issues involved in such situations, freeing him to deal with parties to a conflict in a neutral manner. Thomas G. Weiss, 'Overcoming the Somalia Syndrome – "Operation Rekindle Hope?"' *Global Governance*, (May–August 1995): pp. 181–3.
34. Ibid., p. 168.
35. Ibid., p. 164.
36. James Ingram, 'The Future Architecture for International Humanitarian Assistance', in Weiss and Minear, eds, p. 174.
37. Ibid., pp. 175–9.
38. Ibid., p. 183.
39. UN official, November 1993.
40. UNHCR official, November 1993.
41. Ingram, p. 187.
42. Ibid., p. 190.
43. Ibid., pp. 190–1.
44. UNHAC would be the replacement for the Emergency Relief Coordinator established by General Assembly Resolution 46-182, which was supported by DHA. Recently, others have also proposed consolidation of UN humanitarian assistance activities. See John Borton, Emery Brusset and Alistair Hallam, 'Humanitarian Aid and Effects', Study 3 of the Joint Evaluation of Emergency Assistance to Rwanda, *International Response to Conflict and Genocide: Lessons from the Rwanda Experience,* in the *Journal of Humanitarian Assistance* [Online], (March 1996), Available: http://131.111.106.147/policy/pb022.htm.
45. 'Renewing the United Nations: A Programme for Reform'.
46. Leon Gordenker and Thomas G. Weiss, 'Humanitarian Emergencies and Military Help: Some Conceptual Observations', in Thomas G. Weiss, ed., *Humanitarian Emergencies and Military Help in Africa,* (New York: St. Martin's Press, 1990): pp. 14–16. See also Thomas G. Weiss, 'A Research Note about Military-Civilian Humanitarianism: More Questions than Answers', *Disasters*, 21 (2 1997): pp. 95–117. Weiss makes a distinction between logistics (relief delivery) and security (protection).
47. Ibid., pp. 16–18.
48. International Peace Academy, *Peacekeeper's Handbook*, (New York: Pergammon Press, 1984): p. 236.

49. It is because of the tension between the military and humanitarian aspects that Alan James argues that, to the extent possible, humanitarian activities should be administratively separate from military activities. Alan James, 'Humanitarian Aid and Peacekeeping Operations', in Eric A. Belgrad and Nitza Nachmias, eds, *The Politics of International Humanitarian Aid Operations*, (Westport, CT: Praeger: 1997).
50. See Childers, in Ferris, ed., p. 65.
51. On recent proposals to enlarge the Security Council, see Bruce Russett, Barry O'Neill, and James Sutterlin, 'Breaking the Security Council Restructuring Logjam', *Global Governance*, 2 (January-April 1996): pp. 65–80.
52. Ibid., p. 64.
53. Thomas G. Weiss, David P. Forsythe, and Roger A. Coate, *The United Nations and Changing World Politics*, (Boulder, CO: Westview Press, 1994): p. 84, 92.
54. For one such proposal see 'Towards a Rapid Reaction Capability for the United Nations', Government of Canada, Department of Foreign Affairs and International Trade [Online], (September 1995), Available: http://www.dfait-maeci.gc.ca/english/news/newsletr/un/rap1.htm.
55. See UNHCR, p. 134.

Bibliography

Adelman, Howard. 'Refuge or Asylum: A Philosophical Perspective'. *Journal of Refugee Studies* 1 (1 1988): 7–19.

Adelman, Howard. 'Humanitarian Intervention: The Case of the Kurds'. *International Journal of Refugee Law* 4 (1 1992): 4–38.

Adelman, Howard and Astri Suhrke. 'Early Warning and Conflict Management: Genocide in Rwanda'. Study 2 of the Joint Evaluation of Emergency Assistance to Rwanda. *International Response to Conflict and Genocide: Lessons from the Rwanda Experience.* In the *Journal of Humanitarian Assistance* [Online]. (March 1996) Available: http://131.111.106.147/policy/pb021.htm.

Akhavan, Payam. 'Lessons from Iraqi Kurdistan: Self-Determination and Humanitarian Intervention Against Genocide'. *Netherlands Quarterly of Human Rights* 11 (1 1993): 41–62.

Allen, Charles A. 'Civilian Starvation and Relief During Armed Conflict: The Modern Humanitarian Law'. *Georgia Journal of International and Comparative Law* 19 (Spring 1989): 1–85.

Allot, Philip. *Eunomia: New Order for a New World.* New York: Oxford University Press, 1990.

Analytic Report of the Secretary-General on Internally Displaced Persons. Commission on Human Rights, Economic and Social Committee of the United Nations. E/CN.4/1992/23. 1992.

Anderson, Benedict. *Imagined Communities: Reflections on the Origin and Spread of Nationalism.* New York: Verso, 1991.

Anderson, Walter Truett. *Reality Isn't What It Used to Be: Theatrical Politics, Ready-to-Wear Religion, Global Myths, Primitive Chic, and Other Wonders of the Postmodern World.* San Francisco: HarperSanFrancisco, 1990.

Ashley, Richard K. 'Untying the Sovereign State: A Double Reading of the Anarchy Problematique'. *Millennium: Journal of International Studies* 17 (Summer 1988): 227–62.

Ayittey, George B.N. *Africa Betrayed.* New York: St. Martin's Press, 1992.

Ayres, B. Drummond, Jr. 'Flow of Illegal Aliens Rises as the Peso Falls'. *The New York Times* (4 February 1995): 6.

Barry, Brian and Robert E. Goodin, eds. *Free Movement: Ethical Issues in the Transnational Migration of People and Money.* University Park, PA: Pennsylvania State University Press, 1992.

Bartelson, Jens. *A Genealogy of Sovereignty.* Cambridge: Cambridge University Press, 1995.

Brett, Rachel. 'Human Rights and the OSCE'. *Human Rights Quarterly* 18 (3 1996): 668–93.

Bauböck, Rainer. *Transnational Citizenship: Membership and Rights in International Migration.* Brookfield, VT: Edward Elgar Publishing Company, 1994.

Bazyler, Michael J. 'Reexamining the Doctrine of Humanitarian Intervention in Light of the Atrocities in Kampuchea and Ethiopia'. *Stanford Journal of International Law* 23 (Summer 1987): 547–619.

232

Beitz, Charles R. 'Bounded Morality'. *International Organization* 33 (Summer 1979): 405–24.

Belgrad, Eric A. and Nitza Nachmias, eds. *The Politics of International Humanitarian Aid Operations.* Westport, CT: Praeger: 1997.

Bell-Fialkoff, Andrew. 'A Brief History of Ethnic Cleansing'. *Foreign Affairs* 72 (Summer 1993): 110–21.

Ben-Israel, Hedva. 'Nationalism in Historical Perspective'. *Journal of International Affairs* 45 (Winter 1992): 367–97.

Bettati, Mario. 'The Right of Humanitarian Intervention or the Right of Free Access to Victims?' *The Review* 49 (1992): 1–11.

Biersteker, Thomas J. and Cynthia Weber, eds. *State Sovereignty as Social Construct.* Cambridge: Cambridge University Press, 1996.

Bodin, Jean. *On Sovereignty: Four Chapters from the Six Books of the Commonwealth.* Translated by Julian H. Franklin. Cambridge: Cambridge University Press, 1992.

Borton, John, Emery Brusset, and Alistair Hallam. 'Humanitarian Aid and Effects'. Study 3 of the Joint Evaluation of Emergency Assistance to Rwanda. *International Response to Conflict and Genocide: Lessons from the Rwanda Experience.* In the *Journal of Humanitarian Assistance* [Online]. (March 1996). Available: http://131.111.106.147/policy/pb022.htm.

'Bosnia War Displaces Millions'. *The Associated Press.* [Online]. (13 March 1994). Available USENET: clari.news.gov.international.

Breton, Thierry. *The Pentecost Project.* Mark Howson, trans. New York: Henry Holt and Company, 1987.

Brink, Marjolein, Mutiara Pasariboe, Philip Muus, and Lieke Verstrate. *Reception Policies for Persons in Need of International Protection in Western European States. Research Project Commissioned by the United Nations High Commissioner for Refugees (UNHCR).* Centre for Migration Research, Department of Human Geography, University of Amsterdam, 1993.

Brown, Peter and Henry Shue, eds. *Boundaries: National Autonomy and its Limits.* Totawa, NJ: Rowan and Littlefield, 1981.

Browne, Malcom W. 'France and Australia Kill Pact on Limited Antarctic Mining and Oil Drilling'. *The New York Times* (25 September 1989): 10.

Buccheit, Lee. *Secession: The Legitimacy of Self-Determination.* New Haven: Yale University Press, 1978.

Buchanan, Allen. 'Self-Determination and the Right to Secede'. *Journal of International Affairs* 45 (Winter 1992): 347–65.

Bukowski, Jeanie J. 'A Community of the Regions? European Integration Reexamined: The Case of Spain'. Presented at the *1993 Annual Meeting of the Midwest Political Science Association.* Chicago, 15 April 1993.

Bull, Hedley, ed. *Intervention in World Politics.* New York: Oxford University Press, 1984.

Bunting, Glenn F. 'Plan for National Guard At Border Gains Support'. *Los Angeles Times* [Online]. (19 October 1993): 3. Available: Nexis.

Cable from General Romeo Dallaire, UNAMIR\Kigali to Baril\DPKO\UNations, New York, regarding 'Request for Protection for Informant'. 11 January 1994.

'California Welfare Cuts Banned'. *The Associated Press.* [Online]. (4 May 1994). Available USENET: clari.news.immigration.

Callenbach, Ernest. *Ecotopia.* New York: Bantam Books, 1975.

234 *Bibliography*

Camilleri, Joseph A. and Jim Falk. *The End of Sovereignty?: The Politics of a Shrinking and Fragmenting World*. Brookfield, VT: Ashgate Publishing Company, 1992.

Carens, Joseph H. 'Aliens and Citizens: The Case for Open Borders'. *The Review of Politics* 49 (Spring 1987): 251–73.

'Caribbean: Caricom Countries Pledge Support for Invasion of Haiti'. *Inter Press Service* [Online]. (30 August 1994): Available: Nexis.

Chazan, Naomi, ed. *Irredentism and International Politics*. Boulder, CO: Lynne Rienner Publishers, 1991.

Chisolm, Michael and David Smith, ed. *Shared Space, Divided Space: Essays on Conflict and Territorial Organization*. London: Unwin Hyman, 1990.

Chopra, Jarat. 'The New Subjects of International Law'. *Brown Foreign Affairs Journal* (Spring 1991): 27–30.

Chopra, Jarat. 'Peace-Maintenance: The Last Stage of Development'. *Global Society* 11 (2 1997): 185–204.

Chopra, Jarat. 'The Space of Peace-Maintenance'. *Political Geography* 15 (3/4 1996): 335–57.

'Chronology of Conflict in Former Yugoslavia'. *Reuters* [Online]. (5 October 1995). Available USENET: clari.world.organizations.

'Common But Differentiated Responsibility: A Model for Enhanced International Refugee Protection Within Interest Convergence Groups'. Refugee Law Research Unit, Centre for Refugee Studies, York University. March 1996.

Conference on Security and Cooperation in Europe. 'The Challenges of Change – Helsinki Summit Declaration' [Online]. (July 1992). Available: gopher://gopher.nato.int/Other International Organizations/CSCE/Backgrounds/Follow-up & Summit Documents/1992 Helsinki – The Challenges of Change.

Conference on Security and Cooperation in Europe. Fifth Meeting of the Committee of Senior Officials, Journal No. 1, Annex 2. Prague. 1992.

Corea, Gamani. 'Global Stakes Require a New Consensus'. *ifda Dossier* 78 (July/September 1990): 73–86.

Crawford, James. *The Creation of States in International Law*. New York: Oxford University Press, 1979.

Crawford, Scott and Kekula Crawford. 'Self-Determination in the Information Age' [Online]. (3 May 1995). Available: http://www.cernet.edu.cn/HMP/PAPER/230/html/paper.html.

Cristescu, Aureliu. *The Right to Self-Determination: Historical and Current Development on the Basis of United Nations Instruments. Study Prepared by Aureliu Cristescu, Special Rapporteur of the Sub-Commission on Prevention of Discrimination of Minorities*. New York: United Nations, 1981.

Czempiel, Ernst-Otto and James N. Rosenau, eds. *Global Changes and Theoretical Challenges: Approaches to World Politics for the 1990s*. Lexington, MA: Lexington Books, 1989.

Damrosch, Lori Fisler, ed. *Enforcing Restraint: Collective Intervention in Internal Conflicts*. New York: Council on Foreign Relations, 1993.

Delupis, Ingrid Doimi di. *International Law and the Independent State*. New York: Crane, Russak, 1974.

DeMars, William. *Helping People in a People's War: Humanitarian Organizations and the Ethiopian Conflict*. Dissertation, Department of Government and International Studies, University of Notre Dame, 1993.

Deng, Francis M. 'Protecting the Internally Displaced: A Challenge for the United Nations'. Study by Francis M. Deng, Representative of the Secretary-General on Internally Displaced Persons. United Nations, 1993.

Deng, Francis M. *Protecting the Dispossessed: A Challenge for the International Community*. Washington, DC: The Brookings Institution, 1993.

DerDerian, James and Michael J. Shapiro, eds. *International/Intertextual Relations: Postmodern Readings of World Politics*. Lexington, MA: Lexington Books, 1989.

Donini, Antonio. 'Beyond Neutrality: On the Compatability of Military Intervention and Humanitarian Assistance'. *The Fletcher Forum* (Summer/Fall 1995): 31–45.

Donnelly, Jack. 'Human Rights, Humanitarian Intervention and American Foreign Policy'. *Journal of International Affairs* 37 (Winter 1984): 311–28.

Dowty, Alan. *Closed Borders: The Contemporary Assault on Freedom of Movement*. New Haven: Yale University Press, 1987.

Dyer, Gwynne. 'Beyond Haiti; Armies in the Western Hemisphere Take Note: Coups Will Not Be Tolerated'. *The Gazette (Montreal)* [Online]. (20 September 1994): B3. Available: Nexis.

Eide, Asborne, Gudmundur Alfredsson, Göran Melander, Lars Adam Rehof and Allan Rosas, eds. *The Universal Declaration of Human Rights: A Commentary*. Oxford: Scandanavia University Press, 1992.

Espiell, Héctor Gros. *The Right to Self-Determination: Implementation of United Nations Resolutions. Study Prepared by Héctor Gros Espiell, Special Rapporteur of the Sub-Commission on Prevention of Discrimination of Minorities*. New York: United Nations, 1980.

'Ethnic Conflicts Worldwide'. *Current History* 92 (April 1993): 167–8.

Etzioni, Amitai. 'The Evils of Self-Determination'. *Foreign Policy* 89 (Winter 1992–93): 21–35.

Fairley, H. Scott. 'State Actors, Humanitarian Intervention and International Law'. *Georgia Journal of International and Comparative Law* 10 (Winter 1980): 29–63.

Falk, Richard. *Explorations at the Edge of Time: The Prospects for World Order*. Philadelphia: Temple University Press, 1992.

Falk, Richard. *Revitalizing International Law*. Ames, IA: Iowa State University Press, 1989.

Falk, Richard A. *A Study of Future Worlds*. New York: The Free Press, 1975.

Farley, Lawrence T. *Plebiscites and Sovereignty: The Crisis of Political Illegitimacy*. Boulder: Westview Press, 1986.

Fein, Helen, ed. *Genocide Watch*. New Haven: Yale University Press, 1992.

Ferris, Elizabeth G., ed. *The Challenge to Intervene: A New Role for the United Nations?* Uppsala: Life & Peace Institute, 1992.

Finnemore, Martha. 'Constructing Norms of Humanitarian Intervention'. Presented at the *1994 Annual Meeting of the International Studies Association*. Washington, DC, 29 March–1April 1994.

Forbes, Ian and Mark Hoffman, eds. *Political Theory, International Relations, and the Ethics of Intervention*. New York: St. Martin's Press, 1993.

Frelick, Bill and Barbara Kohnen. 'Filling the Gap: Temporary Protected Status'. Washington, DC: U.S. Committee for Refugees, 1994.

Fukuyama, Francis. 'The End of History?' *The National Interest* 16 (Summer 1989): 3–18.

Galtung, Johan. *The True Worlds: A Transnational Perspective*. New York: The Free Press, 1980.

Gellner, Ernest. *Nations and Nationalism*. Ithaca: Cornell University Press, 1983.

'German Gov. and Church At War'. *The Associated Press* [Online]. (14 May 1994). Available USENET: clari.news.conflict.

'Germans Break Laws To Give Aid'. *The Associated Press* [Online]. (10 May 1994). Available USENET: clari.news.immigration.

'Germany Tightens Laws on Asylum'. *Facts on File World News Digest* [Online]. (3 June 1993). Available: Nexis.

Gibney, Mark. *Strangers or Friends: Principles for a New Alien Admission Policy*. Westport, CT: Greenwood Press, Inc., 1986.

Giddens, Anthony. *The Consequences of Modernity*. Stanford: Stanford University Press, 1990.

Gillespie, Thomas R., 'Unwanted Responsibility: Humanitarian Intervention to Advance Human Rights'. *Peace & Change* 18 (July 1993): 219–46.

Golden, Tim. 'U.S. Blockade of Workers Enrages Mexican Town'. *The New York Times* [Online]. (1 October 1993): 3. Available: Nexis.

Goldsborough, James O. 'California's Foreign Policy'. *Foreign Affairs* (Spring 1993): 88–96.

Gordon, Joshua. 'East Asian Censors Want to Net the Internet'. *The Christian Science Monitor* [Online]. (12 November 1996). Available: http://www.csmonitor.com.

'Governors Seek Aid for Aliens'. *The Associated Press* [Online]. (22 June 1994). Available USENET: clari.news.immigration.

'Great Exoduses Since WWII'. *The Associated Press* [Online]. (16 July 1994). Available USENET: clari.news.immigration.

Greenwald, Jeff. 'The Unrepresented Nations and Peoples Organization: Diplomacy's Cutting Edge'. *Whole Earth Review* 77 (Winter 1992): 32–6.

Grenier, Guillermo J. and Alex Stepick III. *Miami Now! Immigration, Ethnicity, and Social Change*. Gainesville, FL: University of Florida Press, 1992.

Guild, Elspeth. *The Developing Immigration and Asylum Policies of the European Union: Adopted Conventions, Resolutions, Recommendations, Decisions and Conclusions*. The Hague: Kluwer Law International, 1996.

'Haiti Accord Greeted with Relief in Latin America'. *Reuters North American Wire Service* [Online]. (19 September 1994). Available: Nexis.

'Haiti: Latin America Leaders Breathe Sigh of Relief'. *Inter Press Service* [Online]. (19 September 1994). Available: Nexis.

Halperin, Morton H. and David J. Scheffer, with Patricia L. Small. *Self-Determination in the New World Order*. Washington, DC: Carnegie Endowment for International Peace, 1992.

Hannum, Hurst. *Autonomy, Sovereignty, and Self-Determination: The Accommodation of Conflicting Rights*. Philadelphia: University of Pennsylvania Press, 1990.

Harff, Barbara. *Genocide and Human Rights: International Legal and Political Issues*. Vol. 20, No. 3. Monograph Series in World Affairs. Denver: University of Denver, 1984.

Hashmi, Sohail H. 'Is There an Islamic Ethic of Humanitarian Intervention?' *Ethics & International Affairs* 7 (1993): 55–73.

Hathaway, James C. 'Reconceiving Refugee Law as Human Rights Protection'. *Journal of Refugee Studies* 4 (2 1991): 113–131.

Hathaway, James C. 'The Emerging Politics of Non-Entrée'. *Refugees* (December 1992): 40–1.

Hathaway, James C. and John A. Dent. *Refugee Rights: Report on a Comparative Survey*. Toronto: York Lanes Press, 1995.

Hechter, Michael. *Internal Colonialism: The Celtic Fringe in British National Development*. Berkeley: University of California Press, 1977.

Hehir, J. Bryan. 'Intervention: From Theories to Cases'. *Ethics & International Affairs* 9 (1995): 1–13.

Heinze, Eric. 'Beyond Parapraxes: Right and Wrong Approaches to the Universality of Human Rights Law'. *Netherlands Quarterly of Human Rights* 12 (4 1994): 369–91.

Helman, Gerald B. and Steven R. Ratner. 'Saving Failed States'. *Foreign Policy* 89 (Winter 1992–93): 3–20.

Helton, Arthur C. 'The Legality of Providing Humanitarian Assistance Without the Consent of the Sovereign'. *International Journal of Refugee Law* 4 (3 1992): 373–5.

Henz, Paul B. 'Eritrea: The Endless War'. *The Washington Quarterly* 9 (Spring 1986): 23–36.

Hinsley, F. H. *Sovereignty*. New York: Cambridge University Press, 1986.

Hobbes, Thomas. *Leviathan*. Richard Tuck, ed. Cambridge: Cambridge University Press, 1991.

Hobsbawm, Eric. *Nations and Nationalism Since 1780: Programme, Myth, Reality*. New York: Canbridge University Press, 1990.

Hobsbawm, Eric. 'Who's Fault-Line Is It Anyway?' *New Statesman and Society* 5 (24 April 1992): 23–6.

Hoffman, Stanley. 'A New World and its Troubles'. *Foreign Affairs* 69 (Fall 1990): 115–22.

Horowitz, Donald L. *Ethnic Groups in Conflict*. Los Angeles: University of California Press, 1985.

Huntington, Samuel P. 'The Clash of Civilizations?' *Foreign Affairs* 72 (Summer 1993): 22–49.

Internally Displaced in Africa: Assistance Challenges and Opportunities. Washington, DC: Refugee Policy Group, 1992.

International Peace Academy. *Peacekeeper's Handbook*. New York: Pergamon Press, 1984.

Jackson, Robert. *Quasi-States: Sovereignty, International Relations, and the Third World*. New York: Cambridge University Press, 1990.

James, Alan. *Sovereign Statehood*. London: Allen & Unwin, 1986.

'Joint Evaluation of Emergency Assistance to Rwanda. *International Response to Conflict and Genocide: Lessons from the Rwanda Experience*'. In the *Journal of Humanitarian Assistance* [Online]. (March 1996). Available: http://131.111.106.147/jpb.htm.

Jones, Barry and Michael Keating, eds. *The European Union and the Regions*. Oxford: Clarendon Press, 1995.

Jones, Bruce D. '"Intervention without Borders": Humanitarian Intervention in Rwanda, 1990–94'. *Millennium: Journal of International Studies* 24 (2 1995): 225–49.

Joyner, Christopher C. and Sudhir K. Chopra, eds. *The Antarctic Legal Regime*. Dordrecht, The Netherlands: Martinus Nijhoff Publishers, 1988.

Kalshoven, Fritz, ed. *Assisting Victims of Armed Conflicts and Other Disasters*. Dordrecht: Martinus Nijhoff Publishers, 1989.

Kellas, James G. *The Politics of Nationalism and Ethnicity*. New York: St. Martin's Press, 1991.

Keohane, Robert. *Sovereignty, Interdependence and International Institutions*. Center for International Affairs, Harvard University, Working Paper 1. 1991.

Khan, L. Ali. *The Extinction of Nation-States: A World without Borders*. The Hague: Kluwer Law International, 1996.

Kitschelt, Herbert. 'New Social Movements in West Germany and the United States'. *Political Power and Social Theory* 5 (1985): 273–324.

Kouchner, Bernard and Mario Bettati. *Le Devoir d'ingerence: peut-on les laisser mourir?* Paris: Denoël, 1987.

Kriesi, Hanspeter. 'The Interdependence of Structure and Action: Some Reflections on the State of the Art'. *International Social Movement Research* 1 (1988): 249–68.

Kuehls, Thom. *Beyond Sovereign Territory: The Space of Ecopolitics*. Minneapolis: University of Minnesota Press, 1996.

Kutner, Luis. 'World Habeas Corpus and Humanitarian Intervention'. *Valparaiso University Law Review* 19 (Spring 1985): 593–631.

Laberge, Pierre. 'Humanitarian Intervention: Three Ethical Positions'. *Ethics & International Affairs* 9 (1995): 15–35.

LaFranchi, Howard. 'America Puts Up Chain-Links Along a Once-Friendly Border'. *The Christian Science Monitor* [Online]. (13 February 1996). Available: http://www.csmonitor.com.

Lagos, Gustavo and Horacio H. Godoy. *Revolution of Being: A Latin American View of the Future*. New York: The Free Press, 1977.

Lapidoth, Ruth. 'Sovereignty in Transition'. *Journal of International Affairs* 45 (Winter 1992): 325–46.

Laski, Harold. *A Grammar of Politics*. London: George Allen & Unwin, Ltd., 1941.

Lefort, Claude. *The Political Forms of Modern Society: Bureaucracy, Democracy, Totalitarianism*. ed. John B. Thompson. Cambridge, MA: The MIT Press, 1986.

Lewy, Guenter. 'The Case for Humanitarian Intervention'. *Orbis* 37 (Fall 1993): 621–32.

Lijphart, Arend. *Democracy in Plural Societies*. New Haven, CT: Yale University Press, 1977.

Lillich, Richard B., ed. *Humanitarian Intervention and the United Nations*. Charlottesville: University of Virginia Press, 1973.

Loescher, Gil. *Refugee Movements and International Security*. London: Brassey's for the International Institute for Strategic Studies, 1992.

Loescher, Gil and John A. Scanlan. *Calculated Kindness: Refugees and America's Half-Open Door, 1945 to the Present*. New York: The Free Press, 1986.

Ludden, Jennifer. 'Quebec May Loosen Tough Laws Restricting English Use' [Radio Transcript]. *NPR: Morning Edition* [Online]. (24 May 1993). Available: Nexis.

Luke, Timothy. 'The Discipline of Security Studies and the Codes of Containment: Learning From Kuwait'. *Alternatives* 16 (Summer 1991): 315–44.

Luper-Foy, Steven, ed. *Problems of International Justice*. Boulder, CO: Westview Press, 1988.

Lyons, Gene M. and Michael Mastanduno, eds. *Beyond Westphalia? State Sovereignty and International Intervention*. Baltimore: The Johns Hopkins University Press, 1995.

MacFarlane, S. Neil and Larry Minear. *Humanitarian Action and Politics: The Case of Nagorno-Karabakh*. Occasional Paper No. 25, Thomas J. Watson Institute for International Studies, Brown University, 1997.

MacLeod, Andrew 'A Dis-United Kingdom?' *The Christian Science Monitor* [Online]. (15 September 1997). Available: http://www.csmonitor.com.

Makinda, Samuel M. *Seeking Peace from Chaos: Humanitarian Intervention in Somalia*. International Peace Academy, Occasional Paper Series. Boulder, CO: Lynne Rienner Publishers, 1993.

Mapuranga, M.T. 'Mass Movements of People in the Nineties: Problems, Prospects and New Challenges – A View from Africa'. Presented at the *North South Round Table on Movements of People in the 1990s: Challenges for Policy Makers*. 15–17 December 1991.

Markakis, John. 'Nationalities and the State in Europe'. *Third World Quarterly* 11 (October 1989): 119–30.

Martin, David A. 'Effects of International Law on Migration Policy and Practice: The Uses of Hypocrisy'. *International Migration Review* 23 (Fall 1989): 547–78.

Mart́nez, Oscar J. *Troublesome Border*. Tuscon: University of Arizona Press, 1988.

Mathews, Jessica T. 'Power Shift'. *Foreign Affairs* 76 (January/February 1997): 51–66.

Mathews, Jessica Tuchman. 'Redefining Security'. *Foreign Affairs* 68 (Spring 1989): 162–77.

Mayall, James, ed. *The Community of States: A Study in International Theory*. London: George Allen & Unwin, 1982.

Mayall, James and Mark Simpson. 'Ethnicity is not Enough: Reflections on Protracted Secessionism in the Third World'. *International Journal of Comparative Sociology* XXXIII (January–April 1992): 5–25.

Mazrui, Ali A. *A World Federation of Cultures: An African Perspective*. New York: The Free Press, 1976.

Meissner, Doris. 'Managing Migrations'. *Foreign Policy* 86 (Spring 1992): 66–83.

Melucci, Alberto. 'The New Social Movements: A Theoretical Approach'. *Social Science Information* 19 (2 1980): 199–226.

Mendlovitz, Saul H., ed. *On the Creation of a Just World Order*. New York: The Free Press, 1975.

Metzl, Jamie F. 'Information Technology and Human Rights'. *Human Rights Quarterly* 18 (November 1996): 705–46.

Michelmann, Hans J. and Panayotis Saldatos, eds. *Federalism and International Relations: The Role of Subnational Units*. Oxford: Clarendon Press: 1990.

Midlarsky, Manus I. *The Internationalization of Communal Strife*. New York: Routledge, 1992.

Mill, John Stuart. *Essays on Equality, Law, and Education*. John M. Robson, ed. Toronto: University of Toronto Press, 1984.

Mills, Kurt. *Humanitarian Intervention: Responding to the Situation in Ethiopia*. Joan B. Kroc Institute for International Peace Studies, University of Notre Dame, Occasional Paper 3:OP:3. 1992.

Minear, Larry. *Humanitarianism Under Siege: A Critical Review of Operation Lifeline Sudan.* Trenton, NJ: Red Sea Press, 1991.

'Moi Tells UN to Move Refugees in Kenya to Other Countries'. *Agence France Press* [Online]. (19 January 1994). Available: Nexis.

Montville, Joseph V., ed. *Conflict and Peacemaking in International Societies.* Lexington, MA: Lexington Books, 1990.

Motyl, Alexander J. 'The Modernity of Nationalism: Nations, States and Nation-States in the Contemporary World'. *Journal of International Affairs* 45 (Winter 1992): 307–23.

'Movements of People in the 1990s: Challenges for Policy Makers'. *Report of the North South Round Table on Movements of People in the 1990s: Challenges for Policy Makers.* 15–17 December 1991.

Moynihan, Daniel Patrick. *Pandaemonium: Ethnicity in International Politics.* New York: Oxford University Press, 1993.

Myhre, Jeffrey D. *The Antarctic Treaty System: Politics, Law, and Diplomacy.* Boulder, CO: Westview Press, 1986.

Nardin, Terry and David R. Mapel, eds. *Traditions of International Ethics.* Cambridge: Cambridge University Press, 1992.

'NATO Strikes At Serb Base'. *The Associated Press* [Online]. (26 May 1995). Available USENET: clari.world.organizations.

Natsios, Andrew S. 'Food Through Force: Humanitarian Intervention and U.S. Policy'. *The Washington Quarterly* 17 (Winter 1994): 129–44.

'New Law Gives German Border Force More Power'. *The Reuter European Community Report* [Online]. (24 June 1994). Available: Nexis.

'The News in Brief' *The Christian Science Monitor* [Online]. (22 September 1997). Available http://www.csmonitor.com.

'Notes on the Preventive Zone Concept'. UNHCR Memorandum. 1992.

'OAU Questions Exclusively African Force for Rwanda'. *Reuters* [Online]. (5 May 1994). Available USENET: clari.world.africa.

Offe, Claus. 'New Social Movements: Challenging the Boundaries of Institutional Politics'. *Social Research* 52 (Winter 1985): 817–868.

Ogata, Sadako. 'Emergencies, Displacement and Solutions'. Presented at the *North South Round Table on Movements of People in the 1990s: Challenges for Policy Makers.* 15–17 December 1991.

Ogata Sadako, 'Address to the Conference on Humanitarian Intervention, Sovereignty and the Future of International Society'. Dartmouth College. 18 May 1992.

Onuf, Nicholas Greenwood. 'Sovereignty: Outline of a Conceptual History'. *Alternatives* 16 (4 1991): 425–46.

'Operation Gatekeeper' Starts'. *The Associated Press* [Online]. (1 October 1994). Available USENET: clari.news.immigration.

Papademetriou, Demetrios G. *Coming Together or Pulling Apart: The European Union's Struggle with Immigration and Asylum.* Washington, DC: Carnegie Endowment for International Peace, 1996.

Passel, Jeffrey S., Frank D. Bean, and Barry Edmonston, eds. *Undocumented Migration to the United States: IRCA and the Experience of the 1980s.* Lanham, MD: University Press of America, 1990.

Pease, Kelly-Kate and David P. Forsythe. 'Humanitarian Intervention and International Law'. *Austrian Journal of Public and International Law* 45 (1993): 1–20.

Perlez, Jane. 'No Unity on Balkans at Europe Summit'. *The New York Times* (7 December 1994): 8.

Pinard, Maurice. 'The Dramatic Reemergence of the Quebec Independence Movement'. *Journal of International Affairs* 45 (Winter 1992): 471–97.

Plattner, Denise. 'Assistance to the Civilian Population: The Development and Present State of International Humanitarian Law'. *International Review of the Red Cross* (May–June 1992): 249–63.

Pogge, Thomas W. 'An Institutional Approach to Humanitarian Intervention'. *Public Affairs Quarterly* 6 (January 1992): 89–103.

'Poll Finds Anti-Immigrant Bias'. *The Associated Press* [Online]. (23 May 1994). Available USENET: clari.news.immigration.

Porter, Gareth and Janet Welsh Brown. *Global Environmental Politics*. Boulder, CO: Westview Press, 1991.

Post-Gulf War Challenges to the UN Collective Security System: Three Views on the Issue of Humanitarian Intervention. Washington, DC: United States Institute of Peace, 1992.

Premdas, Ralph R., S.W.R. de A. Samarsinghe, and Alan B. Anderson, eds. *Secessionist Movements in Comparative Perspective*. New York: St. Martin's Press, 1990.

Prunier, Gérard. '"Opération Turquoise": A Humanitarian Escape from a Political Dead End'. Paper presented at the workshop on *Genocide in Rwanda: International Responsibilities and Responses*. Washington, DC, 8–9 December 1995.

Rakowska-Harmstone, Teresa. 'Chickens Coming Home to Roost: A Perspective on Soviet Ethnic Relations'. *Journal of International Affairs* 45 (Winter 1992): 519–48.

Ramsbotham, Oliver and Tom Woodhouse. *Humanitarian Intervention in Contemporary Conflict: A Reconceptualization*. Cambridge, MA: Polity Press, 1996.

Ratner, Steven R. 'The Cambodia Settlement Agreements'. *The American Journal of International Law* 87 (January 1993): 1–41.

Reed, Laura W. and Carl Kaysen, eds. *Emerging Norms of Justified Intervention: A Collection of Essays from a Project of the American Academy of Sciences*. Cambridge, MA: Committee on International Security Studies, AAAS, 1993.

Reich, Robert B. *The Work of Nations: Preparing Ourselves for 21st-Century Capitalism*. New York: Vintage Books, 1992.

Reisman, Michael W. 'Sovereignty and Human Rights in Contemporary International Law'. *American Journal of International Law* 84 (October 1990): 866–76.

'Renewing the United Nations: A Programme for Reform'. Report of the United Nations Secretary-General [Online]. A/51/950. 16 July 1997. Available: http://www.un.org/reform.

'Reno Says No Reduction of Illegal Immigrants'. *Reuters* [Online]. (7 October 1993). Available: Nexis.

'Rio Group: Presidents Call for Haitian Regime to Step Down'. *Inter Press Service* [Online]. (10 September 1994). Available: Nexis.

Roberts, Adam. 'Humanitarian War: Military Intervention and Human Rights'. *International Affairs* 69 (July 1993): 429–49.

Rodley, Nigel, ed. *To Loose the Bands of Wickedness: International Intervention in Defense of Human Rights.* London: Brassey's Defense Publishers, 1992.

Rosenau, James N. 'Individual Aspirations and Collective Outcomes: Notes for a Micro-Macro Theory of World Politics'. Presented at the *1992 Annual Meeting of the American Political Science Association.* Chicago, IL, 3–6 September 1992.

Rosenau, James N. 'Normative Challenges in a Turbulent World'. *Ethics & International Affairs* 6 (1992): 1–19.

Rosenau, James N. 'The Relocation of Authority in a Shrinking World'. *Comparative Politics* 24 (April 1992): 253–72.

Rosenau, James N. 'Sovereignty in a Turbulent World'. Presented at the *Conference on National Sovereignty and Collective Intervention.* Dartmouth College. 18–20 May 1992.

Rosenau, James N. 'The State in an Era of Cascading Politics: Wavering Concept, Widening Competence, Withering Colossus, or Weathering Change?' *Comparative Political Studies* 21 (April 1988): 13–44.

Rosenau, James N. and Ernst-Otto Czempiel, eds. *Governance without Government: Order and Change in World Politics.* New York: Cambridge University Press, 1992.

Rosenau, James N. and Hylke Tromp, eds. *Interdependence and Conflict in World Politics.* Brookfield, VT: Gower Publishing Company, 1989.

Rosenau, Pauline. 'Once Again Into the Fray: International Relations Confronts the Humanities'. *Millennium: Journal of International Studies* 19 (1 1990): 83–110.

Rosenau, Pauline. *Postmodernism and the Social Sciences: Insights, Inroads, and Intrusions.* Princeton: Princeton University Press, 1992.

Rotberg, Robert I. and Thomas G. Weiss, eds. *From Massacres to Genocide: The Media, Public Policy, and Humanitarian Crises.* Washington, DC: The Brookings Institution, 1996.

Rotella, Sebastian. 'Texas Border Crackdown Stems Tide, Raises Tensions'. *Los Angeles Times* [Online]. (2 October 1993): 1. Available: Nexis.

Rupesinghe, Kumar, ed. *Internal Conflict and Governance.* New York: St. Martin's Press, 1992.

Russett, Bruce. Barry O'Neill, and James Sutterlin. 'Breaking the Security Council Restructuring Logjam'. *Global Governance* 2 (January–April 1996): 65–80.

Said, Edward W. and Christopher Hitchens, eds. *Blaming the Victims: Spurious Scholarship and the Palestinian Question.* New York: Verso, 1988.

Sandalow, Marc. 'INS Chief Says Illegals' Goal Isn't Welfare'. *The San Francisco Chronicle* [Online]. (30 October 1993): 1. Available: Nexis.

Scheffer, David. J. 'Toward a Modern Doctrine of Humanitarian Intervention'. *University of Toledo Law Review* 23 (2 1992): 253–92.

Schlager, Erika B. *Conflict Resolution in the CSCE.* Joan B. Kroc Institute for International Peace Studies, University of Notre Dame, Occasional Paper 5:OP:4. 1993.

Schoenberger, Karl. '"Cascadia" Borders on the Future'. *Los Angeles Times* [Online]. (1 November 1993): 1. Available: Nexis.

Seigel, Robert. 'Quebec Residents Do Battle Over Language'. [Radio Transcript]. *NPR: All Things Considered* [Online]. (3 June 1993). Available: Nexis.

Simons, Marlise. 'Massive Ozone and Smog Defile South Atlantic Sky'. *The New York Times* (12 October 1992): 1, 6.

Simons, Marlise. 'Winds Toss Africa's Soil, Feeding Lands Far Away'. *The New York Times* (29 October 1992): 1, 6.

Smith, Jackie, Charles Chatfield, and Ron Pagnucco, eds. *Transnational Social Movements and World Politics: Solidarity Beyond the State*. Syracuse: Syracuse University Press, 1997.

Smooha, Sammy and Theodore Hanf. 'The Diverse Modes of Conflict-regulation in Deeply Divided Societies'. *International Journal of Comparative Sociology* XXXIII (January–April 1992): 26–47.

Sornarajah, M. 'Internal Colonialism and Humanitarian Intervention'. *Georgia Journal of International and Comparative Law* 11 (Winter 1981): 45–77.

Soysal, Yasemin. *Limits of Citizenship: Migrants and Postnational Membership in Europe*. Chicago: University of Chicago Press, 1994.

Spegele, Roger D. 'Richard Ashley's Discourse for International Relations'. *Millennium: Journal of International Studies* 21 (2 1992): 147–82.

Spruyt, Hendrik. *The Sovereign State and Its Competitors: An Analysis of Systems Change*. Princeton: Princeton University Press, 1994.

Stanger, Roland J., ed. *Essays on Intervention*. Ohio State University Press, 1964.

'Swedes Hide Bosnian Refugees'. *The Associated Press* [Online]. (23 March 1995). Available USENET: clari.news.immigration.

Tefft, Sheila. 'China Attempts to Have Its Net and Censor It Too'. *The Christian Science Monitor* [Online]. (5 August 1996). Available: http://www.csmonitor.com.

Telöken, Stefan. 'The Domino Effect'. *Refugees* (December 1993): 38–40.

'The Temporary Protection of Refugees: A Solution-Oriented and Rights Regarding Approach'. Refugee Law Research Unit, Centre for Refugee Studies, York University. July 1996.

Teson, Fernando R. *Humanitarian Intervention: An Inquiry into Law and Morality*. Dobbs Ferry, NY: Transnational Publishers, Inc., 1988.

Torrelli, Maurice. 'From Humanitarian Assistance to "*Intervention on Humanitarian Grounds*"?' *International Review of the Red Cross* (May–June 1992): 228–48.

'Towards a Rapid Reaction Capability for the United Nations'. Department of Foreign Affairs and International Trade. Government of Canada [Online]. September 1995. Available: http://www.dfait-maeci.gc.ca/english/news/newsletr/un/rap1.htm.

'Turkish Kurds Seek Refuge in North Iraq'. *Reuters*. [Online]. (22 May 1994). Available USENET: clari.news.immigration.

Twining, William, ed. *Issues of Self-Determination*. Aberdeen: Aberdeen University Press, 1991.

United Nations. *The Limits of Sovereignty*. United Nations Department of Public Information, 1992.

United Nations. *The United Nations Treaties on Outer Space*. New York: United Nations, 1984.

'United Nations Assistance Mission in Rwanda'. Program on Peacekeeping Policy, George Mason University [Online]. Available: http://ralph.gmu.edu/cfpa/peace/unamir.html.

United Nations High Commissioner for Refugees. *A New Approach in the Horn of Africa: The Preventive Zone Concept*. 1992.

United Nations High Commissioner for Refugees. 'Message from the High Commissioner to all staff on UN Reform'. 14 July 1997.

United Nations High Commissioner for Refugees. *REFWORLD* [Online]. Available: http://www.unhcr.ch/refworld/refworld.htm.

United Nations High Commissioner for Refugees. *The State of the World's Refugees: The Challenge of Protection.* New York: Penguin Books, 1993.

United Nations High Commissioner for Refugees. *The State of the World's Refugees: In Search of Solutions.* New York: Oxford University Press, 1995.

United Nations High Commissioner for Refugees. *UNHCR's Role in Protecting and Assisting Internally Displaced People.* Central Evaluation Section Discussion Paper, EVAL/IDP/13. 1993.

United Nations High Commissioner for Refugees. *UNHCR's Operational Experience with Internally Displaced Persons.* 1994.

United States. Agency for International Development. Bureau for Humanitarian Response. Office of U.S. Foreign Disaster Assistance. 'Rwanda – Civil Strife/ Displaced Persons'. Situation Report No. 3, Fiscal Year 1995, 30 January 1995. Available: http://www.intac.com/PubService/rwanda/OFDA/OFDA-8.html.

'U.S. Bombs Bosnian Serbs'. *The Associated Press* [Online]. (10 April 1994). Available USENET: clari.news.fighting.

US Committee for Refugees. *World Refugee Survey – 1992.* Washington, DC: US Committee for Refugees, 1992.

US Committee for Refugees. *World Refugee Survey – 1993.* Washington, DC: US Committee for Refugees, 1993.

US Committee for Refugees. *World Refugee Survey – 1994.* Washington, DC: US Committee for Refugees, 1994.

US Committee for Refugees. *World Refugee Survey – 1996.* Washington, DC: US Committee for Refugees, 1996.

van der Stoel, Max. 'Preventing Conflict and Building Peace: A Challenge for the CSCE'. *NATO Review* 42 (August 1994): 7–12.

Vincent, R. J. *Nonintervention and International Order.* Princeton: Princeton University Press, 1974.

van Dijk, Pieter. 'A Common Standard of Achievement: About Universal Validity and Uniform Interpretation of International Human Rights Norms'. *Netherlands Quarterly of Human Rights* 13 (2 1995): 105–21.

von Glahn, Gerhard. *Law Among Nations: An Introduction to Public International Law.* 5th edn. New York: Macmillan Publishing Company, 1986.

Walker, R.B.J. and Saul H. Mendlovitz, ed. *Contending Sovereignties: Redefining Political Community.* Boulder, CO: Lynne Rienner Publishers, 1990.

Walker, Sam. 'Beefier Border Patrol Hasn't Weakened Allure of a US Job'. *The Christian Science Monitor* [Online]. (12 December 1996). Available: http:// www.csmonitor.com.

Walzer, Michael. *Just and Unjust Wars.* New York: Basic Books, 1977.

Walzer, Michael. 'The Moral Standing of States: A Response to Four Critics'. *Philosophy & Public Affairs* 9 (Spring 1980): 209–29.

Walzer, Michael. 'The New Tribalism: Notes on a Difficult Problem'. *Dissent* 39 (Spring 1992): 164–71.

Warner, Daniel. *An Ethic of Responsibility in International Relations.* Boulder, CO: Lynne Rienner Publishers, 1991.

Warner, Daniel and James Hathaway. 'Refugee Law and Human Rights: Warner and Hathaway in Debate'. *Journal of Refugee Studies* 5 (2 1992): 162–71.

Weiner, Myron. 'Peoples and States in a New Ethnic Order?' *Third World Quarterly* 13 (2 1992): 317–33.

Weiss, Thomas G., ed. *Humanitarian Emergencies and Military Help in Africa.* New York: St. Martin's Press, 1990.

Weiss, Thomas G. 'Overcoming the Somalia Syndrome – "Operation Rekindle Hope?"' *Global Governance* (May–Aug. 1995): 171–87.

Weiss, Thomas G. 'A Research Note about Military-Civilian Humanitarianism: More Questions than Answers'. *Disasters* 21 (2 1997): 95–117.

Weiss, Thomas G. *The United Nations and Changing World Politics.* Boulder, CO: Westview Press, 1994.

Weiss, Thomas G. and Jarat Chopra. 'Sovereignty Is No Longer Sacrosanct: Codifying Humanitarian Intervention'. *Ethics & International Affairs* 6 (1992): 95–117.

Weiss, Thomas G. and Jarat Chopra. 'Sovereignty Under Seige: From Intervention to Humanitarian Space'. Presented at the *Conference on National Sovereignty and Collective Intervention.* Dartmouth College. 18–20 May 1992.

Weiss, Thomas G. and Larry Minear, eds. *Humanitarianism Across Borders: Sustaining Civilians in Times of War.* Boulder, CO: Lynne Rienner Publishers, 1993.

Weiss, Thomas G. and Amir Pasic. 'Reinventing UNHCR: Enterprising Humanitarians in the Former Yugoslavia, 1991–1995'. *Global Governance* 3 (January–April 1997): 41–57.

Wendt, Alexander. 'Anarchy Is What States Make of It: The Social Construction of Power Politics'. *International Organization* 46 (Spring 1992): 391–425.

Wheeler, Nicholas J. 'Pluralist or Solidarist Conceptions on International Society: Bull and Vincent on Humanitarian Intervention'. *Millennium: Journal of International Studies* 21 (3 1992): 463–87.

Wiener, Antje. *Building Institutions: The Developing Practice of European Citizenship.* Dissertation, Department of Political Science, Carleton University. 1995.

World Conference on Human Rights. *The Vienna Declaration and Programme of Action.* United Nations Department of Public Information, 1993.

Wright, Jane. 'The OSCE and the Protection of Minority Rights'. *Human Rights Quarterly* 18 (1 1996): 190–205.

Wright, Robin. 'The Outer Limits?' *The Los Angeles Times* (25 August 1992): 1, 4.

Wright, Robin. 'The New Tribalism All Over the World'. *Sacramento Bee* [Online]. Forum. (13 June 1993): F1. Available: Nexis.

Wriston, Walter B. 'Technology and Sovereignty'. *Foreign Affairs* 67 (Winter 1988–9): 63–75.

Wriston, Walter B. *The Twilight of Sovereignty: How the Information Revolution is Transforming Our World.* New York: Charles Scribner's Sons, 1992.

Zolberg, Aristide R. 'The Next Waves: Migration Theory for a Changing World'. *International Migration Review* 23 (Fall 1989): 403–30.

Zolberg, Aristide, Astri Suhrke, and Sergio Aguayo. *Escape From Violence.* New York: Oxford University Press, 1989.

INTERVIEWS

Bellamy, Daniel. Head of Desk, Desk II, Regional Bureau for Europe, United Nations High Commissioner for Refugees. Interviewed on 28 October 1993.

Bornet, Jean-Marc. Delegate General, International Committee of the Red Cross. Interviewed on 4 November 1993.

Brett, Rachel. Associate Representative, Friends World Committee for Consultation, Quaker United Nations Office. Interviewed on 10 November 1993.

Bwakira, N. Director, Regional Bureau for Africa, United Nations High Commissioner for Refugees. Interviewed on 2 November 1993.

Crisp, Jeff. Senior External Affairs Officer, Central Evaluation Section, United Nations High Commissioner for Refugees. Interviewed on 26 October 1993.

Durieux, Jean-François. Chief, Promotion of Refugee Law, Division of International Protection, United Nations High Commissioner for Refugees. Interviewed on 11 November 1993.

Grossrieder, Paul. Deputy Director of Operations, International Committee of the Red Cross. Interviewed on 3 November 1993.

Hall, Raymond. Chief of Secretariat, Division of External Relations, United Nations High Commissioner for Refugees. Interviewed on 28 October 1993.

Henneman, Jan. Intra-European Affairs Coordinator, Regional Bureau for Europe, United Nations High Commissioner for Refugees. Interviewed on 1 November 1993.

Jastram-Balian, Kate. Senior Human Rights Liaison Officer, Division of International Protection, United Nations High Commissioner for Refugees. Interviewed on 28 October 1993.

Jury, Alan. Counsellor, Refugee and Migration Affairs, Permanent Mission of the United States, Geneva. Interviewed on 4 November 1993.

Kent, Randolph. Coordinator, Inter-Agency Support Unit, Department of Humanitarian Affairs, United Nations. Interviewed on 8 November 1993.

Khan, Irene. Executive Assistant to the High Commissioner, United Nations High Commissioner for Refugees. Interviewed on 2 November 1993.

Kristoffersson, Ulf. T. Coordinator, Horn of Africa, Kenya, Sudan and Uganda, Regional Bureau for Africa, United Nations High Commissioner for Refugees. Interviewed on 29 October 1993.

Lambo, David. Coordinator for Southern Africa, Regional Bureau for Africa, United Nations High Commissioner for Refugees. Interviewed on 26 October 1993.

Mayne, Andrew. Desk Officer, Desk IV, Regional Bureau for Asia and Oceana, United Nations High Commissioner for Refugees. Interviewed on 10 November 1993.

Okoth-Obbo, G. Senior Legal Adviser, Africa, Division of International Protection, United Nations High Commissioner for Refugees. Interviewed on 1 November 1993.

Pasquier, André. Special Representative of the President, International Committee of the Red Cross. Interviewed on 9 November 1993.

Plattner, Denise. Legal Adviser, International Committee of the Red Cross. Interviewed on 9 November 1993.

Riera, José. Senior External Affairs Officer, Division of International Protection, United Nations High Commissioner for Refugees. Interviewed on 1 November 1993.

Schack, Bo. Senior Regional Legal Adviser, Regional Bureau for Asia and Oceania, United Nations High Commissioner for Refugees. Interviewed on 4 November 1993.

Sokiri, Andrew R. Deputy Director, Regional Bureau for Africa, United Nations High Commissioner for Refugees. Interviewed on 29 October 1993.

Thoolen, Hans. Coordinator, United Nations Voluntary Fund for Technical Cooperation in the Field of Human Rights, Center for Human Rights. Interviewed on 3 November 1993.

Verwey, Anton. Deputy Director, Regional Bureau for Europe and North America, United Nations High Commissioner for Refugees. Interviewed on 26 October 1993.

Wagenseil, Steven. First Secretary, Permanent Mission of the United States, Geneva. Interviewed on 4 November 1993.

Walker, Peter. Disaster Policy Department, International Federation of Red Cross and Red Crescent Societies. Interviewed on 3 November 1993.

Index

248

Index